CUSTER AND ME

Robert M. Utley. *Courtesy Eastern National Park and Monument Association.*

CUSTER AND ME

A Historian's Memoir

Robert M. Utley

UNIVERSITY OF OKLAHOMA PRESS : NORMAN

This book is published with the generous assistance of The McCasland Foundation, Duncan, Oklahoma.

Library of Congress Cataloging-in-Publication Data

Utley, Robert Marshall, 1929–
    Custer and me : a historian's memoir / Robert M. Utley
      p.   cm.
    Includes bibliographical references (p.   ) and index.
    ISBN 0-8061-3638-3 (alk. paper)
      1. Utley, Robert Marshall, 1929– 2. Historians—United States—
    Biography. 3. Custer, George Armstrong. 1839–1876. 4. Custer,
    George Armstrong, 1839–1876—Influence. 5. United States—
    Historiography. 6. Civil service—United States—Biography.
    7. United States. National Park Service—Biography. I. Title.

    E175.5.U85A3 2004
    973.8'2'092—dc22

                                                        2004046035

For my sister, Nancy

CONTENTS

ILLUSTRATIONS

PREFACE

THIS BOOK IS NOT just about Custer and me, although that is a theme that pervades it and appears intermittently from beginning to end. I have had other relationships and experiences in life that I want to write about. Those interested only in Custer may want to jump over those sections of my narrative. Those readers interested in the U.S. Army of the 1950s, the National Park Service, the national historic preservation program, the writing and publishing of narrative history, or autobiographical details may jump over Custer and stick with these passages. For the latter constituencies as well as the Custer following, I feel I have something of interest or even value to say.

I began this memoir in 1998, at the urging of Martha Kohl of the Montana Historical Society. I have worked on it only sporadically, in spare moments and with one lapse of almost two years. Additional incentive to stay with it came from my wife, Melody Webb, who had undertaken her own memoir (*A Woman in the Great Outdoors: Adventures in the National Park Service,* University of New Mexico Press, 2003). As with all my books, she has been a source of inspiration and valued professional criticism.

This is a memoir, not an autobiography. The distinction is important because a memoir sets forth the author's memory of what happened, not necessarily what actually happened. My memory, however, has been strengthened by correspondence files dating from the 1940s and a journal I began in 1972 and have maintained sporadically ever since.

For the purist, I am aware that the title is ungrammatical. Even so, I like it.

A number of my friends and former coworkers who read early chapters urged me to continue the project. I am especially indebted to Paul Andrew Hutton, Charles E. Rankin, Larry Sklenar, and Jerome Greene for the big push that brought it to completion. All four read part or all of the manuscript; and at the University of Oklahoma Press I am indebted to editor-in-chief Chuck Rankin and, for exceptional editorial skills, Steven Baker and Marian J. Stewart. Thanks also to John Doerner, historian at the Little Bighorn Battlefield National Monument. To all I express my deepest appreciation.

Custer and Me

CHAPTER 1

I HAVE LIVED WITH George Armstrong Custer for more than sixty years. For some of those years he dominated my life. For others, he prowled somewhere in the shadows, ready to pounce again when least expected and reassert his presence if not his domination.

I am not alone in bearing this burden, if such it is. Thousands of men, women, and children in the United States, and even in a score or more other nations, are similarly encumbered. The phenomenon exempts no ethnicity (even American Indian), no gender, no social or economic class, no age group. More than a thousand of the faithful unite in an organization replete with all the trappings of a professional association. Part fraternal, part scholarly, part absurdity, fully passionate, the Little Big Horn Associates publish a quarterly magazine and a monthly newsletter, and they meet each year to offer learned disquisitions, argue arcane issues, and recapture—some in meticulously accurate costume—a man, an event, and a time from a remote past. I am a member.

Beyond the buffs, practically everyone has heard the name *Custer*. For most, the name summons at least a fleeting image of a soldier who died fighting Indians. His true role in history cannot account for the nearly universal name recognition. For that explanation, one must probe the murky realms of mythology and folklore. Beneath the layers of legend, however, a living human being, possessed of a remarkable range of human faults and virtues, made his brief mark on the history of the United States.

Born in 1839 into a God-fearing but rowdy farm family, "Autie" Custer divided his youthful years between the Ohio farm and the home of his elder half-sister in Monroe, Michigan. At the U.S. Military Academy at West Point, he excelled in equitation and the martial skills but in academics and deportment balanced constantly on the brink of expulsion. As the Civil War broke out in 1861, he received his commission as second lieutenant, ranking thirty-fourth in his graduating class of thirty-four.

With other trained professionals, Lieutenant Custer found himself in demand as a staff officer. As such he served, and impressed, generals George B. McClellan and Alfred Pleasanton. But no one, least of all the young subaltern, anticipated the stunning good fortune that befell him and two of his fellow junior officers in June 1863, on the very eve of Gettysburg. Captain Custer, Fifth Regular Cavalry, found himself suddenly Brigadier General Custer, U.S. Volunteers. At the head of the Michigan Cavalry Brigade, he made his debut at Gettysburg. With repeated slashing saber charges, he helped throw back Jeb Stuart's Confederate cavalry and laid the groundwork for a meteoric rise in the esteem of his superiors and the affections of the public. Bedecked with loops of gold braid and flowing scarlet tie, with brushy mustache and red-gold hair falling to his shoulders, the exuberant "Boy General" slashed his way through one bloody battle after another. He was twenty-five and a major general when, out of the morning mists near Appomattox Station, he received the white towel that signaled General Robert E. Lee's decision to surrender the Army of Northern Virginia.

The war over and the Volunteers mustered out, General Custer bore his wife of two years, Elizabeth Bacon Custer, to the Kansas frontier to assume the lieutenant colonelcy of the newly formed Seventh Cavalry of the regular army. In the next ten years, in Kansas, the Indian Territory, Dakota, and Montana, the Boy General made a name for himself as Indian fighter, sportsman, hunter, and outdoorsman. By 1876 he was famous, ambitious, blissfully wedded, and depending on one's point of view, well liked or detested, but seemingly destined some day to be a general once again.

Then on June 25, 1876, history merged with legend to award George Armstrong Custer immortality. The Battle of the Little Bighorn cut short a career that would have gained occasional mention in histories of the Civil War and the western frontier. Instead, it made the slain Custer's name a household word then and forever after—an icon in the public imagination, at times bright, at times tarnished, but never in danger of decay.

How can a man long dead haunt the lives of so many people? How can a man both venerated and abominated in his own time still command so much veneration and abomination in a generation ten times removed from his? How can Japanese who read translations of my writings—or for that matter, French, Italians, Poles, or Czechs—find even a narrow bridge to that distant time, place, and culture that can convert them into Custer addicts?

Of the afflicted, many do not know, or cannot explain, why. Others will offer many and diverse reasons. For myself, I know only how it started and how it is ending. In between, many things happened that may help illumine the question. Whether they do or not, they tell much about Custer and me.

Memory of my introduction to George Armstrong Custer does not predate the age of twelve. But through some medium now forgotten, he may have figured in my fantasies earlier. In the late 1930s, my friends and I in the little Indiana community of Dayton (population eight hundred) interminably played "gun." David Crouse lived in much the largest house in town, and his spacious lawn, featuring a tree-shaded cabin that stored tools, served as fort and battleground. When we advanced in formation against the enemy—American flag held aloft, simulated bugle tooting the charge, toy rifles and pistols cracking with guttural explosions from our throats—we must have drawn inspiration from some movie featuring cavalry charging on Indians.

"Gun" had its penalties. Once, a group of girls passing my house caught us in the midst of a shootout. Among them was Joy Rohler, who, although she did not know it, was my girlfriend. They heaped laughing ridicule on such juvenile nonsense, and I was paralyzed with acute embarrassment. Other times, when I spent a night with friends on outlying farms, I gloried in the new dimensions the barn afforded for "gun." The farm boys humored me only sporadically. They also thought "gun" pretty juvenile and could not conceal their lack of enthusiasm.

Radio as well as the movies inspired "gun." Before I knew of General Custer, the Lone Ranger suggested many variations of the game. He and his faithful Indian companion, Tonto, brought the six-shooter and its silver bullets to bear on western lawlessness with deadly effect. The most stirring episodes united the Lone Ranger with the U.S. cavalry and often climaxed with the sound of hoof beats mingled with the bugle's staccato charge. Perhaps more significant, the *William Tell* Overture and other of the opera's musical themes planted in me a love of classical music that matured long after the Lone Ranger and Tonto had slipped into the youthful past.

The movies, however, proved far more influential than radio. On the screens of the Paramount and Mars Theaters in Lafayette, an eight-mile drive from Dayton on State Highway 38, those wonderful and improbable adventure films of the late 1930s played daily. As often as once a week, Dad packed Mother, me, and my younger sister Nancy into our 1934 Chevrolet and drove to the city for a movie, often followed by a stop for a frozen custard. Who of my generation can forget *The Plainsman, Union Pacific, Stanley and Livingstone, Four Feathers, The Charge of the Light Brigade,* and *Northwest Mounted Police?*

The last in particular furnishes a vivid memory. My fourth-grade report card traced a dismal scholastic record each month through the winter of 1938–39. One with especially bad marks came to my father's attention on the same Friday he had promised to take us to see *Northwest Mounted Police.* Those Cs and Ds in everything from arithmetic to deportment loosed a wrath gathering for six months. No movie tonight, he decreed, arousing intense dismay and tearful entreaties. Probably with some coaching from Mother and Nancy, he fell back on a scheme full of humiliation. If I walked the three blocks to the house Miss Hymes shared with another teacher and poured forth promises of reform sufficient to win her permission, we would go. Miss Hymes was probably as embarrassed as I by this little drama, and she readily consented. We went.

Watching *Northwest Mounted Police* today on VCR, I recall the horror of that day. And I wonder if what I see now was worth what I endured then.

The movie that propelled me into a lifetime of Custer addiction emerged from Hollywood shortly after my twelfth birthday. I was babysitting for a next-door neighbor when I picked up the issue of *Life* magazine dated December 8, 1941. The cover bore a picture of Lieutenant General Douglas MacArthur, our new Far East commander, and featured a photographic tribute by Margaret Bourke-White to this military potentate, ensconced in his Manila penthouse confidently planning the defense of the Philippines should the Japanese dare attempt an invasion.

But the handsome general in the gilded hat shrank to insignificance when I reached the "Movie of the Week." Errol Flynn and Olivia de Havilland starred as George and Elizabeth Custer in *They Died with Their Boots On.* Old photos and the ubiquitous Anheuser-Busch painting *Custer's Last Fight* lent historical realism to the page of publicity stills from the film that promised an exciting adventure "from West Point to points West."

That magazine, of course, appeared a few days before the cataclysmic date on its cover, and only a few days more before the genius of Douglas MacArthur received its first rude challenge. But it set a young mind engrossed with the frontier cavalry on a course decisively influenced by the boozy Hollywood warrior's portrayal of the swashbuckling cavalier. (Several years ago my wife, Melody Webb—of whom more later—paid $45 for a copy of that issue of *Life* and gave it to me for my birthday. It is a cherished memento of a turning point in my life.)

Edging into adolescence, I no longer depended on my father for transportation to film land. Saturday mornings I boarded a Greyhound bus for the trip into Lafayette, reported to Mr. Elmore for my cornet lesson, killed time until the theaters opened, loaded up on popcorn and candy, and sat through the feature movie two or even three times before climbing on a southbound bus to return home. Flynn and de Havilland seared themselves into my mind's eye, planted themselves deeply in my psyche, and treated me repeatedly to the thrilling denouement of the Last Stand. That they piled historical absurdity on top of historical travesty I learned only later. For in 1942, especially in the climate of military celebration created by World War II, I found my obsession.

I went to Lafayette's public library, an imposing classical temple on a hill a few blocks from the Paramount Theater. The card catalogue offered several entries under *Custer.* The one I checked out first was a huge tome bound in black, indicating enough usage to have prompted the library to have it rebound. The title was *A Complete Life of General George A. Custer;* the author, Frederick Whittaker, identified himself as "Brevet Captain Sixth New York Veteran Cavalry." The publication date, December 1876, recorded an awesome achievement—650 pages of biography published in less than six months after the protagonist's demise. The dedication set the tone for the treat those 650 pages held in store for me: "To the American People, whose Liberties He so Gallantly Defended, and Especially to the American Cavalry, Past and Present, whose Greatest Pride and Brightest Ornament He Was, I Dedicate this Memoir."

What a thrill those pages provided. Here were printed words that, to a receptive young mind, sang of incontestable historical accuracy. Here was a George Armstrong Custer fully the glorious hero portrayed by Errol Flynn. I read of his rowdy youth in Ohio and Michigan; of his sorry record at West Point; of his brilliant Civil War career as dashing "Boy General" of cavalry; of his marriage to the angelic Elizabeth Bacon; of his Indian campaigns; and of the Last Stand, where, betrayed by cowardly subordinates, he stood with his men to the last even though an Indian scout offered a chance to escape.

How moving were those final paragraphs of Whittaker's great work of history:

> Truth and sincerity, honor and bravery, tenderness and sympathy, unassuming piety and temperance, were the mainspring of Custer, the man. As a soldier there is no spot on his armor, as a man no taint on his honor.

We have followed him through all his life, and passed in review boy, cadet, lieutenant, captain, general, and Indian fighter, without finding one deed to bring shame on soldier or man. People of the land he loved, my task is ended. Would it had been committed to worthier hands. Four simple lines, written by an unknown poet, form his best epitaph.

> Who early thus upon the field of glory
> Like thee doth fall and die, needs for his fame
> Naught but the simple telling of his story,
> The naming of his name.

I was born in the early morning hours of October 31, 1929, in the tree-shaded, white-frame hospital of Bauxite, Arkansas. The architecture mimicked most of the other buildings in the little town, business and residential alike, because it was a company town. Here the Aluminum Company of America mined the bauxite ore central to the manufacture of its product. My father, Don Williams Utley, practiced his profession in ALCOA's chemical laboratory. My mother, Valeria Haney Utley, a beautiful but troubled woman, had difficulty just managing a household. Children— Nancy Jane arrived in 1934—would inflict additional mental and emotional stresses that neither Nancy nor I sensed until many years later.

Mother came out of a hellishly abusive childhood, replete with drunkenness, beatings, brothers who ran away and vanished forever, and older sisters who shuttled Valeria from one household to another for rearing. I never knew my maternal grandparents. Somehow Mother succeeded in entering the Arkansas State Teachers College at Conway. There she met Dad, then studying chemistry at neighboring Hendrix College.

Dad's family background could hardly have been more different. Joseph Simeon "Sim" Utley and his wife, Vivian Williams Utley, ranked among Little Rock's first families. Grandpa had been a prosecuting attorney, a state senator, and the attorney general of Arkansas. High in the leadership of the state Democratic Party, he later became a distinguished circuit judge. Grandma had her own world, as an artist and in various women's organizations. Their worlds intersected in the Asbury Methodist Church and in the big frame house at 2404 Schiller Avenue. Grandma took almost no responsibility for their home's upkeep. That was the province of the faithful Carrie. Like most southern families of moderate or better means, my grandparents ceded the house and its kitchen to a "colored" maid.

I worshipped my grandfather, a big gray-haired man with a passion for fried chicken and pitcher after pitcher of ice tea. He looked exactly like a judge should look. He planted in me an ambition to study law and become a judge. More enduringly, he shared with me his own love of history. Only long after his death did I learn some of his flaws. I am still outraged that he demanded that my father study for the Methodist ministry and, when confronted with a defiant switch to chemistry at Hendrix, cut off all financial support. Dad borrowed the money to finish college from Aunt Lillian, who came from a well-to-do family and need not have burdened him with monthly payments of principal and interest that took nearly fifteen years to pay off—especially since my grandfather had saved his lawyer brother, her husband, from a prison term for some financial or legal skullduggery.

For my parents my arrival on Halloween of 1929 could not have been less timely. Only a week earlier the crash on Wall Street had set off the terrible depression of the 1930s. Precariously, Dad clung to his chemist job at ALCOA, although an oppressive frugality ruled the household and added to my mother's already fragile hold on reality. As he did all his life, Dad covered for Mother's problems, and he tried to be a good parent. Honest, principled, imbued with a healthy work ethic, a man devoted to his family yet a stern disciplinarian, he remained until his last few years a somewhat distant figure. Only then—too late, really—did we achieve a true rapport. I think my second wife formed the connecting bridge.

We lived in one of a dozen company houses fronting the street. On the other side of the street, clumps of huge trees shaded a "run" that trickled beneath a stone bridge bearing the gravel road to Benton. Our house was a modest two-bedroom frame structure with front porch, a garage devoted to Dad's wood-working tools since we had no automobile, and an ample yard. A big black woman, Mary, did the wash, cleaned the house, and helped with the kids. Without Mary, Mother could not have coped, especially in the few years her Grandma Brown lived with us. Wispy, incredibly ancient, blind, she passed her days on the front-porch swing. I am remembered for running my tricycle wheels over her feet and pushing her snuff stick into her mouth.

My best friend in Bauxite was Reyman Branting. Since his father superintended the bauxite mines, Reyman came from circumstances far more opulent than mine. He lived in a company house, too, a gleaming white mansion set atop the highest hill in town. A dense ten-foot hedge surrounded the estate and isolated it from the lower orders of the ALCOA family. Black men tended the manicured lawns and gardens. Black women in starched whites tended the inside. We played at Reyman's home, not mine, and these interludes afforded a study in glaring contrasts.

Sometimes our family rode the Missouri Pacific's "puddle jumper," a unit containing both motive power and passenger seats, to Little Rock to visit Grandma and Grandpa. Sometimes I got to go by myself and live with them for several days. "Bobmarshall," they and everyone else called me, as ordained by southern custom. "Nancyjane" identified my sister. Like Grandpa, I loved Carrie's fried chicken. For that reason, still a source of perplexity, all my relatives pronounced me destined for the Methodist ministry—a prospect truly frightening.

Halfway through the first grade at the Bauxite school, ALCOA summoned Dad to a new job at the company's central chemical laboratory in New Kensington, Pennsylvania. Dad went in advance, leaving to Mother the task of shepherding two children in a midwinter voyage that must have been as daunting to her as it was sensational to them. "Look, Mother," I exclaimed as a white-jacketed porter helped us aboard a Pullman car, "the train has beds!"

We lived in a dingy old rental house on Keystone Drive, clearly a blot on a neighborhood of otherwise nice homes. In contrast to Arkansas, New Kensington was cold and snowy and heavy with the soot of coal-burning locomotives and the steel mills of nearby

Pittsburgh. Worse, I encountered a sudden culture shock. For the balance of the first grade, a stern Miss Hill had little patience for my southern ways and southern drawl. She talked so fast I could not keep up. Relief came in the second grade, with a warm and friendly Miss Anderson, who went out of her way to help this little immigrant from the South adjust to new ways. At the same time, Mr. Marsh's "Living World Science Club" introduced me to a caring man and some of nature's wonders.

We lived on Keystone Drive from early 1936 until the summer of 1937. Then we moved across town to an even dingier rental home on North Street, but closer to the chemical laboratories. Here, in a heavily ethnic neighborhood, I went through the third grade, ruled by a severe clone of Miss Hill. She rewarded misbehavior with a ruler slap on the hands or, worse, nose placed in a circle drawn on the blackboard at a tip-toe elevation. North Street brought pink eye, mumps, and measles; an allowance of a nickel a week; radio serials such as *Little Orphan Annie, Dick Tracy, The Shadow,* and the first of the *Lone Ranger* episodes; "Big-Little Books," my favorite of which featured Don Winslow of the navy; our first automobile, the 1934 Chevrolet; and a small but growing collection of toy lead soldiers, no doubt reflecting interest in the Spanish Civil War and certainly foreshadowing "gun" of a few years later.

The summer of 1938 marked the end of the Pennsylvania years with a move I have never regretted. ALCOA transferred Dad to its new plant in Lafayette, Indiana. It was a clean flat land, with fields of corn and wheat and a people much more congenial. We settled first in the city, and I began fourth grade there. But by October we had moved out to Dayton. Again we lived in a modest rental house—$25 a month, frozen there by World War II rent controls until my father insisted on paying more.

Here, a month late, I entered fourth grade. Here Miss Hymes gave me permission to see *Northwest Mounted Police.* And here, in that memorable year of 1942, I first saw Errol Flynn as General Custer in *They Died with Their Boots On* and first read Frederick Whittaker's *Complete Life of General George A. Custer.*

CHAPTER 2

THE LAFAYETTE PUBLIC LIBRARY yielded other books about Custer. I especially liked *A Boy Rides with Custer,* by Zoa Grace Hawley. Most disconcerting—indeed, infuriating—was *Glory Hunter,* by Frederic F. Van de Water. Published in 1934, on the crest of one of the debunking waves of American biography, *Glory Hunter* presented a Custer at the opposite pole from Whittaker's paragon of all virtues. Voraciously pursuing glory, this Custer exhibited in his every act gross flaws of character and intellect. A military incompetent, cruel martinet, ego-driven publicity hound, incorrigible insubordinate, at the Little Bighorn he sacrificed nearly 250 lives on the altar of insatiable ambition.

This could not be the true Custer. Again and again I read that worn library copy of Whittaker's *Life of Custer.* For a teenager seeking idols in wartime America, Whittaker authored the gospel. I despised Van de Water, the more so as I discovered that his influence on later books surpassed even Whittaker's. I have long since outgrown Whittaker, but I am still contemptuous of Van de Water. Years later I took delight in finding a review of the book by General Hugh S. "Iron Pants" Johnson, who headed Franklin Roosevelt's National Recovery Administration. "As history," Johnson wrote late in 1934, "this book is just adverse advocacy. As biography, it is merely muckraking. As military criticism, it sounds like the musings of a daisy-crunching doughboy." Those are judgments I still share.

Although I read exhaustively, childish fantasies still exerted their power. Sister Nancy, a tomboy, willingly helped act them out. We costumed her as General Custer. With black and yellow construction paper, I fashioned general's shoulder straps, a double row of buttons, and coils of sleeve braids, and we pasted them on my navy pea jacket. A floppy hat bore a paper representation of the cavalry's crossed sabers against a black oval. We pasted stripes of yellow crepe paper on the outer seams of her blue jeans, which she stuffed into her cowboy boots. A piece of wood sawed in the shape of the cavalry's butt-forward holster and painted black hung from a belt buckled over the pea jacket. A huge sword that had somehow found its way into the family's possession completed the armament. We mounded some pillows, covered them with a blanket, and stuck a feather into one end. With one foot on this mock Sitting Bull, the sword grasped in her right hand with point resting on the slain Indian, her left hand holding a big paper mustache against her lip, Nancy created a historic tableau for her brother's camera.

All was not Custer during those early teen years. I read other books too, among them most of the Sherlock Holmes mysteries. Ten-cent comic books—Captain Marvel, Superman, Batman—afforded pleasure even after they were banned from the household: I read them at David Crouse's. I went to the movies at least once a week. My cinematic taste was strictly limited to adventures, preferably military; I had no use for musicals. I worked at my cornet, not too successfully. I fashioned model airplanes from balsa wood and tissue paper, not very expertly, and hung them on my bedroom walls to gather dust. I even ventured briefly into the Boy Scouts of America, drawn no doubt by the chance to dress in a uniform. I progressed from Tenderfoot to Second Class, but First Class eluded me because I convinced myself that I had covered more than the required fourteen miles of a hike, then accepted a ride—lamentably with the scoutmaster's son.

The Methodist Church continued to play a large part in family life. Mother, who played the piano in our living room, became the church organist. I am sure that at an early age I became a nonbeliever, but the parents demanded attendance at Sunday school every Sunday and church twice a month. I protested repeatedly, to no avail. I think Dad gave up somewhere in my last years of high school. For himself, he remained a faithful and strong presence in the Methodist Church for the rest of his life, even after my mother decided to become a Christian Scientist. Never a fundamentalist, Dad brought a rationalist, scientific influence to bear on every church he attended. But in his son, the church had forever lost a communicant.

To Dad's disappointment and exasperation, I continued to bring home report cards that branded me a poor scholar.

Dayton's big brick school building housed all twelve grades and served Sheffield Township. Each of the first six grades had its own room and teacher. Grades seven through twelve occupied rows of desks in a spacious "assembly room" that served as a home base. A wine-colored curtain hid the stage at the front of the room. One began the final six years at a desk next to the wall and worked, row by row and year by year, across the room to the windows, the preserve of the seniors. From the assembly room each morning, we scattered to various classrooms throughout the building for instruction, returning for study hours.

As Dayton High School served a rural area, it did not count a large student body. My senior graduating class numbered only seventeen. This made for relatively small classes and, with a cadre of reasonably competent teachers, an education as good as the big school in Lafayette.

David Crouse and I, with perhaps one or two others, lived in Dayton. The rest were farm kids, hauled from home and back each day by yellow "hacks." The school year ended in April because the boys had to get into the fields for spring planting. They were big muscular fellows with fine physiques developed by farm labor. They excelled in basketball, the passion of school and community alike, the fuel of raging rivalries among all the schools of Tippecanoe County, and the means to male honor and stature.

In this society I was the bookish, puny town boy. Class pictures always posted me on a flank because everyone else towered over me. My arms and legs displayed no muscles. Not only could I not compete in basketball, but I had little interest in any sport (and still don't). One year—my sophomore, I think—my father forced me to go out for basketball. I failed miserably, emerging from each practice so humiliated that I finally prevailed on Dad to let me quit. One morning, halfway up the big staircase to the second floor, I stopped the coach, Mr. Siler, and told him. His sarcastic acknowledgment only intensified my despair. An acute sense of physical inadequacy dogged me until the U.S. Army showed me some things about myself that I had not known.

Although contemptuous of my flight from basketball, Mr. Siler, more than any other teacher, afforded opportunities to climb above my seemingly fated mediocrity. A Quaker, a lifelong bachelor, tall and ramrod stiff with demeanor to match, he taught English as well as coaching basketball. His cherubic face occasionally betrayed a hint of a smile, but he ruled his classroom with iron discipline.

For a time Mr. Siler took his evening meals at our home. I suspect he and Dad conspired to launch me on the basketball court, and when that did not work, they probably discussed other ways I might be prodded out of mental if not physical lethargy. In Siler's classroom, although I never mastered the art of diagramming a sentence, I began to sense the rhythms of the English language and, however clumsily, to write essays that gained more than a passing mark.

Mr. Siler also directed the junior and senior plays. He gave me the lead in the junior play, and I did well enough to be chosen for the lead in the senior play, *Charley's Aunt*. Bedecked in Victorian finery, with wig and fluttering fan, I created an uproarious title role. Those performances, accompanied by a sudden surge in academic performance, transformed a nobody into a somebody. Faculty and students alike, and not least my demanding father, gave evident approval despite the paucity of athletic prowess.

Girls were another matter. The basketball stars got the prettiest, and they had the self-confidence to know what to do. In the family car, the boy picked up the girl, went to Lafayette for a movie, had a hamburger and fries at a drive-in, spent an hour parked at a wooded byway "necking," then went home. They hinted or even boasted of sexual conquests, although I think that rarely happened.

By my junior year, I too had a driver's license and access to a family auto—in 1940 Dad had bought a new Chevrolet. But I lacked the nerve even to ask for a date, much less to know how to behave on one. Somehow I summoned the courage to approach Pat Moyer, a pretty sophomore who was probably too reserved for the extroverted farm boys. For two years we "went steady," which safeguarded us both from rejection and from a reputation as social oddities. The relationship ended the night of my senior prom, when I discovered she had no intention of giving up the dictates of her Catholic religion.

In these last years of high school, moreover, I found a job, part-time in winter, full-time in summer. Mr. Widmer had earned a degree in pharmacy at Purdue University in 1899 and ever since had run Widmer's Drug Store in Dayton. By 1944 he was a shrunken little bachelor with wispy gray hair and a wispy voice that he never raised even in reprimand. I dispensed ice cream sundaes, sodas, and malts and sold candy and cigarettes (although in these war years we hid the best of both for special customers: Marvels at eleven cents a pack occupied the display case while the Luckies and Camels at fifteen cents remained beneath). Widmer's was also a hardware store and the evening gathering place, around a battered table, of the town's old men, who talked of crop prospects and vented their hatred of Franklin Delano Roosevelt. Mr. Widmer started me at twenty-five cents an hour and raised it in 1946 to thirty-five cents.

Travel, possible even during the war, broadened my horizons. In the summer of 1941, in our new Chevrolet, the family drove to Arkansas to visit relatives, then continued to New Orleans and Pensacola before returning home. In December 1943 we endured the agonies of wartime train travel to go back to Arkansas for Grandpa's funeral. Grandma had died a year earlier, but Dad went alone for that occasion. The outpouring of tributes to my grandfather only heightened my pride in his achievements and my determination to follow in his footsteps.

I also had a love affair with buses, Greyhound buses. The route between Indianapolis and Chicago ran in front of Widmer's Drug

Store, and whenever possible I went to the front steps to wave to the driver. Greyhounds took me to Lafayette and back and even to a boldly adventurous exploration of Chicago. Twice, I bused alone to Arkansas to visit my relatives. I took on full responsibility for working with Greyhound officials to organize every detail of the senior class trip to Washington, D.C., which was a triumph. By then, however, the bus trip that critically influenced my future had already occurred, in 1946.

In fact, I had two portentous trips in the summer of 1946. The war had ended, and gas rationing no longer limited travel. Dad's roommate at Hendrix had been Raymond Gregg, who now served as park naturalist at Rocky Mountain National Park in Colorado. In June we drove there to visit the Greggs and sample the park. Rocky Mountain, together with Mount Rushmore and Badlands on the way home, introduced me to the National Park Service.

Rocky Mountain also afforded a minor rite of passage. We drove the park's spectacular Trail Ridge Road, which surmounts the Continental Divide and descends to Grand Lake on the western slope. Dad let me drive. Surrounded by towering peaks, the road clung precariously to the sides of steep ridges, gorges plunging from the very edge of the pavement. We climbed above the tree line and entered a swirling blizzard. Snow covered the road and reduced visibility to the hood ornament. Mother cowered in the back seat, but Dad grimly let his newly licensed sixteen-year-old meet the challenge. I did. For years after, we boasted of Bob's achievement that day on the spine of the continent.

The momentous bus trip occurred in August 1946. I had saved enough money clerking at Widmer's to buy a bus ticket back to the West, especially to the hill where Custer and his troopers died. The National Park Service also had jurisdiction over Custer Battlefield National Monument, Montana. I wrote to the superintendent asking how to get there. His reply intimated that there was really no good way unless one had an auto; but he promised if I took the morning train down to Crow Agency from Billings, he would meet me on his mail run and drive me to the battlefield, three and one-half miles distant. My bus ticket projected a grand tour of the West by way of Chicago, Minneapolis, Butte, Salt Lake City,

Denver, Kansas City, and St. Louis. I took the superintendent up on his offer and arranged for the side trip from Billings to Custer Battlefield.

Late on that consequential August morning, the Burlington's southbound passenger train puffed to a stop at the Crow Agency station. On the platform as I stepped down stood a man in the gray and green uniform of the National Park Service. He was tall and blocky, with a long red face and hawk nose shaded by the flat brim of his "Montana Peak" Stetson. His shirt pocket bore the round gold badge of a park superintendent, but what immediately caught my eye was a watch chain looped over his right trousers pocket, from which hung the blue and gold regimental crest of the Seventh Cavalry. He introduced himself in a parade ground voice with a pronounced Boston accent. He was Captain Edward S. Luce, superintendent of Custer Battlefield National Monument.

We climbed into the cab of a black prewar Chevrolet pickup bearing a white U.S. government shield on each door. We crossed U.S. Highway 87 and drove down the graveled main street to the post office. Grocery store, lunchroom, and other businesses faced across the street toward a spacious square shaded by huge cotton-wood trees. Only partly visible beyond the trees were big white-frame buildings—the administrative offices, hospital, warehouse, and tribal council hall of the Crow Indian Agency. Blanketed Crow women and men with braided hair and high-crowned, feathered hats moved about the village, on foot, in battered cars and pickups, and on horseback.

As we waited for the mail to be posted, Captain Luce spoke in graphic and droll absolutes about the town and its citizens. He liked and respected Superintendent Lippert, whom the Indian Bureau had placed in charge of the Crow Reservation; and he liked and respected Reverend Bentley and his family. The latter's domain was the white Baptist church whose steeple rose above the town and whose interior Luce had probably never seen. Toward the Crows, however, Luce directed a patrician condescension—interesting and colorful people, but lazy, dirty, drunken, and immoral.

We drove south on Highway 87 across the Little Bighorn River, then turned to ascend a winding road to the high, treeless ridges overlooking the valley. Before leaving the valley, we passed a small cabin and gas pumps bearing signs identifying it as a souvenir shop. This was run by Mary Jane Williams, Luce said, whose family he tossed off contemptuously as beneath notice. "Prairie Mary," he called her, pronounced in his Boston tongue "Prayrie Mayrie."

We passed through a black steel gate holding an arch that silhouetted black metal letters spelling "Custer Battlefield." Beyond, a neatly trimmed hedge partly obscured a small stone dwelling and stone bandbox. Within lay the immaculately maintained green carpet of Custer Battlefield National Cemetery. A narrow roadway lined with pine trees ended at a tall white flag pole flying the national colors. Ranks of white grave stones aligned with military precision marched outward from the flag pole.

The little stone house had been built in 1894 as the cemetery custodian's home and office. A covered passage connected its rear with a shop, above which were quarters for the maintenance chief. Behind them stood a stone garage.

The stone house still served the purpose for which it was built. The small front room, entered from a roofed porch, contained the superintendent's desk, a table for the visitor register, and a few exhibits. Above the table hung an oil painting of General Custer. Beneath it were crossed cavalry carbines, in the angle of which hung a framed collection of portraits of officers who had died at the Little Bighorn. In one corner an exhibit case displayed a fringed buckskin jacket and breeches that had belonged to Custer. I do not recall any artifacts representing the Indians.

Mrs. Luce—Evelyn, or as he called her in jest, "Mrs. McGilli-cuddy"—turned out to be the big blustery man's opposite. Younger than he by perhaps a dozen years, quiet, courteous, kindly, thought-ful, self-effacing though clearly a vital figure in managing the park, she welcomed me with a ham sandwich and a coke.

Afterward, Luce drove me to the hilltop where Custer and the last of his men perished. A granite monument rose from the mass grave of the dead troopers. It bore the name of each, with an inscription on the base recording its purpose:

In Memory of
The Officers and Soldiers Who Fell near This Place
Fighting with the 7th United States Cavalry
Against Sioux Indians
On the 25th and 26th of June
A.D. 1876

The hill capped by the monument marked the northern tip of "Battle Ridge." On its western slope, just below the monument, clustered about fifty white marble headstones, official U.S. government issue. A few bore names, including those of George A. Custer and his brother Thomas W., but most recorded simply "Unknown Soldier, 7th U.S. Cavalry, fell here June 25, 1876." Each marked where a trooper had fallen in battle and been buried until removed to the mass grave. Below in a deep coulee, and south on both sides of Battle Ridge, gravestones glistened white amid the brown late-summer grass. Seemingly scattered at random, they too marked where soldiers had fallen.

"Custer Hill," as it came to be called, commanded a sweeping view. Below, the Little Bighorn River, its course traced by cottonwood trees, snaked down a valley two to three miles wide, the locale of the Sioux and Cheyenne village that Custer sought to attack. Benchlands rose beyond, extending to a horizon etched by the Bighorn Mountains. In the foreground, a hundred yards or so below the bunched markers of Custer Hill, the five-acre national cemetery lay in brilliant green contrast to the dry plains grass dappled with blue-gray clumps of sagebrush.

The monument, the gravestones tracing ragged battle lines and the final stand, the wrinkled brown landscape, and the vista embracing a hundred miles of plains and mountains combine in a powerful evocation of one of history's most compelling tragedies. It stirred me deeply on first sight, as it has ever since. Rare is the visitor not similarly affected.

Cap Luce's running commentary competed with the emotions evoked by the scene's grandeur. He drove me along Battle Ridge to Calhoun Hill; through a gate and down to the mouth of Medicine

Tail Coulee, opening on the cool, shaded waters of the Little Bighorn; up a winding trace to Weir Point; and on to the Reno-Benteen
Battlefield. Here, atop ravine-scored bluffs rising steeply from the
river, Major Marcus A. Reno and Captain Frederick W. Benteen
formed a perimeter defense and fought off the warriors who had
wiped out Custer. Luce guided me among the positions and
pointed out, in the valley below, where Reno had first attacked
the Indian village, where he had withdrawn to a timbered river
bend, and where in bloody panic he and his men had fled over
the open valley and the river to gain the bluff tops.

Back at the Custer Battlefield, Luce let me wander. I roamed
among the markers, climbed ridges and descended ravines, and
jumped wildly every time buzzing grasshoppers reminded me of
the captain's warning about rattlesnakes. As the late-afternoon
sun cast shadows that threw the rugged landscape into bold relief,
I walked in the cemetery, reading names that recorded history
from the Indian wars to World War II. The cemeteries of frontier
forts had been moved here as the garrisons marched away. Luce
joined me for the evening ritual of lowering and folding the flag.

Mrs. Luce had me take supper with them. Together they drove
me to Crow Agency and saw me aboard the evening bus back to
Billings. What a powerful set of impressions I took with me. What
an enduring set of memories I had acquired. And in the Luces I
had found adults to respect, admire, and I hoped, be my friends
beyond this day. I still marvel that these dedicated public servants
took under their care a sixteen-year-old kid, an utter stranger, who
had bought a bus ticket from Indiana to Custer Battlefield. On
that day, unknown to all of us, they set my life on a new course.

CHAPTER 3

I wrote to the Luces from Salt Lake City and again as soon as I reached home. I wrote to thank them, but also for another reason. Visitors to the battlefield received a threefold leaflet bearing Custer's portrait on the front that told briefly of the battle and the battlefield. I read and reread it. What especially caught my eye and roused exciting visions was a statement that during the summer months the battlefield employed "historical aides" to tell visitors the story of the battle. Before even beginning my senior year in high school, before even turning seventeen, I asked Captain Luce if I could be a historical aide the following summer. He replied that he would like to have me but that regulations set a minimum age of twenty-one.

I continued to write my new friend. All through that winter of my last year in high school, we exchanged letters. He could easily have brushed me off with the first; but patiently, perhaps because he was flattered, perhaps because he sensed himself as a mentor, he answered my every letter, sometimes with several pages of single-spaced typescript. He instructed me on the fine points of Custer and the battlefield, and he provided addresses of used-book dealers from whom I might build my own library of Custeriana. At last I had my very own copy of Whittaker's *Complete Life of General George A. Custer.*

I worked part-time for Mr. Widmer that winter and expected to continue full-time through the summer of 1947, after graduation from high school. I had already laid plans to follow my grandfather's professional path and enter nearby Purdue University in the fall. Then came a long letter from Luce, dated May 12, 1947. It stunned and thrilled. There was a "slight possibility" he could hire me. After three acutely anxious weeks, the word arrived: come.

By mid-June, for the second time, I stepped from the Burlington's morning train to the platform of the Crow Agency station. And there to greet me, for the second time, was that big man for whom, over the past nine months, I had come to have something close to veneration.

Luce had made some advance arrangements for me. He had persuaded Indian Bureau officials to rent me a room in a two-story frame house that sat across from the hospital and that housed some of the nurses. He had convinced Mike Baca, who ran the Crow Lunch, to open earlier so I could get breakfast; I would take my evening meals there too. The Crow Lunch left much to be desired, both in the fare and in hours of operation; at times I went without breakfast. For lunch, I kept a few items in Mrs. Luce's refrigerator and prepared my own at a little table in the breezeway connecting the house to the shop. For transportation, I had my feet. Morning and evening, except when a kindly tourist noted the uniform and took me aboard, I made the hour's hike between Crow Agency and the battlefield.

Finally I assembled my uniform from the Park Service contractor: green trousers and tie, gray shirt. I couldn't afford the $20 Stetson, so substituted a war-surplus olive green sun helmet. Luce issued me brass collar ornaments and a silver badge proclaiming my status as a "U.S. Park Ranger."

Thus clothed in unprecedented authority, I took station on Custer Hill next to the monument. Every day, in the blazing Montana sun, I met all who came, told them as little or as much as they wanted to know about the battle, and answered their questions.

Most compelling, I got to know—and stand in awe of—Captain Luce. He talked a lot about himself. Some of his history, I learned later, rested on less than solid foundations, but I questioned nothing, only marveled. He had been born into a patrician Boston family; his grandfather, Admiral Stephen Luce, had founded the Navy War College. Edward went to Harvard Medical School but got himself expelled for engaging in professional boxing. In 1907, ignoring parental displeasure, he enlisted in the Seventh Cavalry. As a headquarters clerk at Fort Riley, Kansas, he took down the reminiscences of the four surviving officers who had fought at the Little Bighorn. Luce served two hitches, including a tour in the Philippines, and ultimately rose to first sergeant of Troop B.

I delighted in his story of the brief interlude between enlistments. He returned to Massachusetts and, to taunt his disapproving family, took a job as assistant motorman of a streetcar plying the route in front of the family home. Chief Motorman Spellman would become Francis Cardinal Spellman—at least so Luce claimed. One day when the young man was dozing on a bale of hay in the car barn, a familiar tune issuing from the instrument of an organ grinder roused him. It was "Garryowen," the regimental battle song of the Seventh Cavalry. Luce awoke looking at a monkey that reminded him of the captain of Troop E, flipped a nickel into the tin cup, and rushed off to reenlist.

In retrospect, some of his wonderful stories seem embroidered if not altogether invented. Was he really aboard a troop transport torpedoed in World War I, cast on a rocky island with Ty Cobb, and rescued by the German submarine itself? Underlying the stories, however, as I confirmed much later, was a foundation of truth, however elastic. Luce did serve in the Seventh Cavalry. He may have fought with Mexican revolutionaries along the border. He was commissioned a quartermaster captain in World War I. That he commanded a battalion of black machine gunners I doubt, but the tales he told of that outfit were hilarious. That he engaged in a grim tableau of hide-and-seek with a German officer, both with pistols drawn and a barn between them, may also have been fictional. Probably he did suffer, as he contended, from a German gas attack, which led to his retirement at war's end.

In the 1920s, Luce said, he gravitated to Wall Street and became a "quarter of a millionaire" before the crash. He also worked with retired general Nelson A. Miles, Elizabeth Custer, and Montana's

Senator Thomas J. Walsh in a vain effort to persuade Congress to authorize a museum at the battlefield to house the widow's extensive collection of her husband's memorabilia. Luce talked little of the 1930s, but for a time in 1938 he returned to the Seventh Cavalry, at Fort Bliss, Texas, to work in the regiment's historical records, which he would one day see deposited at the Custer Battlefield for the use of researchers. He also wrote a book, *Keogh, Comanche and Custer,* which he published privately in 1939 and which did not reveal him as a very good historian.

Meanwhile, Custer Battlefield, along with other historic places under the War Department's jurisdiction, had been marked for transfer to the National Park Service. Probably through his Seventh Cavalry connections, Cap Luce got himself designated the first National Park Service superintendent. For a time he learned cemetery administration at Arlington National Cemetery—he told me he had been assistant superintendent. Early in 1941 he and Evelyn moved into the little stone house in the Custer Battlefield National Cemetery. For the first time he donned the uniform of the National Park Service.

Six years later I put on the same uniform. I did very well that first summer, as the Luces gently but firmly instructed me in my new responsibilities and made patient allowance for the immaturity of their young historical aide. As the captain wrote my father on September 7, 1947, Bob "made himself, in the jitterbug jargon— 'solid' not only with the Park Service but with all with whom he came in contact." And he added: "We want him back here next year. If he wants to come."

If he wants to come! He surely did. I came back every summer during college, for a total of six from 1947 to 1952. In the summers of 1948 and 1949, I had a companion—none other than my childhood friend from Bauxite, Reyman Branting, then studying engineering at Rensselaer Polytechnic in Troy, New York. At my behest, Luce made him a historical aide, too. In 1950 and 1951 a Purdue classmate of mine, Jim DeCamp of Cincinnati, took Branting's place. The final summer I came alone.

For the 1948 summer Luce arranged with the Indian Bureau to rent Branting and me half of the "Teacherage," a rundown duplex where schoolteachers lived in the winter. We had two rooms, a bathroom, a kitchen, and a screened porch. We had no refrigerator and only a huge black cooking range, fired by coal, that did not function well. Once I baked a cherry pie all night before it could be pronounced done, though scarcely edible.

We made close friends with two range specialists on the reservation payroll, Rayne Pilgeram and a giant, soft-spoken Crow Indian named Albert Perkins. As an Indian, Al was not constrained by hunting laws, and we four often dined on grouse and pheasant. Saturday nights we drove in Rayne's Ford to Hardin, fifteen miles up the highway. At the Hilltop Tavern we would have a perfectly broiled T-bone steak and french fries, amply washed down with the spirits that attracted throngs of cowboys and Russian beet farmers to the popular watering place.

Jim DeCamp and I had the Teacherage for the summer of 1950, but the next year it was unavailable. Ever resourceful, Luce arranged for us to set up cots on the stage of the high school gymnasium. The athletes' shower rooms furnished a bath, and across the basketball court was a kitchen, with modern appliances, including a refrigerator. For the first time we could cook in style. To celebrate that, after overcoming repeated resistance, we persuaded the Luces to be our dinner guests. We served Cap's favorite highball (bourbon and ginger ale), turned out quite nice steaks with potatoes, and ended with a pie we baked ourselves. The only thing missing was a bottle of wine.

I grew up in a strictly dry household. Neither liquor nor tobacco had any place in the family. My parents could not conceive that their children would ever allow alcohol to pass their lips. In 1948, however, Dad was transferred to ALCOA's East St. Louis laboratory, leaving me on my own for room and board during the balance of my enrollment at Purdue. From fellow students at Addie Meador's boardinghouse, most of whom were war veterans, I discovered that alcohol did not seem the evil declared by my father.

Cap Luce's example surely had a bearing on my plunge. Frequently on one of my days off, he would let me ride with him and Evelyn to Billings, sixty miles to the north, for their shopping. Actually, Evelyn did the shopping. Luce would take me with him to the bar in the Northern Hotel, where he was a frequent enough customer to have his own bottle of Southern Comfort tucked away on a corner shelf. We would crawl onto the bar stools. Luce would call for his usual and loudly announce, so everyone could hear, "and give the boy a Coca Cola; he's not old enough to drink."

The summer after I turned twenty-one, in 1951, we duly made our way to the Northern Hotel bar. Before he could open his mouth, however, I boomed out an order for a bourbon and soda and instructed the bartender to give my companion a Coke, for he was not old enough to drink.

Luce smoked long Pall Malls in a cigarette holder. One summer, to Mrs. Luce's intense disapproval, I showed up smoking Pall Malls. Not for twenty years could I break the addiction. Luce could not at all. Ordered to quit smoking after a heart episode, he clung secretly to his Pall Malls, trying to hide the reality from Evelyn. Each evening, after dinner, he went out to water the flowers and talk with the rabbits, each of which bore the name either of a Greek philosopher or a long-remembered comrade in the Seventh Cavalry. Then, hidden by trees or buildings, he would light up. Evelyn, of course, knew exactly what he was up to, as she later told me, but decided that he would smoke less if he had to do it in secret. Occasionally, she would come outside and call to him, thus giving enough warning for him quickly to douse the cigarette and kick it under a pine tree.

For my last year, 1952, none of the earlier housing arrangements was possible. I had a room above the Crow Lunch next to the one occupied by a friendly Crow widow, Martha Long Neck. Blanketed and moccasined like most of the older Indian women, she was a good neighbor and a good friend. Mike Baca's cooking had not improved, however, although I made do as I had six years earlier.

Also in these later years I became more properly uniformed. When Reyman Branting left, he sold me his Stetson hat, that distinctive mark of the national park ranger. For inclement weather I had bought a billed cap similar to those policemen wear, a headgear no longer sported in the Service. And, most stylish of all, I had the uniform contractor make me an Ike jacket, that waist-length

garment popularized by General Eisenhower in the war. On the
lapels my mother embroidered in yellow thread the USNPS emblem
we wore in brass on our shirt collars. It was distinctly nonregu-
lation and would not be tolerated in today's Park Service.

The late 1940s were frantic for the national cemetery, as World
War II dead were removed from overseas cemeteries and returned
home. We reburied many of them in the Custer Battlefield National
Cemetery—on one day fourteen.

Full military honors accompanied each reinterment. The army
sent a firing squad and a bugler from Fort Douglas, Utah. More
often than not, the bugler could not bugle. He had simply said he
could to escape garrison drudgery. I could bugle, and soon, using
the cemetery's long cavalry trumpet, I sounded taps for all the burials.

Most of the returns occurred during the summer of 1948, and
in such numbers as to strain the small monument staff to the
limit. Not only did I play taps, but Reyman Branting and I pitched
in with the cemetery laborers to help dig the graves and, later, to
fill them in. Luce quipped that Utley not only prepared their
beds but sang them to sleep and tucked them in.

In my daily hikes to and from work, I usually paused at the little
souvenir shop in the valley below the ridge-top park. This was the
place run by the big, hearty, fun-loving woman Luce had contemptuously dismissed as "Prayrie Mayrie." Mary Jane Williams had a
considerable brood of children and a husband somewhat defi-
cient in ambition and energy. Her shop brought in most of the
family income. She was a hospitable, generous woman, unde-
serving of Luce's ridicule. We became good friends and remained
so until her death years later from cancer.

She stocked pop and candy, the usual array of tacky souvenirs,
postcards, and a few publications about the battle. At the battlefield,
in addition to the free leaflet, we sold a sixteen-page brochure,
written by the Luces, for fifteen cents. We also stocked postcards,
especially made for us by a Billings photographer. Although we
sold these items, the inventory and profits belonged to the nonprofit
Custer Battlefield Historical and Museum Association, formed a
few years earlier by Luce and some Billings friends. The meager
profits paid for needed items the government would not fund.

Gradually the thought dawned that perhaps I could write a history of the battle, somehow get it published, and have Mary Jane sell it at the Battlefield Souvenir Shop. She thought that a grand idea. Through my freshman and sophomore years at Purdue, as time permitted, I labored on a manuscript. I even persuaded my old high school mentor, Mr. Siler, to look it over and help me get it right.

At Mary Jane's shop, near the end of my first summer tour, I met a fellow Hoosier—R. C. "Rock" Jenkins, a prosperous businessman from Orleans, in southern Indiana—and his wife. I had no sooner returned home than he wrote to invite me for a weekend visit to talk about Custer and the history of the West. He had a large collection of frontier photographer David Barry's historic photographs as well as other western memorabilia. I went and we had a grand time.

As we corresponded over the next year, I told him about my manuscript and asked him to read it. He liked it and encouraged my ambition to see it in print. Hoping I might plant an idea in his mind, I replied that money was the only problem. Rock told me to find a printer, and he would lend me the money. I did, in Lafayette, and by the spring of 1949 I had a thousand copies of *Custer's Last Stand: With a Narrative of Events Preceding and Following.* It contained fifty-two slick-paper pages, pictures of officers and Indians, and a couple of crudely drawn maps. A yellow card stock cover bore the title, my drawing of crossed sabers with a seven in the angle, and those stirring words "Copyright 1949 by the author." Rock Jenkins paid the bill, $365.

What a stirring experience to see one's words in print for the first time! Glaringly amateurish, laden with purple prose and strings of adjectives, reflecting Luce's adoration of Custer and abhorrence of Reno and Benteen, it is not a work that I now, more than half a century later, look back on with pride.

But Mary Jane thought it was a great sales item, and it did sell well, especially when she told customers that its author was the boy they talked with up at the battlefield. Today the Park Service would pronounce the enterprise a flagrant conflict of interest. No one objected then. Luce was proud of his protégé, an author at nineteen. Eventually, Mary Jane sold the entire printing, at seventy-five cents each. I paid off the loan from Rock Jenkins and made a few dollars' profit. Today, a copy occasionally turns up in used-book catalogues for several hundred dollars.

Another who read and commented on my draft text was R. G. Cartwright. "Cartie" was an athletic coach at the high school in Lead, in South Dakota's Black Hills. A short, balding little fellow with horn-rimmed spectacles, he spent a lot of time trying to work through the puzzles of the Custer Battlefield. I met him the first summer, and we walked the battlefield for hours as he told of his years of study and the theories to which they had led. He knew war firsthand, having been a battlefield dispatch runner in World War I. Where Luce was dogmatic, Cartie was always open-minded and objective. I learned much about history from him. He had no ambition to publish, only to satisfy in his own mind what had happened and why.

Cartie invited me to stop in Lead for a visit on my way home that fall of 1947. I rode a bus to Lead and spent a couple of days with him and his wife, who made no secret of her total lack of interest in Cartie's obsession. We retraced Custer's trail through the Black Hills with the expedition of 1874, visited the graves of Wild Bill Hickok and Calamity Jane in Deadwood's Mount Moriah Cemetery, and examined the exhibits in the Deadwood Museum. But the highlight of the days with Cartie was a front-porch visit with one of his oldest friends—Charles A. Windolph.

Charlie was ninety-seven that year. A German immigrant who signed up in the cavalry to learn English, Windolph found himself a private in Captain Benteen's H Troop on June 25, 1876. Charlie told of his admiration for Benteen, of lying in a shallow trench on Reno Hill as the Indians fired from all sides, of Benteen walking the lines seemingly oblivious to the bullets lacing the hilltop and pausing by Charlie. "Stand up here, Charlie," he commanded, "and look at all those Indians." He was scared, Charlie remembered, but he stood up. Although hit in the leg by a Sioux bullet, he acquitted himself well enough in the fight that Benteen gave him a battlefield promotion to sergeant. Listening to the old man reach back in time with memories still vivid gave me a treasured personal glimpse of history. I had sat on the front porch talking with a man who had actually fought in the Battle of the Little Bighorn.

Three years later Charles Windolph died, the last white survivor save one of the Battle of the Little Bighorn. That summer of 1950 I again rode the bus down to Lead. Cartie entrusted me with a treasure trove of artifacts to carry back to Custer Battlefield: Windolph's discharge papers, signed by Captain Benteen; Windolph's Medal of Honor, awarded for bravery at the Battle of the Little Bighorn; and the Purple Heart that recognized his wound on Reno Hill.

Cap Luce ran Custer Battlefield National Monument the way he had once run the Seventh's B Troop as its top sergeant. Only Evelyn's gentle counsel qualified his absolute rule over his 750-acre domain. He and his staff, including his historical aides, expressed in every action his dedication to protection and care of the battlefield and service to the public. No visitors left without as full an understanding and appreciation of the historical values of the area as they wished—and a feeling too that they had been well treated. No trash or even scrap of paper was allowed for long to deface the area. The ten-acre national cemetery received loving care. Every corner of Custer Battlefield bore evidence of the superintendent's scrutiny and rigid standards.

National Park Service bureaucrats never entirely adjusted to the superintendent they had inherited from the War Department. He decided what he wanted and went for it with disarming but unremitting persistence—as he demonstrated in getting me hired at the age of seventeen. When he failed to have his way in the Omaha regional office, he would drop in on the Washington office during the annual autumn vacation he and Evelyn took in the East. Often the Washington officials, charmed by his blandishments, saw merits the regional officials had overlooked. Although kept constantly off balance by his unorthodoxies, the Park Service came to view Cap Luce almost as an institution—the colorful, warmly hospitable, endlessly entertaining, and above all vigilant guardian of the hill charged to his custody.

If he could have this effect on career veterans of the Park Service, imagine the effect he had on me. I idolized the man and his wife. I fiercely defended him when maintenance workers labeled his stories invented. In my youthful innocence, I detected no flaw in his character, though ample flaws he exhibited for those who looked. I detected none in Evelyn either, and none were there. In retrospect, I credit Cap Luce and Evelyn with as much influence as my parents in shaping my character and charting the path I would follow into adulthood. Perhaps more.

CHAPTER 4

ONE BRIGHT SUNDAY MORNING in 1948, I had the early shift—to open the battlefield at seven o'clock. As I trudged the final steep slope to the entrance gate, a big Buick pulled to the side of the road in front of me. It was one of those postwar models, with bulging fenders that swept from the front wheel well to the rear. I was invited to ride for the short distance remaining.

The driver was a slight balding fellow with a Clark Gable mustache, horn-rimmed glasses, a soft voice, and a friendly manner. His attractive black-haired wife (a French Canadian) sat beside him. I climbed into the back seat next to their young daughter. The driver introduced himself as Dr. Lawrence Frost, a podiatrist from Monroe, Michigan. He headed the county historical society, whose interests centered on the city's most famous son, George Armstrong Custer. More to the point, the Frosts were close friends of the Custer descendants. Three brothers, George, Tom, and Boston, had been killed at the Little Bighorn, leaving only Nevin, the farmer who stayed on his farm, to carry forward the line of Emanuel Custer. Although a close student of the Custers, Dr. Frost had never visited the battleground where those three brothers, with a nephew and a brother-in-law, had perished.

I never disturbed the Luces' early morning leisure unless for compelling reason, especially Sunday mornings. I believed, however, that the Frosts constituted such a reason. They did. The captain and Evelyn warmly welcomed these emissaries from Custer's hometown.

The friendship was cemented a year later, in October 1949, when the Luces stopped in Monroe on their annual eastern jaunt. Dr. Frost introduced them to the resident Custer clan, the aging son and daughter of Nevin and two granddaughters, and all got along famously. Luce wrote me about them all, adding that two grandsons of Nevin—grandnephews of the general—were on active duty with the army. One, Charles, was an infantry major at Fort Lewis, Washington. The other, Brice, had recently served on occupation duty in Japan as, with ironic coincidence, lieutenant colonel of the Seventh Cavalry, and in a further irony, he now commanded the reserve unit in Billings, Montana.

The pause in Monroe lengthened when the captain came down with viral pneumonia. He nearly died before recovering enough to leave the hospital for a bed in the Park Hotel. Day after day he lay in that room staring at the ceiling. Gradually he became obsessed with the belief that the plaster ceiling verged on collapse. Evelyn ridiculed the notion but gave in to his demand for another room. The next day the ceiling fell in.

As Evelyn nursed the captain back to health at a beachside hotel in Florida, I resolved to visit Monroe myself. Between semesters of my junior year at Purdue, in February 1950, I bused to Monroe. I too stayed in the Park Hotel. Larry Frost welcomed me, but as tour guides I picked up two other Custer enthusiasts, H. B. Berry and his son John. Berry served as a corrections officer at the federal prison in Milan, Michigan. He took two days' leave to squire me around. He and John saw to it that I met all the Monroe Custers and visited all the Custer sites—the Custer homes, the cemetery with its many Custers, the Presbyterian church where Libbie and Autie were married in 1864, the impressive equestrian statue of the general, and the treasures of the local historical society. It was a wonderful as well as educational experience, thanks to the helpful hospitality of Berry, Frost, and the Custer clan.

Soon after reporting for duty at Custer Battlefield for the fourth summer, in June 1950, I rode to Billings with the Luces. Besides the usual visit to the Northern Hotel bar, the captain took me to the army reserve headquarters and introduced me to Lieutenant Colonel Brice C. W. Custer. I thought him the most magnificent soldier I had ever seen. With ramrod posture, graying hair, stern visage, the infantry's crossed rifles and his rank's silver oak leaf on his collar points, his chest ablaze with ribbons and the Combat Infantryman Badge, he stood as the epitome of World War II battlefield leadership. Yet he was also a genial, kindly man with a keen sense of humor.

I remember June 25, 1950, for three reasons. It was the seventy-fourth anniversary of the Battle of the Little Bighorn. It was the day the North Koreans invaded South Korea, an event not without an ultimate effect on me. And on this day Brice Custer showed up with his two sons. The older, Second Lieutenant George Armstrong Custer III, had overseas orders and wanted to tour the battlefield before leaving. The younger, Brice, Jr., was an engineering student at Michigan State University. We had a great tour, especially as I worshipped the very name *Custer* and had only a few months earlier met the Monroe Custers, including Brice's father.

Brice and his jovial wife, Lenore, made several visits to the battlefield that summer. The most memorable occurred in mid-July, for Larry Frost showed up too. The trio of Luce, Frost, and Custer bonded instantly and solidly in a friendship always fun loving and frequently studded with harrowing practical jokes—the sort for which the boisterous sons of Emanuel Custer had gained notoriety. Almost always the captain and Brice conspired against "Dr. Foot, the Frost Doctor"—much as Autie and Tom had conspired against brother Boston and other household guests. Once, Luce and Brice conducted a mock trial of Frost for some trumped-up offense, found him guilty, and stretched his neck in a rope noose flung over the limb of a cottonwood tree.

On July 15 my colleague, Jim DeCamp, and I accompanied Luce, Frost, and Custer on an expedition up Reno Creek—the Seventh Cavalry's approach route to the battleground—to the divide between the Rosebud and Little Bighorn watersheds. We intended to climb the "Crow's Nest," the mountain peak from which General Custer first scanned the Little Bighorn Valley at dawn on

June 25, 1876. Luce, with his bad heart, guarded the truck while the rest of us started the climb. Brice did not quite make the summit, but Jim and I prodded a jaded Frost to the top and duly recorded the feat on film. Going down, we found Brice, in another uncanny evocation of his great uncle, propped against a fallen tree indulging the famed "Custer catnap."

Two days later, July 18, we joined in a historic ceremony. At last Congress had appropriated funds for constructing a museum and visitor center on the Custer Battlefield. We would turn the first spadeful of earth. Hardin's Veterans of Foreign Wars and American Legion posts furnished a color guard and firing squad. Luce, Frost, and Custer made speeches. Then Brice dug a shovel into the sandy soil and marked the beginning of construction. I stepped forward to sound taps. Jim DeCamp had teased me while I practiced for this assignment, so Luce found a second trumpet and made him sound a distant echo. July 18, 1950, also marked the day on which Brice Custer received his promotion to full colonel.

August 1950 brought Paramount Pictures to Billings to film *Warpath*, a B Western about the Little Bighorn. James Millican played Custer. Much of the adult Crow population disappeared from their homes to don feathers and breech clouts and shoot at blue-clad extras from Hardin and Billings. Luce had a brief cameo as a cavalry captain. But most appropriately, when Millican/Custer appeared at the head of his column, the bearer of the regimental standard riding beside him was none other than Brice C. W. Custer, sporting the two stripes of a cavalry corporal rather than the silver eagles of his new rank.

Those were exciting, engrossing summers, the high point of each college year. I did not do very well at Purdue the first two years. Incurable militarist that I was, however, I loved ROTC (Reserve Officers' Training Corps), and in my second year I even sewed on the stripes of a staff sergeant. I eagerly looked forward to entering senior ROTC and emerging with the beautiful pinks and greens of an army second lieutenant. Alas, the medics found my blood pressure an unacceptable 155/84, and I had to give up the ambition.

At some point the idea took root that I should finish four years at Purdue and get a bachelor's degree before entering law school at Indiana, instead of transferring after three years. And at some point beyond that, as I took more and more history courses, the notion of abandoning history for law became increasingly distasteful. I did stay for the fourth year at Purdue, and probably by then the only ambition I entertained was to become the permanent park historian at Custer Battlefield National Monument—if and when such a position were established.

At Purdue all my history professors found me an outstanding student, and they consistently gave me high marks for term papers and course work. The professor I recall most vividly was Louis Martin Sears. He was a huge, elderly, intimidating man with a burr haircut, horn-rimmed glasses, and a frightening habit of suddenly, while lecturing, bending to present himself face-to-face with a dozing student and shout a question or admonition. Dr. Sears was a bachelor who had a room at the Student Union Building during the school year and spent each summer at the Cosmos Club in Washington, D.C. He could be observed in the cafeteria each morning, hidden behind his copy of the *Chicago Tribune*. His political views coincided with those of the paper's editor and publisher, Colonel Robert R. McCormick. With McCormick, Dr. Sears suffered a consuming hatred of Franklin Roosevelt, which he made no effort to soften in the classroom. Under the Sears influence, doubtless fortified by Indiana's senatorial delegation of Capehart and Jenner and my own congressman, Charles Halleck, I too became a vocal right-winger. Captain Luce's conservative views reinforced the trend.

I caught the notice of Dr. Sears in his survey course in American history. I told him the textbook's brief treatment of the Battle of the Little Bighorn was all wrong. He invited me to stand before the class and tell what really happened. I did, and thereafter, as I took more of his courses, Dr. Sears came to consider me his protégé. When he invited me to dine with him at a Lafayette restaurant, however, I grew apprehensive. As a lifelong bachelor, he stirred campus gossip about his sexual orientation, and I worried that I might be an object of more than professional interest. The fears proved groundless. Except for his influence on my early political convictions, he proved a splendid mentor and probably played a major role in finally turning me from law to history.

Whatever the timing, by my senior year I had resolved to enter graduate school at Indiana University and begin work on a master's degree in history. Beyond that, I also resolved, I would quit asking my draft board for educational deferment and play whatever part in the Korean War the government might decree.

June 25, 1951, marked the seventy-fifth anniversary of the Battle of the Little Bighorn. Cap Luce and the Hardin American Legion Post had succeeded in promoting a star-studded commemoration. The governor came down from Helena to join with an array of brass representing all the military services. The army's Lieutenant General Albert C. Wedemeyer, recently a controversial China hand, gave the principal address. President Truman sent Fleet Admiral William D. Leahy, FDR's chief of staff during the war. Dewey Beard (Horn Cloud), a youth at the Little Bighorn and a warrior at Wounded Knee, stood in behalf of the Sioux.

For Cap Luce and me alike, however, the awesome attraction was the assemblage of high-ranking brass. All those glittering stars so excited Luce that he drove the government car without releasing the emergency brake, which caught fire.

Brice Custer was there, of course, together with another colonel whom I came to admire and ultimately treasure as a friend: William A. "Wild Bill" Harris. Representing the Seventh Cavalry, Colonel Harris had just returned from Korea, where he had commanded the regiment from September 1950 to April 1951. Years later, after he had retired a major general and settled in San Antonio, he welcomed me whenever my travels took me there. Over dinner at his club, he regaled me with stories of his adventures in Korea. Like Custer, he cultivated a distinctive persona, marked by a walking cane, a cavalry saddle on the hood of his jeep, and a large plywood cutout of the Garryowen regimental crest mounted on the bumper.

Harris had led the Seventh in the dash northward after the break-out from the Pusan Perimeter. "Billy" told me he had assumed command of a dispirited, ineffective outfit. Taught to believe that they fought to hold back the communist scourge, the men could not relate to that, he said. So he told them what they really were fighting for was the honor of the Seventh Cavalry and the memory of General Custer and the Little Bighorn. Fixing loyalties to the regiment aided immensely, together with Harris's own fiery brand of leadership. Also, he cared deeply for his men and gained an enviable reputation for constant preoccupation with the comfort and wants of his soldiers. Under Harris the Seventh turned in a distinguished combat record in Korea.

Despite damp, chilly weather, the anniversary observance drew some seventy-five hundred people, who watched General Wedemeyer lay a wreath at the monument, then gathered at the rostrum in the national cemetery for the program. Proudly adorned with my Stetson "flat hat," I mingled with the crowd as honor guards, flag ceremonies, and speeches paid homage to America's military heritage. Several feathered warbonnets dotted the horde of dignitaries who crowded the rostrum, colorful yet token reminders of another heritage, a heritage overwhelmed that day by the array of generals, admirals, and political luminaries.

That autumn of 1951 I settled into a little rooming house in Bloomington, Indiana, a few blocks from the campus of Indiana University. I resolved to win my master's degree in history in two semesters, which I did. Oscar Osborne Winther, the faculty's specialist in the history of the American West, became my major professor. I found him gentle, kindly, and likable, but not especially helpful. He was an abominable lecturer and a mediocre writer, but his scholarship was widely recognized in the profession. For years I benefited from the label of "Winther student."

To his credit, he grudgingly allowed me to write a master's thesis about Custer, a concession that met with frosty skepticism among others of the history faculty. It would be a historiographical study: a history of the history of the Battle of the Little Bighorn. I dug into the origins of what would become a mighty, self-perpetuating engine of history and legend, exploring the contributions of the newspapers, contemporary military commentators, popular writers, the Indians themselves, and of course the most powerful influence of them all, Frederick Whittaker.

"The Custer Controversy: An Historiographical Study of the Battle of the Little Bighorn for the Period 1876 to 1900" was several cuts superior to my 1949 brochure, but it still reeked of amateurism. Even so, I survived the interrogation of a faculty committee that could not quite take seriously a scholarly work on so superficial a subject as General Custer.

I left Bloomington in June 1952 with my thesis, my parchment, and a Selective Service rating of 1-A. I also left with an understanding that, when my military obligation had been discharged, I would come back and study under Dr. Winther for a Ph.D. in history. He at least thought that, despite my fixation on General Custer, I had the makings of a good historian. In those days, as now, that meant the potential to rise to the exalted rank of full professor of history on a university faculty. I was not sure that was what I wanted to do with my life.

The Luces welcomed me back for my final summer at Custer Battlefield. Now, however, it was *Major* Luce, not Captain Luce. I never quite understood how the promotion came about, but I think Brice Custer convinced Luce that he could use the rank he had attained in the army reserves in the 1920s. My first alert to the new protocol came to me at Indiana University in the form of a Lynchburg, Virginia, newspaper. In October 1951 Luce and Brice Custer had journeyed to Appomattox Courthouse, a unit of the National Park System, to present several artifacts from the Elizabeth B. Custer Collection at Custer Battlefield. Most notable among the items intended for display in the museum at Appomattox were the white towel that had been borne to General Custer in token of General Lee's decision to surrender and the small table on which the surrender document had been signed. General Sheridan had bought the latter from the owner of the house and presented it to Libbie Custer. Also transferred were the battle flags of two Virginia regiments captured by Tom Custer, George's brother, in the battles that led to Lee's surrender.

The newspaper that reached me bore a front-page photo of Luce, Brice, and the Appomattox superintendent holding the surrender flag. The accompanying article detailed the ceremonies and summarized Luce's speech. Bold black headlines proclaimed "Major Luce Voices Hope for World Peace." And so I returned to Custer Battlefield to work my final summer for a newly self-promoted chief.

June 25, 1952, did not draw the throng that had celebrated the seventy-fifth anniversary a year earlier. Despite a cold rain, however, twelve hundred people turned out for a more significant ceremony— dedication of the visitor center and museum for which we had turned the first spadeful of earth two years earlier. Brice Custer came, as did Colonel Billy Harris. This year the military celebrity wore four stars—General Jonathan M. Wainwright, the "Skinny Wainwright" of Corregidor fame who had spent the war years in a Japanese prison camp.

The new building lay at the foot of Custer Hill, between the monument above and the national cemetery below. Later generations of park planners would correctly judge it an intrusion on the historic scene. But it liberated us from the tiny office in the stone house and provided ample office space, a sales counter, and a museum. A glass viewing room and deck on the monument side commanded a sweeping view of the battlefield and provided me with a large topographical model on which to base my talks. No more greeting visitors under the blazing Montana sun at the monument—a loss in interpretive effectiveness, as it later seemed.

The museum—one of only two funded by Congress in the decade following the war—was the creation of Ned J. Burns, chief of the Park Service Museum Branch, who proudly attended the opening. Everyone admired the result—his last, it turned out, before an untimely death. Two meticulously detailed dioramas drew the most acclaim, one of Reno's retreat from the Little Bighorn bottoms, the other of the last stand itself. Display cases exhibited Custer's uniforms and other personal memorabilia lovingly preserved for this very purpose by Libbie Custer. Other exhibits portrayed the weapons and uniforms of the frontier army (including Charlie Windolph's Medal of Honor) and traced the story of the campaign leading to the Little Bighorn. The Sioux and Northern Cheyennes had a few exhibits, too, but they paled in contrast to the splashes of army blue and gold.

Because of the rain, the program had to be held in the observation room, with onlookers crowded under the surrounding portico peering through the glass. A highlight was the introduction of General Wainwright, who presented Luce with an 1866 Winchester repeating rifle. His father, adjutant of the First Cavalry at Fort Custer in 1887, had taken it from a Crow warrior in the Sword Bearer religious upheaval of that year. Reputedly, a Sioux or Cheyenne warrior had dropped the weapon during the Battle of the Little Bighorn, and the Crow had picked it up on the battlefield shortly after the fight. As cameras recorded the presentation, I stood just to Luce's right—and just outside the photograph. The Winchester found its way into a display case of Indian arms.

Before departing, General Wainwright also presented Major Luce with a bottle of Scotch whiskey. Immediately dubbed the "Wainwright bottle," it was tucked into a far corner of the top shelf of the kitchen cupboard, to be tapped only on the most special occasions.

This summer I had no university registration deadline. The only deadline I faced came courtesy of the Tippecanoe County Selective Service Board: report for induction into the United States Army at Butte, Montana, on October 12, 1952—three weeks shy of my twenty-third birthday. The Luces decided to take their annual pilgrimage to the East in September. For a full month, therefore, as the crowning climax of my experience on that haunting Montana hilltop and as an ultimate accolade of the Luces' confidence in me, I served as acting superintendent of Custer Battlefield National Monument.

In those postwar years, the dominant theme at Custer Battlefield mirrored the dominant theme in my young life. The generals and admirals who showed up for ceremonies, the colonels who came regularly to consort with *Major* Luce, stood as symbols of the story we told on Custer Hill, in the little stone house in the national cemetery, and finally in our grand new museum itself. It was the story of a "cavalier in buckskin," as I would later title a biography of Custer, a dashing and flamboyant hero who led brave cavalry to their doom in the lofty cause of opening the West to civilization. It was a story that exalted America's military heritage, so recently ennobled tenfold on the battlefields of Europe and the Pacific and destined for half a century of celebration in the global struggle with communism.

The Indians of course played a part in this story—the Sioux and Cheyennes as the enemy who had wiped out Custer, the Crows and Arikaras as the scouts and auxiliaries in the war against their tribal enemies. But in our telling, these Indians emerged less as real people than as cardboard cutouts, impersonal foils for blue-coated frontiersmen battling to clear the way for sturdy westering pioneers. Our perspective was that of those who won the West, not those who lost the West.

Later generations would look in contempt on the story we told and demand a "balance" that easily strayed beyond to an opposite imbalance. I was part of those later generations and, endowed with new insights and perspectives, participated in the quest for balance. But I have never looked back in contempt or shame. We were products of our time and place, reflecting the larger society. We thought and behaved just as our later critics would have thought and behaved had they been our contemporaries.

Major and Evelyn Luce, Brice Custer, Billy Harris, Larry Frost, Cartie, Reyman Branting and Jim DeCamp, Rayne Pilgeram and Al Perkins, as well as the adventures and personal growth of those years at Custer Battlefield—all stand forth to this day in retrospect as defining people and events. I would change nothing about them even if I could.

CHAPTER 5

THE INDUCTION STATION IN Butte, Montana, was as worn and dismal as the rotting old mining town itself. The crowd of draftees lined up naked to endure the first of the indignities that would soon become routine to the new way of life. Each of us presented every feature of our anatomy for the impersonal probings of the medics. I desperately wanted to return to Custer Battlefield, and I thought, just maybe, high blood pressure would allow me to retreat from an increasingly scary future. But a reading too high for ROTC apparently did not disqualify one for service as an infantry rifleman. With others, now clothed again, I raised my right hand and swore the oath that transformed me into a recruit in the United States Army.

The Milwaukee Railroad deposited us in Seattle, Washington, and an olive-drab bus conveyed us to nearby Fort Lewis. The recruit reception center gave further introduction to the new way of life: my beautiful black hair shorn to the skull; my arms and posterior riddled with inoculations; uniforms, fatigues, and other equipment tossed across a counter to fill a duffel bag; a portrait snapped in the new uniform against the backdrop of an American flag to be sent home; and "donation" of a considerable quantity of blood for some wounded soldier in Korea.

Finally, after chow in a mess hall, we dragged ourselves to our barracks with visions of collapsing on the double-decked bunks. But here we met our barracks sergeant, a truly sadistic brute just back from Korea. He kept us up long past midnight scrubbing the latrine, mopping the floors, and standing at attention by our bunks as he bestrode the aisle shouting insults and obscenities. For most of us, the labors of day and night combined with a diminished blood supply proved too much. Several of us fainted, I among them.

Fort Lewis introduced me to KP—kitchen police. My first such experience found me assigned to "Pots and Pans," the very worst of the mess-hall chores, especially under the glare of a tyrannical mess sergeant. The aura of all those immaculately uniformed officers at Custer Battlefield seemed remote indeed. Pots and Pans left me with a pervasive sense that this was no life for a gentleman. To be a gentleman, however, one also had to be an officer. Over that greasy, grimy sink, amid stacks of greasy, grimy kettles, I resolved to become an officer and a gentleman.

An antiquated C-46 flew us south to California, where we wound up at Camp Roberts, a sprawling base in the rough brown hills north of Paso Robles. Camp Roberts was the home of the Seventh Armored Division, reconstituted as a training outfit for infantry riflemen. It would be my home for a year. First, because my papers disclosed more than the usual education, I entered an eight-week training cycle, designed to provide the rudiments of soldiering for those destined for office jobs. Near the close of the eight weeks, however, my name somehow found its way to a list of men reassigned to a sixteen-week cycle, designed to prepare men for shipment to Korea as infantry riflemen.

Thus I learned to fire M-1 rifles, carbines, pistols, light and heavy machine guns, light and heavy mortars, and anti-tank rocket launchers; to toss hand grenades; and to wield the bayonet. The instructor explained that the troughs on either side of the blade allowed your victim's blood to exit and thus eased the bayonet's withdrawal. By that time, I wondered what I had gotten myself into.

I especially recall the two-week bivouac that capped the sixteen-week cycle. We pitched our pup tents in the remote ruggedness of the Hunter-Liggett Military Reservation. Here word reached us that Joseph Stalin had died. Here too we geared up for a fourteen-mile hike, I toting the heavy tripod of a machine gun in addition to my pack and rifle. We ended on a hilltop and dug in for a perimeter defense against a nighttime attack by the "Aggressors," a force maintained to confront trainees with live enemies. As dusk fell, I ate a C ration of cold pork and beans, then made my way to the foot of the hill to heed a call of nature. I had no sooner dropped my pants and squatted than the woods exploded. Trees surrounding the base of the hill had been wired with explosives to simulate a mortar bombardment preparatory to an enemy attack. The chore unfinished, I scrambled back to my foxhole and fired off countless clips of blank cartridges to help my comrades repel the Aggressor attack.

Determined to become an officer and gentleman, I had applied for Officer Candidate School (OCS). In Sixth Army, in contrast to all other continental army commands, one had to attend an infantry leaders' course before assignment to OCS. That meant another eight weeks, these even more tightly packed with rigorous training and stern discipline. A blue helmet liner and black arm brassard with a yellow star burst marked us as the elite of Camp Roberts. I had begun to look on myself as a gung-ho soldier, and a pretty good one at that.

An event delightfully revealing of the ethic of leaders' course occurred when a Swedish general visited Camp Roberts. A contingent of us "blue bonnets" formed the welcoming honor guard. We starched and ironed our khakis to perfection, spit-polished our combat boots, and waxed and buffed our helmets. Nothing could be permitted to mar the starched excellence of our khakis. The pockets had been starched shut, admitting nothing. We ate lunch standing up because sitting would crease the trousers. For the same reason, other trainees lifted us onto a platform and then into the bed of a truck, where we rode standing to the huge parade ground where the general's plane would land. There a length of string was stretched on the pavement to align our glistening boots in exact precision, then withdrawn. In due course the general's light plane landed and taxied to our position. We snapped to attention and presented arms. He dismounted, trooped the line, and then was driven off to whatever reception awaited him. Our mission performed, we returned to the company area. This time, we had to climb into the truck bed unaided and at last broke the wall of starch that encased our midsection.

By the time I completed leaders' course, the summer of 1953 was well advanced. The war in Korea had stalemated in an armistice that ended the fighting. The demand for infantry platoon leaders—in combat the most endangered of species—had plummeted, and the OCSs had their quota of graduates drastically reduced. I joined the General Subjects Committee of Division Faculty to lecture basic trainees on the evils of communism and to don the uniform of an Aggressor major to interrogate trainee "prisoners-of-war" and try to bully them into revealing more than their name, rank, and serial number. I often succeeded.

As the need for replacements in Korea diminished, Camp Roberts began to phase out. Division Faculty shrank. I wound up in a holding company, riding shotgun on stockade prisoners. On the very eve of the base's closure in October, possibly because I had to be sent somewhere, I finally received orders posting me to infantry OCS at Fort Benning, Georgia—the "Benning School for Boys."

In Cheyenne, Wyoming, I detrained and boarded a Frontier Airlines DC-3 for a bumpy flight to Billings and thence bused down to Crow Agency. Major and Evelyn bedded me in the upstairs front bedroom of the old stone house. They were glad to see me. Because I was now a soldier, moreover, and a prospective officer at that, Luce conferred on me a rare honor—a draught from the Wainwright bottle.

Pausing in St. Louis to visit my parents, I entrained for Columbus, Georgia. On November 30, 1953, I reported at headquarters of the Tenth Officer Candidate Company in the Harmony Church area of Fort Benning. I thought the demands of leaders' course had prepared me for OCS. I was wrong. A cloud of "tactical officers" descended on each arriving bus of new candidates. The "tacs" were as nattily uniformed as we had been at leaders' course; mine even carried a swagger stick. They wore varnished black helmet liners adorned with a white stripe, the blue "Follow Me" emblem of the Infantry School, and the insignia of their rank. Aiming to eliminate all who could not take it, they hounded us day and night with shouted commands that pushed us to, and sometimes beyond, our physical and psychological limits.

OCS no longer manufactured the "ninety-day wonders" of World War II. The course now lasted six months. Moreover, Korea no longer had an insatiable appetite for second lieutenants, and so the standards had been lifted to "board out" all but the number that could be absorbed by the peacetime army. Tacs wrote out "ORs" (observation reports) for the most trivial misstep—an indignity Cadet Custer endured repeatedly at West Point. Close to two hundred candidates composed our class in November 1953. Fifty-two received their commissions in May 1954.

My tac, Lieutenant Charles Story, decided at once that I had a "defiant look" in my eyes, and he spent the first eight weeks trying to provoke me into taking a swing at him. Defiance was the last thing my eyes held. I grimly put up with the constant abuse and strove to meet every demand. Tacs barked "Drop for fifty!" on the slimmest pretext, or none at all. I had never been able to do legal pushups and so offered a prime target.

As the weeks passed, the abuse began to take on hints of humor, although never betrayed by even the suggestion of a smile. On Easter morning, the tacs turned us out for an egg hunt, a mad scramble powered by all the punitive devices in their ample arsenal.

As candidates by the score fell victim to stacks of ORs, the survivors bonded in a fierce determination to prevail and in a camaraderie that even infected the tacs, though they never relaxed their stern demeanor or permitted the slightest lapse in discipline. In the final weeks we "turned blue"—became Senior Candidates sporting blue helmets like those at the Camp Roberts leaders' course.

Tough as the harassment was, it served only as backdrop to the advance training that produced an infantry platoon leader—weapons again, maps again, tactical problems, PT, PT, and more PT. I had never shone at "physical training" in high school or in basic training, and I did not now. But I discovered for the first time that my physical limitations need not be the only element in the equation. A forced march under full field pack in the Georgia heat and humidity thinned the ranks even of muscular athletes, but I never dropped out. The will to go on proved as important as the physical ability to do so.

By "Blue Bonnet" time, I had no doubt that I would graduate. Then came a harrowing order: your medical records have to be updated before commissioning; report for an exam. I was so scared that it shot my blood pressure even higher than its normal high. The medic tried several times, but the number would not drop. Within two weeks of those gold bars, I saw all the hell of six months a wasted ordeal. In the allotted box, the medic inked in the number and handed the form to me. I looked and saw that he had entered a figure a full twenty points lower than the instrument reading, comfortably under the ceiling. I hope that dear man has had a good life.

Graduation exercises took place in the main post theater on May 26, 1954. The program bore the names of one Honor and Distinguished Graduate and two Distinguished Graduates, all three of whom could receive commissions in the regular army if they wished. My name appeared as a Distinguished Graduate. Dad and Mother had driven down from St. Louis for the occasion. Mother pinned the gold bars on my shoulders.

I had two choices for my first assignment. The Intelligence Committee wanted me to join the faculty of the Infantry School as an instructor. More amazing, the OCS command wanted me to don a varnished black helmet and serve as a tactical officer. Perhaps puffed with my new status as an infantry officer, I chose the latter, even though far more demanding and challenging. After a month's leave with my parents, I moved into a room at the Bachelor Officers Quarters, put on the grim visage and affected the terrifying bearing of a tac, and set forth to transform candidates into officers. A fellow tac was the same Lieutenant Story who had tried to goad me into striking him six months earlier.

I probably did not make a very good tac. Our company commander had a firm rule that no tac would ever be seen smiling by a candidate. That was hard for me. Also, while I could terrorize as well as anyone, I felt sorry for my victims. In short, I became too compassionately involved with my men, too remorseful of the necessity to board out those who could not make the grade.

Since the tac had to set the example, to *appear* superior in every way to every candidate, I found the physical demands daunting. After several weeks of ease, I drew the duty one morning of taking the company on a predawn five-mile run. The men ran with rifles at port arms, while I carried nothing but myself. In the final mile I grew so exhausted and nauseous that I knew I could not go on. Yet neither could I show the candidates anything but a super-human exterior. I shouted, "Last man to the company area gets fifty pushups!" They broke formation and ran while I dropped back to identify the winner of the pushups—and to heave the contents of my stomach. Sometimes hypocrisy is the only solution.

I wanted out, but everyone assured me that no one ever got out of the OC Regiment.

While at Fort Benning, I received a letter from Colonel Billy Harris, then studying at the Army War College. Luce had told him that I had emerged from OCS a Distinguished Graduate, and Harris urged me to apply for a regular army commission. Off and on through my young life, I had thought I wanted to be a pro-fessional soldier. Now I decided that I would not remain in the army but return to Indiana University for my Ph.D. in history. Harris and Luce alike were disappointed.

Once again, however, Luce changed my life. A recent visitor to the battlefield was Lieutenant Colonel Roy E. Appleman, en route from Korea back to Washington, D.C. Appleman had been a combat historian in World War II and had written the army's official history of the Battle of Okinawa. Before and after the war he had been a National Park Service historian, most recently in the Richmond regional office. He had been recalled to active duty to write an official army history of the first year of the Korean War. Luce told him about me and urged him to get me into the army's Office of the Chief of Military History.

Appleman tried but failed. One day, however, he happened to be in the Historical Section of the Joint Chiefs of Staff (JCS), then headed by an old cavalry colonel. Appleman dropped my name at a propitious time. The Historical Section had about a dozen slots for field-grade officers, but it had become a dead end for any field grade who wished to rise higher. The chief of the section, therefore, began filling the field-grade billets with junior officers educated as historians. I fit the need nicely. I drove to Atlanta to be interviewed by Bell Irvin Wiley, the distinguished Civil War historian who also served as an advisor to the JCS historians. I passed his scrutiny.

One day in September 1954 I was summoned to regimental headquarters and reported to the executive officer, Lieutenant Colonel Troutman. He handed me a set of orders directing the transfer of Second Lieutenant Robert M. Utley to the Historical Section, Joint Chiefs of Staff, in the Pentagon—"by command of Matthew B. Ridgway, Chief of Staff, U.S. Army."

"I wish you good luck, Lieutenant," Troutman said. "But tell me one thing: how the hell did you do it?"

CHAPTER 6

At Columbus, Georgia, in the summer of 1954, I had bought a new but plain-Jane Chevrolet for $1,500, with payments extended over years that seemed an eternity. It had no radio, in fact had no heater. I drove it to Washington, D.C., parked in the far end of the Pentagon's north parking lot, and hiked with growing apprehension toward the huge five-sided edifice that would be my workplace for three years. On the ramp to the entrance I met several officers who hardly knew how to respond to my snappy Fort Benning salute.

The Historical Section was part of the Joint Staff, which provided staff support for the Joint Chiefs of Staff. Like the chiefs, their staff was unified—made up of personnel from all the services. The army colonel whom Roy Appleman talked to had given way to an air force colonel, who in time would be replaced by a navy captain. The historians also came from different services. For personnel matters I looked to the next ranking army officer in the chain of command, who happened to be a lieutenant general. That came in handy a couple of times.

The chief of the section was a figurehead. His executive officer provided the continuity and actually ran the office. Air force major Norman E. Cawse-Morgon, my senior by perhaps fifteen years, possessed an exceptional intellect, which he took no pains to conceal.

He read deeply in history, mainly medieval history, employed a huge vocabulary with both oral and written precision, and displayed an uncanny skill in manipulating the military bureaucracy to attain his own ends. He was so smart, so brash, and so quick thinking that he made superior officers feel inferior, which they usually were.

Backing Cawse-Morgon were two men of uncommon talent. Captain Wilbur Hoare of the army's Medical Service Corps, a soft-spoken, painfully deliberate scholar of caustic certitude, had the most formal training. Major Ernest "Gus" Giusti, a rotund little Italian American with a bubbling sense of humor and a chest full of ribbons attesting to his combat record as a marine fighter pilot, rounded out the trio. Bill Moody, an air force major, was a likable mediocrity. New like me, navy lieutenant (junior grade [jg]) Norman B. Ferris had been brought in to replace another junior navy officer who had left for Harvard and ultimately prestigious professional status, Ernest R. May.

Not one of these men had the Ph.D. so prized by the historical profession, but they taught me more about historical method and clear expository writing than I had learned in graduate school. Except for Ferris, moreover, who never quite fit in, we became close personal friends. As the only bachelors, "Cawse" and I grew particularly close—he the mentor, I the protégé.

In the tightly controlled security of the Joint Staff, where no one wandered without special clearance, I quickly became a conspicuous oddity. I was the only second lieutenant in an organization containing 250 generals and admirals. Some laughed and waved at me from the entire length of a corridor. Not so humorous was the day I and a young lady from across the hall gamboled into an intersection of corridors to find ourselves almost trampled by a marching phalanx of five men—the entire Joint Chiefs of Staff. I had never seen so many stars on so few officers.

I found myself a basement room in a residence in north Arlington, but that proved too cramped and expensive. Later I teamed up with another navy jg, Bernie Kohn, to share a little apartment in Alexandria. The furnishings were dingy and sparse, and the only defense against Washington's heat and humidity was an exhaust fan in the kitchen window. But Bernie and I got along well, and we made do with our lodgings.

When I reported for my new assignment in September 1954, shock waves from the French debacle at Dien Bien Phu the previous spring still washed over the Pentagon. The chairman of the JCS, Admiral Arthur Radford, had joined with Vice President Nixon in urging President Eisenhower to take up the French struggle against communism in Indochina. I was proud of the outspoken opposition of my own army chief of staff, General Matthew Ridgway, to getting our country involved in a ground war in Indochina. As a veteran infantryman himself, the president needed no coaching on the perils of that course. Instead, the United States assumed the French burden of supplying arms, ammunition, and advice to France's native surrogates in the war against the followers of Ho Chi Minh.

Ever since World War II the Historical Section had confined its studies largely to that conflict—a fine prescription for extinction in any budget or personnel crisis. To his credit, Admiral Radford wondered whether the historians had something to contribute to present rather than past problems. I had no sooner settled at my desk than he asked for a documented, book-length study of the role of the JCS in the Indochina debacle, from the formation of the JCS during the war until the present. We would have access to all the JCS's top secret files, as well as those of the State Department and the Central Intelligence Agency (CIA). The admiral wanted instant action, but settled for what seemed to us an impossible four-month deadline.

We turned to the project with a vengeance. For four months we researched and wrote day and night and over weekends. Cawse, Wilbur, and Gus proved themselves talented historians and stylists who kept calm under intense pressure and turned out chapter after chapter of first-rate history. I was even assigned a chapter— which served mainly as a vehicle for the most humiliating critique I have ever endured. They showed no mercy or gentleness in shredding my work in style, clarity, precision, handling of evidence, and readability. That devastating experience was the most valuable single lesson in my professional growth. These men had done for me what no professor had done in graduate school, and what few professors do to this day.

Exhausted, we met our deadline in time for a joyous New Year's celebration at the close of 1954. Admiral Radford liked our study, and planners throughout the Joint Staff showered us with acclaim. More important, they all declared it a valuable tool in strategic planning. No more World War II. We were in the business of today, our budget and positions secure.

We did other crisis studies. When the Chinese Communists threatened the islands of Quemoy and Matsu in the continuing effort to destroy Chiang Kai-shek on Formosa, we prepared a study. When the Hungarians rose in revolt against their Russian overlords, we prepared another study. We also kept watch on the unfolding saga in Indochina. My assignment was to monitor all the cable traffic from Saigon to State, Defense, and the CIA, as well as other documentation, and every few months write another chapter to add to our basic study. It was an exhilarating project for a young, untested historian to watch history unfold before his eyes and try to fashion it into a factual and analytical narrative. Cawse, Gus, and Wilbur helped immeasurably in shaping my skills of method and style.

They shaped me in another way too. The three formed a hotbed of liberalism that played havoc with the conservative principles Dr. Sears had planted in me at Purdue. The mid-1950s were the heyday of McCarthyism, and anyone who tried to defend the Wisconsin senator's antics or those of such Republican stalwarts as Bricker, Capehart, Jenner, or even Taft and Dirksen invited sarcastic commentary from my intellectual superiors. A daily reader of the *Washington Post*, a great admirer of cartoonist Herblock, I gradually shed my Midwestern biases and drifted away from the political right. Even so, I cast my first presidential vote in November 1956 for Dwight Eisenhower.

Never again, however, was I to vote for a Republican for president. My JCS experience transformed me from a conservative Republican into a liberal Democrat—even a card-carrying member of the American Civil Liberties Union. Such I still am, even though part of a lonely minority in the midst of Republican Texas.

My Pentagon assignment brought me back in touch with the National Park Service, now at the very top echelons. The medium was the Potomac Westerners.

In the decades since 1944, Westerner "corrals" have sprung up in nearly all the major cities of the nation and in many foreign cities as well. Members are men and women (though the women gained admission belatedly) who share an interest in the history of the American West. They come together from all professions and all walks of life for monthly meetings featuring drinks, dinner, and a talk.

National Park Service officials took the lead in launching the Potomac Westerners, and Roy Appleman, now out of uniform and back in the Service's Washington office, made sure I was a charter member. We held our first meeting in January 1955 in the Cosmos Club, that bastion of learning housed in an elegant mansion on Massachusetts Avenue. General Ulysses S. Grant III spoke about his grandfather's California service before the Civil War.

At Westerner meetings I came to know other high officials of the Park Service, among them Chief of Interpretation Ronnie Lee and Chief Historian Herb Kahler, both of whom I had first met as a young aide at Custer Battlefield. I also met Conrad L. Wirth, director of the National Park Service.

Connie Wirth attended with fair regularity through 1955 because he sought support for a bold new program to rescue the parks from the wartime neglect that by the 1950s had left them unprepared for the tremendous postwar surge in travel. He called his plan Mission 66. It was a ten-year program, to be completed by 1966, to upgrade all aspects of the national parks. To sell this ambitious and expensive undertaking to Congress, Wirth needed the support of President Eisenhower. One of the most committed members of our corral, Bradley Patterson, happened to be a special assistant to the president. At the Westerner meetings, Wirth assiduously courted Patterson. In due course, Wirth won the opportunity for a full-blown presentation to the president himself. Ike gave his enthusiastic backing, and Mission 66 propelled the national parks and the National Park Service into a decade of revolutionary change.

Thus in no small measure because of Bradley Patterson, Connie Wirth sat in the audience the night I spoke on Custer and the Battle of the Little Bighorn. It was a good speech for a beginner, well received by the audience in that dark-paneled dining room on the second floor of the Cosmos Club. As the group broke up, I later learned, Connie pulled Herb Kahler to one side and said, "You get that fellow back into the National Park Service." Ironically, Mission 66, with its flood of new money and personnel, would enable Herb to carry out the director's instructions.

Before leaving Indiana University, I had arranged with Oscar Winther to return for work toward a Ph.D. after my military service. Residence in Washington, D.C., afforded opportunities for research in the National Archives and Library of Congress, and so the need arose to settle on a dissertation topic. I dared not ask Winther to let me work on another Custer project, but he did agree to one that at least kept me in the Seventh Cavalry. My dissertation would deal with the Ghost Dance movement on the Sioux reservations of Dakota in 1889–90 and with the tragic clash between the Indians and the Seventh Cavalry on Wounded Knee Creek.

Nights and weekends, therefore, often still in uniform after a day at the Pentagon, I dug into the records of the Indian Bureau and the army housed in the National Archives. Many of these documents had never been seen by historians, as attested by the dried and brittle "red tape" that bound the packets and had to be scraped off to gain access. In the years since 1955, with the skyrocketing emphasis on Indian studies, they have been plumbed again and again and now are all available on microfilm.

Three years of research in the National Archives, the Library of Congress, and the Pentagon's own excellent military library yielded several boxes of meticulously recorded notes. I had most of what I needed for a dissertation on a significant subject—and one not too far removed from General Custer himself.

Not that Custer receded much. I gave two more talks on Custer and the Little Bighorn to the Potomac Westerners—one in tandem with retired major general James G. Ord, grandson of the Civil War Union general. I also wrote the chapter on the Little Bighorn for the corral's book, *Great Western Indian Fights*, published in

1960 by Doubleday and still in print at the University of Nebraska Press. I kept up with all the literature on Custer and of course kept up a correspondence with Major and Evelyn Luce.

For Custer Battlefield 1956 marked the end of an era—a sad end. Luce retired, and he and Evelyn settled in San Diego. The captain cum major had stamped his distinctive personality on every feature of that battlefield, and a large constituency viewed him and the field as inseparable. It was difficult to imagine Custer Battlefield managed by a succession of assembly-line superintendents. Something not only colorful but vital had been lost.

As the fateful day approached, I received a letter from one of his constituency—one who had come after my time but viewed the loss as sadly as I. He was Norman Maclean, professor of English at the University of Chicago, an expatriate Montanan who returned each summer to his mountain cabin in western Montana. His literary fame lay in the future, but he already enjoyed high stature in his profession. He proposed that we collaborate on a tribute to Luce.

The idea of a "collaboration" between a distinguished professor and an utter novice struck me as preposterous. This kindly and unpretentious scholar brushed aside my protests, and we undertook the project. The "collaboration," of course, turned out to be mostly Lieutenant Utley's anecdotes and recollections phrased in Professor Maclean's elegant prose. The article appeared in the summer 1956 issue of *Montana The Magazine of Western History* as "Edward S. Luce, Commanding General (Retired), Department of the Little Bighorn."

The article launched a friendship both professional and personal that deepened over the next two decades. Norman Maclean—this man whose literary immortality would rest on *A River Runs through It* and *Young Men and Fire*—had decided he had to write a book about Custer. I held his hand through fifteen years of agonizing struggle. He simply could not come to grips with the story he wanted to tell. Indeed, he did not really know what story he wanted to tell, other than the Custer Battle as "ritual drama." I never understood that concept and told him so repeatedly. He gave up several times, finally in the mid-1970s. In the end, however, he told the story he wanted to tell, but the protagonists were smoke jumpers rather than cavalry troopers and the hill a blazing canyon slope rather than the height on which Custer perished. In *Young Men and Fire*, Norman Maclean at last realized his ambition to do the Custer story.

Norman Maclean held my hand as I strove to become a narrative historian whose work could command a general as well as scholarly readership. His contribution to *The Last Days of the Sioux Nation* (1963) ran quietly through the entire text. In this and subsequent books, he helped me immensely—gently, patiently, surely. I remember him with gratitude, admiration, and affection.

Advancing into my late twenties, I thought the time overdue for marriage. I had never overcome my awkwardness with women and had developed only a few fleeting attachments. I was still a virgin and lacked the skills to remedy that. I did develop what seemed the right relationship, however, and on May 5, 1956, Lucille Dorsey and I were married in a quaint stone church on a wooded hill near her family farm in western Pennsylvania.

As my military service neared its end, Lucille and I had to decide what next. Oscar Winther expected me back at Indiana University. But Cawse, Wilbur, and Gus wanted me to stay with the JCS. The Historical Section was civilianizing, and Cawse offered me a GS-9 position to don a business suit and keep at the same desk. Marriage cast a new light on the issue, but GS-9, the highest grade I qualified for, did not bring much income. Thinking to end the matter, I told Cawse if I could have a GS-11 I would stay. That master at bureaucratic phraseology succeeded in making the master's degree plus my experience at Custer Battlefield and the JCS equal a Ph.D. and so persuaded the personnel evaluators.

I stayed at the Pentagon as family responsibilities promised to grow with Lucille's pregnancy, which originated in September 1956 somewhere west of Washington as we headed toward her introduction to Custer Battlefield. To my disappointment, she was not impressed with the place where I had spent six life-changing summers. On June 12, 1957, Donald Warner Utley joined the family.

At the Pentagon, no longer fitted out in uniform, I continued my labors for a year. At the same time, Mission 66 won approval in Congress. The National Park Service reactivated the Historic Sites Survey—a prewar program aimed at inventorying the nation's important historic places. One GS-12 historian would be assigned to each of the Service's five regional offices. Herb Kahler offered me Philadelphia. I said I wanted to go to the West. Some quick shuffling yielded Santa Fe, New Mexico.

Early in September 1957, Lucille and I fitted out the backseat of the old Chevrolet with a cushioned platform, packed infant Don into this improvised crib, and headed west on old U.S. 40 and U.S. 66.

CHAPTER 7

No LONGER UNIFORMED, NO longer employed for only three months a year, I had now rejoined the National Park Service with the expectation that it would be my life's work. It was a small but very proud agency in the Department of the Interior, steeped in tradition and set in its ways. It still had a few eccentric characters like Luce, but they were a doomed species as Wirth's Mission 66 launched a steady growth in personnel. Although bent on a career in the Service, I regarded myself as a historian first and a Park Service official second. I sought to maintain my professional independence as a historian, and over the next three decades I succeeded.

Region III, soon to be renamed the Southwest Region, embraced the states of Oklahoma, Texas, New Mexico, Arizona, Utah, and southern Colorado. The superintendents of all the national parks and monuments in this region reported to the regional director, Hugh Miller, a wispy little man who ran the region with a gentle but sure hand and who commanded the affection of all. Hugh also had responsibility for a variety of "external" programs such as recreational and reservoir planning, archeological salvage in the paths of dams and pipelines, state and local cooperation, study of proposed additions to the National Park System, and of course the Historic Sites Survey, now rechristened the National Survey of Historic Sites and Buildings. The last, my responsibility, would soon spawn another, the National Historic Landmark program. Owners of places found by the survey to possess significance to the nation as a whole would receive a certificate and bronze plaque attesting to the distinction.

The Southwest Region had a few big parks such as Grand Canyon, Lake Meade, and Big Bend. But most were small and drew their significance from prehistoric ruins. Mesa Verde, Chaco Canyon, Casa Grande, Montezuma Castle, and little Tuzigoot were but a few among many. Thus the professional component of the regional office, called the Division of Interpretation, was heavy with archeologists. The region was the only one in the service lacking a regional historian, and I went to Santa Fe determined, with Roy Appleman's backing from Washington, to remedy that defect and move myself into the opening.

Because of years of domination by archeologists, who tend to be an independent breed disdainful of authority, the Southwest Region boasted a tradition of doing things its own way. As Washington officials observed only half humorously, the people in Santa Fe happily pursued their own ends "behind the adobe wall."

This was literally true, for we worked in the world's largest adobe office building. The Civilian Conservation Corps built it in 1939 as a beautiful exemplar of the pueblo style of architecture. Hispanic workmen molded thousands of adobe bricks for the massive walls and stuccoed them in the earth colors and soft rounded forms of the Pueblo Indian villages scattered up and down the Rio Grande Valley. The offices opened on a roofed flagstone walkway defining the four sides of a large interior court, landscaped and graced with an adobe fishpond. Vigas supported the ceilings and projected from the roofline above the court. Hispanic craftsmen contributed tin light fixtures and the heavy, ornately carved table and chairs that filled the conference room. The building nestled among piñons and junipers at the foot of the Sangre de Cristo Mountains on the southeastern edge of the city. My office windows commanded a view of the Ortiz and Sandia mountains to the south and the Jemez Mountains to the west. Santa Fe personnel were rightly the envy of every central-office employee of the National Park Service.

Santa Fe, in the years before it was consumed by Texas and Los Angeles money and the boutiques it spawned, offered an appealing place to live. Girded by mountains and displaying a mix of pueblo and territorial architecture, it boasted a European history reaching back to 1610 and a diversity of Spanish, Indian, and Anglo tradition that combined in a rich cultural heritage. Once my only ambition had been to spend my career as park historian at Custer Battlefield. Now I aspired only to spend it as regional historian of the Southwest Region. In young adulthood, one rarely understands that the world never remains the same.

After several weeks in a motel, Lucille, Don, and I moved into a newly purchased home on the northwest edge of the city. It was of wooden frame and cinder block stuccoed in the pueblo style and colored pink and white. The front windows opened a view to the high peaks of the Sangre de Cristos to the east.

The Park Service community proved congenial and warmly welcomed us to Santa Fe. While still in the motel, we had dined at the home of the regional solicitor, Merritt Barton, and before year's end we had been invited to the homes of the regional director and assistant regional director. The Park Service wives met for lunch once a month. That so junior a member of the office could be accorded social equality, and that the Park Service "family" offered such an array of social relationships, surprised us. We liked Santa Fe, and we liked our new friends.

With my coworkers, I discovered that the adobe wall tradition of the Southwest Region had its benefits. I reported to Erik Reed, a Harvard Ph.D. of true genius and an archeologist of high reputation in the profession. Providing almost no oversight, he left me free to chart my own course while he and his colleagues pursued their own professional interests. Unlike the survey historians in the other regional offices, I operated behind an adobe wall that hid some of my activities from Ronnie Lee, Herb Kahler, and others in Washington responsible for the National Survey of Historic Sites and Buildings and the National Historic Landmark program.

Lacking a regional historian and unwilling to battle very hard to get one, the Santa Fe officials had a backlog of historical projects that could be rationalized as falling within the purposes of the National Survey. The most pressing was a study to establish the national significance of Fort Bowie, Arizona, and thus lay the legislative groundwork for getting it into the National Park System. Senator Carl Hayden and Representative Stewart Udall had been pressing both Washington and the region to push forward, so the adobe wall proved unnecessary to get all united in assigning Utley to do the study.

Fort Bowie did not return me to Custer, but it brought me once again to the Indian-fighting army in which he starred. Picturesquely sited in Apache Pass, a rocky, cactus-studded defile separating the Chiricahua and Dos Cabezos mountains of southeastern Arizona, Fort Bowie played a major role in the wars with the Apache chieftains Cochise and Geronimo. Nearby Apache Springs fixed the travel route across the region's deserts and mountains. Even before Fort Bowie's advent, a Butterfield stage station had depended on the waters of the spring, and the Butterfield Trail wended its tortuous way through the pass. The interest of Carl Hayden, powerful chairman of the Senate Appropriations Committee, surely arose in part from the first transcontinental run of a Butterfield stagecoach, which in 1857 brought his father to Arizona.

Not much remained of Fort Bowie, only the roofless stubs of adobe walls and the stone foundations of buildings whose walls had melted away. But the setting reflected everyone's vision of Apache country, and the story was both exciting and significant. I researched in the Arizona Pioneers Historical Society in Tucson, walked the mountainous terrain, and wrote a report that impressed everyone and easily convinced the final judges, the secretary of the interior's Advisory Board on National Parks, Historic Sites, Buildings and Monuments, of Fort Bowie's national significance. It also established Bob Utley as one of the Park Service's promising young historians.

Special studies like Fort Bowie interested me much more than the broader studies we survey historians were paid from Mission 66 funds to carry out. For one thing, a special study could be structured in such a way that part or all constituted a publishable article. Every special study I conducted in my seven years in Santa

Fe found its way into a historical journal and built a professional reputation outside as well as inside the National Park Service.

I had not finished with Fort Bowie. In the middle of the following summer, 1958, Herb Kahler and Roy Appleman showed up in Santa Fe for a tour of parks and prospective landmarks in New Mexico and Arizona. Coincidentally, at the same time, Major and Evelyn Luce drove through en route to their San Diego home. We had a marvelous dinner party at our home in which Luce, as usual, held center stage. Afterward, I drove my Washington superiors across a broad swath of Arizona that ended at Fort Bowie, which neither had ever visited.

After dropping Herb and Roy at the Tucson airport, I headed for home. Dusk found me at Truth or Consequences, New Mexico—which had traded its old name for the one-night performance of a popular radio show. Both in name and decrepitude, T or C was an abomination, but I decided to stop for the night. I called Lucille to let her know that I would be home the next day. In this dreary setting I learned from Lucille that there would be a fourth member of the family. Philip Lee Utley was born in Santa Fe on March 4, 1959.

At Fort Bowie, Roy Appleman had been stunned by what he considered the regional office's ineptitude in drawing boundaries for the proposed new park. Before my arrival, the planners had conducted a study that simply drew a square around the ruins of the fort. Left out were the site of the first fort, Apache Springs, the site of the stage station, the trace of the Butterfield Trail, and the sites of several fights with Indians that formed integral parts of the story. In fact, the route of the trail, the site of the stage station, and the other associated sites had never been professionally studied and identified. Roy Appleman convinced Ronnie Lee that Fort Bowie had to be restudied and the boundaries expanded to include all the significant places. So Utley, to the acute discomfiture of the regional officials, had another Fort Bowie study assigned.

The discomfiture arose not only from the rejection of their first effort but from the prospect of reopening a contentious issue. Old L. C. Knape, whose cattle had grazed among the fort's ruins since 1919, firmly (and probably rightly) declared, "Cows and people don't mix." Except for the fort itself, however, which Knape owned, all the cows in the area grazed on public land. The ranchers opposed any park at all, and the Bureau of Land Management, reluctant to surrender any of its kingdom, sided with them. But if there had to be a park, it must be as small as politically possible.

So no one welcomed my new project. Even so, Mr. Knape gave me every cooperation, sharing the trove of knowledge he had gained by riding these mountains for nearly forty years. He even lent me a horse to speed my field work. I was not a horseman, which the horse knew. On the ascent to Apache Pass, he brushed against every specimen of thorned vegetation within reach of the trail. Nearing the summit, he broke into a gallop. The clipboard I had wired to my belt containing my maps and notes banged against my hip and released a cascade of paper. Literally and figuratively, I averred, Utley's research covered the Butterfield Trail.

This Fort Bowie project was a landmark in my professional growth. Although I had repeatedly walked the Custer Battlefield and pondered what may have happened where, at Fort Bowie and Apache Pass I carefully correlated documentary evidence with the landscape and the surviving physical evidence it contained. I meshed indoor research with outdoor research. To the satisfaction of my superiors in Washington, I identified the Butterfield Trail and stage station and all the other sites at issue. When the proposal made its difficult way through Congress, my expanded boundaries survived intact. On July 29, 1972, I took great pleasure in standing with Congressman Morris Udall on a platform in the midst of the parade ground to dedicate the Fort Bowie National Historic Site.

Meanwhile, Washington expected our region to keep pace with the others in conducting the National Survey. We had divided the history of the United States into a series of themes and subthemes, each to have its own study. The study would contain a narrative history, a descriptive listing of all the historic places in the nation illustrating the theme, and an evaluation of which sites merited the designation of National Historic Landmark. Working closely with state and local experts, each survey historian combed his region for historic properties that illustrated the themes under study. Each coordinated one or more themes, wrote the narrative introductions, and incorporated the site data turned up in his own region as well as those provided by colleagues in the other regions. It was a cumbersome process, but it worked well enough in tandem with the staff historians in Washington, a special "consulting committee" of distinguished academic scholars, and the interior secretary's Advisory Board on National Parks, Historic Sites, Buildings and Monuments. Under the Historic Sites Act of 1935, the secretary, based on the advice of this board, made final determinations of national significance.

Early studies assigned to me to coordinate were "Spanish Exploration and Settlement," "Military and Indian Affairs," "Great Explorers of the West," and "The Texas Revolution and Mexican War" (the last three subthemes of "Westward Expansion"). Such studies afforded several opportunities for professional growth. They challenged my research and writing skills. They required intensive field work that not only gave me detailed knowledge of the history and geography of the Southwest but, like Fort Bowie, involved the application of documentary evidence to the landscape and its cultural evidences of the past. The studies also introduced me to a broad network of people in state and local historical societies and the universities of five states. Finally, the studies had to be defended in periodic meetings in Washington with Ronnie Lee, Herb Kahler, Roy Appleman, and the other staff historians and with the luminaries of the "consulting committee." I traveled extensively—by auto throughout the Southwest, by train and plane to Washington in the years before jetliners.

Survey funds paid my salary, but my true interest remained in the parks, and my true ambition to be regional historian and work with park personnel. I believed the region to be vastly oversupplied with archeological parks, many of which appeared to me, and I think the visiting public, as somewhat redundant. We had only two genuinely historical parks: the old Spanish mission of Tumacacori in southern Arizona and the ruins of the nineteenth-century military post of Fort Union in northeastern New Mexico. The latter had only recently been added to the park system and aroused little interest in the regional office.

My survey work turned up a number of historic places in the region that I believed ought to be in the park system. But in the Southwest Region, except for the handful of natural and recreational parks, archeology ruled. Regional management had no historical ambitions beyond Fort Bowie. This proved especially true after Hugh Miller retired and Thomas J. Allen, a cantankerous old-line ranger, took over as regional director. Tom and I had only two things in common: we both suffered hearing impairment, and we both had a high regard for Roy Appleman. In the Richmond regional office, Tom and Roy had fought fiercely on virtually every historical issue, and Tom had come to admire Roy's outspoken honesty even while ruling against him. Tom, of course, knew that I was Roy's protégé. So we got along personally, although he obstructed me professionally whenever he could.

Which was not always, because I had learned to operate on both sides of the adobe wall. Director Connie Wirth was an unabashed imperialist, determined, under the mantle of Mission 66, to bring as many new parks into the system as could be justified to the secretary's advisory board and Congress. All he needed was persuasive documentation for the board and receptive interest in Congress. I could supply the first and sometimes quietly stimulate local supporters to supply the second. All I needed was a directive to conduct a special study as part of the National Survey. In 1959 and 1960 I worked under three such directives, readily obtained from Washington. In all three, I championed addition to the system. In all three, Tom Allen dissented; but to his credit, he forwarded my findings to Washington, where of course Wirth overrode his regional director. As a result, the region ultimately acquired three new national historic sites. Like Fort Bowie, however, they had to await a presidential administration more aggressive in expanding the National Park System.

The first was the Hubbell Trading Post at Ganado, Arizona. Don Lorenzo Hubbell had established it in 1876 and had built it into one of the leading such posts on the Navajo Indian Reservation. Under Dorothy Hubbell, widow of the old man's son, it still functioned much as it had for decades. The old stone post, house, and barn contained a wealth of blankets, silverwork, and the paintings of artists who had partaken of Don Lorenzo's hospitality. The old trading ritual still unfolded each day, and the trader still acted as mediator between two cultures.

Dorothy Hubbell wanted to retire. Her good friend Edward B. Danson, director of the Museum of Northern Arizona, urged the post's addition to the system. So did two other good friends, senators Carl Hayden and Barry Goldwater. The price tag was considerable because the Navajo blankets and silverwork, together with the art collection, formed an asset that Mrs. Hubbell did not intend to donate. Even so, the first step was a study to determine national significance and park suitability.

Tracing the history of the post was not difficult, especially after poring over reams of water-stained, mice-infested papers thrown into barrels in the barn. Establishing national significance proved harder. I had to show that throughout the West the reservation trader played a historically significant role in Indian-white relations, that on the Navajo Reservation the institution reached its peak of development, and that of all the Navajo trading posts, the Hubbell, in the integrity of its surviving buildings and contents, best represented the institution.

My study, completed in January 1959, found little support in the regional office and none in the history division in Washington. Even my mentor Roy Appleman spoke against my findings. Not so Director Wirth or the advisory board. They bought the evaluation of national significance and placed the Park Service on record as favoring its addition to the system.

The second special study of a proposed park centered on Promontory Summit, Utah, where on May 10, 1869, a motley crowd of construction workers and corporate magnates gathered to drive the last spike in the Pacific Railroad. There could hardly be any debate over the national significance of this event, but for years the regional officials had looked disdainfully on the site—an utterly barren spot marked by an unimposing monument. The Southern Pacific Railroad had long since rerouted the main line to span the Great Salt Lake on a causeway, and the rails had been pulled up as scrap for the war effort. Lacking even a single tree,

Promontory Summit did not accord with my colleagues' notion of what a national park should look like.

But the place had an energetic activist who simply would not give up. Bernice Gibbs Anderson of Brigham City, Utah, poured forth a constant stream of letters to members of Congress and the secretary of the interior and even several of accusatory tone and awesome length to President Eisenhower. With Mission 66 in high gear, it required little effort for Roy Appleman to use Bernice Anderson's strident campaign as the basis for another directive for a special study.

Preoccupied with the little patch of desert where the rails joined, regional officials had never looked beyond. Yet on the slopes on both sides of the summit abundant remains represented a compelling story. The Union Pacific and Central Pacific raced each other for federal subsidies and land grants, and in the final stages, before the government fixed a point of union, their work crews labored side-by-side. The grades, cuts, fills, and trestle footings of both railroads snaked up the rocky sides of the Promontory Mountains, testimony to a rivalry sometimes deadly when one crew failed to warn another before setting off a demolition charge.

The best documentary evidence turned out to be the dispatches filed from the combat zone by correspondents of the San Francisco newspapers. They described what occurred each day in colorful detail that permitted events to be readily connected with features still visible on the ground. I consulted the newspapers in the Stanford University Library, then took my notes to Utah.

This was January 1960. A storm had mantled the region in deep snow. The federal motor pool in Salt Lake City let me have a wheezy old Jeep truck. In Brigham City I picked up Bernice Anderson, an amply proportioned matron on the far side of middle age. Together we set forth to apply the newspaper reports to the grades, cuts, fills, and trestle footings still prominent on the landscape. Somewhere on the western slope, miles from any human, we slid into a snow drift. Even in four-wheel drive, no feat of maneuver could extricate us. Finally I told Bernice we had but one hope: she must place her considerable bulk in the truck bed over the rear axle. She did, and we worked ourselves free.

My report easily established national significance, told an exciting story in terms of landscape and remains still there for all to see, and ended by judging the site of the joining of the rails and the construction evidences on either slope to be eminently suitable for incorporation into the National Park System. Tom Allen, of course, vigorously disagreed, but in Washington my report formed the paper platform on which, at a more auspicious time, the administration and Congress could unite in the creation of the Golden Spike National Historic Site.

Almost overlapping Golden Spike was a third special study, of Fort Davis, Texas. A frontier outpost during the Indian wars, it served as a base for cavalry operations against Apaches and as garrison for the Buffalo Soldiers—the black regiments with white officers who played an important part in the final clashes with Indians. Unlike forts Union and Bowie, Fort Davis's structures were wrecks rather than ruins. Unlike Golden Spike, the surrounding Davis Mountains offered appealing scenery.

Even so, Tom Allen did not look with favor on yet another historical area that might someday come into the park system. With my bias toward the frontier army, I thought it a fine prospect. Local backers had long tried to enlist more than token support from the National Park Service. With a little quiet prodding from me, they weighed in heavily on their congressional delegation, and in February 1960 Senator Ralph Yarborough and Representative J. T. Rutherford introduced legislation in Congress to place the fort in the custody of the National Park Service. That of course required a special study. Completed in June 1960, my report told a dramatic and significant story and set forth appealing ways in which the old fort could be brought back to life. Again, the paperwork had all been set in place for the ultimate enactment of the Yarborough and Rutherford bills.

Working both sides of the adobe wall, I managed to get assigned to three other special studies that took me from the survey themes. One, rationalized as a part of the survey theme study of the Santa Fe Trail, centered on Fort Union National Monument. In the vicinity of the fort, the prairie sod was scarred in all directions by the ruts left by wagons on the Mountain and Cimarron branches of the Santa Fe Trail and by the wagon traffic generated by local military activity. My task, accomplished mainly with old maps, diaries, military reports, and aerial photographs, was to identify and separate from all the other ruts the main traces of the Santa Fe Trail.

Another study traced the military movements and combat sites of the Battle of Glorieta Pass, where in 1862 Union troops turned back the Confederate invasion of New Mexico. This study had no immediate consequence, but more than three decades later the Glorieta Pass Battlefield did in fact become part of the National Park System.

Still another study arose from the fertile imagination of Roy Appleman. He convinced Connie Wirth that Big Bend National Park, Texas, would gain a marvelous tool for interpreting an important aspect of western history by pasturing a herd of longhorn cattle on its thin grasses. The very thought of introducing cattle into a national park, especially one that had hardly recovered from overgrazing before its establishment as a park, appalled park and regional officials and aroused considerable skepticism in me. Nevertheless, my "Longhorns of the Big Bend," completed early in 1962, laid out the historical background, provided me with a fascinating project, and added luster to my professional stature outside the Park Service. Fortunately, the idea itself died with the demise of the Wirth directorate less than two years later.

In 1962, also, I finally attained the goal for which I had come to Santa Fe. The position of regional historian, GS-13, was finally established in the Santa Fe office, and I had no difficulty stepping into it. William E. Brown—hardworking, brilliant of mind, a good researcher and writer—took my place as survey historian. Bill and I cemented a close professional and personal friendship destined to last the lifetime of us both.

Now freed from the survey, except for overseeing Bill Brown, I turned to the parks and proposed parks, concentrating mainly on the latter. I worked with park planners from the service's design and construction office in San Francisco and with regional interpretive specialists on how we would develop and display the new parks if they ever cleared Congress to become part of the park system. I also spent much effort on Fort Union, close to my heart because of its connections to the frontier army.

And in 1964 I did a final special study of a proposed new park. An initiative launched by President Kennedy and carried forward by President Johnson had resolved a long-festering dispute between the United States and Mexico over a tiny tract of land in El Paso, Texas, called Chamizal. As a feature of rechanneling the Rio Grande to fix the new boundary, El Pasoans proposed a memorial park to celebrate the new spirit of amity. My study, "The International Boundary, United States and Mexico," surveyed the history of the entire boundary from the mouth of the Rio Grande to the Pacific Ocean and proposed a Chamizal National Memorial to interpret this story to the public.

As with all my previous special studies, this one constituted but one step—a vital one—in a lengthy process involving the Park Service, the Interior Department, the Bureau of the Budget, and Congress that led finally to the addition of a new historical area to the National Park System. I am proud of my role in the creation of them all—Fort Bowie, Hubbell Trading Post, Golden Spike, Fort Davis, and Chamizal.

Superseding my early ambition to be park historian at Custer Battlefield, I had now realized my ambition to be regional historian of the Southwest Region. I looked forward to spending the rest of my career in this job.

Custer and me at age twenty-four. Custer wears the two stars of a major general. I wear the gold bars of a second lieutenant. *Courtesy of the National Archives and the author.*

Senior Class play
1947
"Charley's Aunt"

I was pretty much a nobody in high school until cast in the role of Charley's Aunt in the senior play. After that I was a somebody. *Courtesy of the author.*

Thanks to Errol Flynn, I became a historian instead of a judge. As World War II got underway, his portrayal of General Custer in the 1942 movie *They Died with Their Boots On* provided an impressionable twelve-year-old with a flawless hero. History instead of the law was the result. Olivia de Havilland played Libbie Custer. *Warner Brothers, courtesy Paul A. Hutton.*

In Memory of
The Officers and Soldiers Who Fell near This Place
Fighting with the 7th United States Cavalry
Against Sioux Indians
On the 25th and 26th of June
a.d. 1876

What an impression those words made on a sixteen-year-old Custer enthusiast when first viewed in August 1946. *Courtesy of the author.*

The view from Custer Hill. For six summers I stood on this hill and talked to every visitor. It looked almost the same in 1998, when Jim Brust took this picture. *Courtesy James Brust.*

Edward S. Luce, superintendent of Custer Battlefield National Monument, 1941–56. When this photo was taken in 1947, he was still Cap Luce. Later, somehow, he became Major Luce. *Little Bighorn Battlefield National Monument.*

Not for two years could I afford the traditional park ranger's "flat hat." Instead, until I came up with $20, I donned a war-surplus sun helmet. *Courtesy of the author.*

Larry Frost and Brice Custer, July 17, 1950, the day before we broke ground for the new visitor center. *Little Bighorn Battlefield National Monument.*

The seventy-fifth anniversary of the Battle of the Little Bighorn, June 25, 1951. At the extreme left center, the ranger's "flat hat" records my presence. *Little Bighorn Battlefield National Monument.*

On a rainy June 25, 1952—the seventy-sixth anniversary of the battle—we dedicated the new visitor center. General Jonathan Wainwright presented Luce with a Winchester rifle picked up at the Little Bighorn by one of the Crow scouts and in turn captured by the general's father in the Crow outbreak of 1887. Looking on was Crow Indian Art Bravo, whose uncle found the rifle on the battlefield. I stood to Luce's right but did not get included in the picture. *Little Bighorn Battlefield National Monument.*

In October 1952 I traded my Park Service uniform for the uniform of a U.S. Army recruit. The smile, at the induction center at Fort Lewis, Washington, was not genuine. *Courtesy of the author.*

From 1964 to 1980 I was a Washington bureaucrat—and a pretty good one too. Here I am in 1973 with my successor as chief historian of the National Park Service, A. Russell Mortensen. I was then director of the Office of Archeology and Historic Preservation. *National Park Service.*

George B. Hartzog, Jr., director of the National Park Service from 1964 to 1972, presents me with some sort of performance award in 1969. *National Park Service.*

I was principal speaker at the centennial of the Battle of the Little Bighorn, June 25, 1976. American Indian Movement activist Russell Means upstaged me with drums, whoops, and an American flag dragged upside down on the pavement to signify distress. Later, after the Indians and the cameras left, I joined Colonel George A. Custer III, his son Chip, and Larry Frost in a wreath-laying ceremony at the monument. *Photographs by R. N. Wathen, Jr., courtesy Little Bighorn Battlefield National Monument.*

Since as writer and bureaucrat I had a foot firmly planted in two worlds, I received three honorary doctorates. This is the University of New Mexico, 1976. *Courtesy University of New Mexico.*

CHAPTER 8

IN SANTA FE I consciously began to pursue a professional course that I have followed ever since: to strive to keep one foot in each of two worlds. One was what has since come to be called "public history," the world of which the Park Service was a part but that also included state and local historical societies, museums, groups of "buffs" such as the Westerners corrals, and freelance writers and "grassroots" historians. All these people strove, like the Park Service, to communicate history to the reading and traveling public. The other was the scholarly world almost entirely centered in the nation's colleges and universities. Scholars in academia communicated mainly with their students and, in their publications, with one another. The few who wanted to reach the general public found their training and professional culture a hindrance.

Reared in the first world, I found my introduction to the second in the injunction of the National Survey of Historic Sites and Buildings to seek counsel on the campuses of each region. I did but discovered that few professors had any knowledge of historic sites or interest in my world. From one who did, however, I learned much about the life I had turned from when I chose to remain with the government rather than return to Oscar Winther's oversight for a Ph.D.

John Alexander Carroll of the University of Arizona hardly typified the college history professor. A conspicuous maverick in the profession and his own institution, Jack Carroll was a tall, slim clothes horse invariably costumed—impeccably and expensively— in Hollywood's image of the western saloon gambler. His slicked black hair and pencil-thin mustache enhanced the illusion. He had come off a Montana ranch, signed on for several hitches in the regular U.S. Navy, and barely escaped the sinking of the USS *California* at Pearl Harbor on December 7, 1941. Yet he not only had the Ph.D., earned after the war, but boasted a Pulitzer Prize in history.

Jack and I formed a close professional and personal friendship. In part this reflected a common fascination with General Custer and the Battle of the Little Bighorn, as unusual at Arizona as at Indiana. Nor did academic elitism keep him from mingling with the Tucson Westerners and contributing an article on the Little Bighorn to their periodical. Unlike many of Jack's associates, I was amused rather than repelled by his eccentricities, and I looked up to him as a fountain of wisdom about the hallmarks of superior historical writing and about the ways of the academic world. He freely shared his knowledge and insights. I discovered that I wanted to gain the respect of his world, move comfortably in it, but not play by its rules.

At the University of Arizona, Jack had founded a handsome and distinguished quarterly journal, *Arizona and the West.* The first issue appeared in the spring of 1959. Ambitious for more than regional influence, he aspired to transform his journal into the primary voice of all historians of the American West. This could not be accomplished in the absence of a regional association of specialists, such as already existed for the South, the Midwest, and elsewhere.

In San Diego in the summer of 1959, Jack discussed his vision of an association of westernists with Donald Cutter, a scholar of the Spanish Borderlands soon to join the faculty of the University of New Mexico in Albuquerque. Jack promptly recruited me for the movement. I brought two assets to the drive: I had strong ties to the "buffs," whom Carroll saw as a distinctive source of strength.

And, since he envisioned the first gathering amid the scenic and historic splendors of Santa Fe, I could be saddled with all the onerous logistical chores that senior scholars disdained.

Quickly an "organizing committee" took shape: Carroll, Cutter, Utley, John Porter Bloom of Texas Western University (soon to join the National Park Service), Walter Rundell of the American Historical Association, Edgar I. Stewart of Eastern Washington College (who contributed nothing but his name), and K. Ross Toole, director of the Museum of New Mexico. Bloom chaired the program committee, which soon acquired enough lustrous names to ensure an appealing menu. Ross Toole, though irreverently scornful of such conferences, offered the Museum of New Mexico as host institution.

In the spring of 1961 we all descended on Detroit to promote the idea at the annual convention of the Mississippi Valley Historical Association. We stirred little enthusiasm, indeed encountered skepticism and even opposition among turf-conscious westernists themselves. But the scheming went forward anyway, and in the golden autumn of 1961 fully three hundred registrants, instead of the expected ninety, turned up in Santa Fe for the First Conference on the History of Western America.

It was, all agreed, a smashing success. The weather and the ambiance were splendid. John Bloom's program emptied La Fonda Hotel's lobby and filled the session rooms. The wealthy White sisters of Santa Fe and General Patrick Hurley served up bounteous drink and distinctive nibblies in settings of exquisite Santa Fe charm. And all parted with a rough consensus, if not perfect unanimity, that an association of westernists was indeed a worthy goal.

But not before some rocky disputation. I wielded the gavel at a "special business meeting" designed to produce a "spontaneous" call for an association. This distinction fell to me because, if the meeting turned sour, I was the only one of the organizers with no reputation to lose.

It nearly turned sour. With a mischievous twinkle in his eye and probably several martinis under his belt, Ross Toole rose and, waving a sheet of paper, announced that this was the script for the meeting and at this juncture it called for him to speak the following lines, which he proceeded to read aloud. When he sat down amid an audience buzzing with unfriendly commentary, Jack Carroll stood and, his face red with anger, mumbled some lame explanations of the process and then delivered his own lines—from memory, not the script.

The script became irrelevant when LeRoy Hafen of Brigham Young University gained the floor. His discourse, partly submerged in the abominable acoustics of the Saint Francis Auditorium, contained sentiments concerning the sanctity of democracy and the effrontery of a little band of promoters subjecting a distinguished assembly to the constraints of a deviously crafted script. I thought I heard, somewhere in the presentation, the word "railroading."

But in truth most who came *did* want a Western History Association. And if it was not actually born at that moment, under my gavel, certainly as the meeting adjourned conception had taken place.

Santa Fe laid the groundwork, producing consensus and, of vital importance, an enlarged organizing committee. Joining the original group were Robert G. Athearn of the University of Colorado, Joe B. Frantz of the University of Texas, Roy Hafen (a shrewd choice), and W. Eugene Hollon of the University of Oklahoma. Heading the list of newcomers, as arranged in a quiet dinner in La Fonda's dining room, was Ray Allen Billington, dean of western historians and soon to be installed at the Huntington Library in San Marino, California. Ray's agreement to serve as president pro tem, and of course as first president, was the crucial ingredient in the propellant that launched the Western History Association. No one else could be so certain of piloting a machine that would fly.

It took off at the Denver meeting in October 1962. The Lord blessed the Denver efforts—quite literally. The headquarters hotel had burned down a few weeks before the conference, which was then squeezed into the big new Hilton in space next to the convention of the Salvation Army. There, as the Reverend John Francis Bannon of St. Louis University put it, "the boss dropped in"—a bearded and robed figure with outstretched arms, gliding down the aisle in Roy Hafen's fur trade session proclaiming himself to be Jesus Christ. We sent him back to the Salvation Army.

Denver launched the Western History Association. Under Ray Billington's presidency, it gained a solid footing in academia and, as Jack Carroll had hoped, among Westerner corrals and other "buff" organizations. (His hopes of expanding the scope of *Arizona and the West*, however, fell victim to state parochialism and professorial aversion to his unconventional ways.) Because of my hard work, my name found its way to the ballot for the first council. To my astonishment, I gained more votes than my opponent, the distinguished Texas professor Joe B. Frantz.

The Santa Fe and Denver meetings gave me high visibility with all the big names in western history. The Western History Association gave me a forum in which to gain at least a toehold in academia without being a part of it. In all the years since 1961, I have not missed a single of the annual conventions of the WHA.

Bureaucratic visibility, however, conferred no more than a toehold. "Publish or perish" ruled in academia, no matter how specialized or even how poorly crafted the publication. One did not rise in faculty rank without a publication record. To win true acceptance, therefore, I had to publish.

In addition to my amateurish first publication on the Custer Battle in 1949, I had succeeded in having two articles published in *North Dakota History*, neither of which was worthy of much notice. Some of my special studies for the Park Service, recast as articles, found acceptance in such journals as the *New Mexico Historical Review, Arizona and the West, Arizoniana, Utah Historical Quarterly,* and *El Palacio*. But the demands of my Park Service job, combined with the domestic demands of a household with two small boys, left little time for research and writing.

Frustrated, I vowed to use the notes I had taken for my doctoral dissertation as grist for a series of articles for professional journals. Lucille balked at that, declaring that I had the makings of a full book, and only a full book would catch the attention of the professors. She bought me a portable electric typewriter for my birthday, we converted the family room into a study, and I set to work on a book about the Ghost Dance and Wounded Knee. As it unfolded, both Cawse-Morgan and Norman Maclean read chapters and offered critical commentary. The university presses of Oklahoma and Nebraska expressed interest.

When the Santa Fe conference on western history convened in October 1961, I had all but committed the manuscript to Nebraska. But David Horne of Yale University Press told me he thought my subject admirably suited for his new Western Americana Series. That so prestigious a press could even be interested dazzled me. The vision of Yale's imprimatur on my book made the Santa Fe conference all the more magical. I promised to send David the manuscript.

If that were not enough of an ego boost, at the conference Paul Bailey, head of Westernlore Press in Los Angeles, approached me about my master's thesis. Major Luce and two other old friends, Hugh Schick and Mike Harrison, had told him about me. By now, I knew the thesis to be badly flawed stylistically and, ending with the nineteenth century, incomplete. Even so, I promised Paul I would revise it and let him see it.

In 1962 Westernlore Press published *Custer and the Great Controversy: Origin and Development of a Legend.* In 1963 Yale University Press, as the third of the Western Americana Series, published *The Last Days of the Sioux Nation.* Both were well received, but the latter gave me the reputation I sought then and have aimed for ever since—as a writer of narrative history that not only appeals to the general reader but also wins the approval of the professors. A laudatory review by Ray Billington helped greatly. Both books have remained in print ever since.

Custer and the Great Controversy bore a dedication: "To the Luces, for many cherished memories of Custer Hill." That deeply touched the old man and Evelyn. We had never ceased exchanging letters and keeping in touch with each other's lives. Twice in my travels I parked the government car in Yuma, Arizona, and flew to San Diego for a visit of several days. In his retirement years, Luce grew increasingly bitter toward the National Park Service. Successor personnel at the battlefield waged a relentless campaign to defame his name and administration, and bumbling in the Interior Department botched the presentation of his Distinguished Service Award.

Even as he read the dedication in *Custer and the Great Controversy,* his health had begun to fail. He died in November 1963.

Evelyn continued to teach school and, after retirement, took up residence in a Modesto home for the elderly, where at this writing (2003) she still lives, aged ninety-one. Each year at Christmas, we exchange greetings.

The Last Days of the Sioux Nation not only planted one foot in the scholarly world (acceptance could never be total, I would learn, without the "terminal degree") but also established a close tie with Yale University Press. David Horne asked me to write a foreword for a reissue of Britton Davis's *The Truth about Geronimo*, first published in 1920 and long out of print. Davis had been a cavalry officer and Indian scout commander during the wars against the Apache leader, and his memoirs had become a minor classic. With my foreword, drawn largely from my work on Fort Bowie, the new edition appeared in 1963, the same year as *Last Days*.

More daunting was a request to "make publishable" the memoirs of General Richard Henry Pratt, founder and long-time superintendent of the Carlisle Indian School in Pennsylvania. The Pratt family had donated the general's papers to Yale University Library on the condition that the press publish his memoirs, which were voluminous, repetitive, and full of long quotations available elsewhere. Without sacrificing Pratt's genuine contributions to history, I scaled back the manuscript, supplied a foreword and annotations, and in 1964 added still another listing to my bibliography. *Battlefield and Classroom: Four Decades with the American Indian* earned me the gratitude not only of Yale but of the Pratt family, and it received favorable reviews in the scholarly journals. (The University of Nebraska Press published a new edition in 1987 and the University of Oklahoma Press in 2004.)

While still working on the Pratt volume, in April 1963 I appeared on the program of the Mississippi Valley Historical Association in Omaha, presenting a paper drawn from the newly published *Last Days*. In Omaha I ran into an old friend, Professor Louis Morton of Dartmouth College. I had known him in Washington as the army's chief civilian historian. Lou had now been commissioned by the Macmillan Publishing Company, then the most prestigious trade publisher of history, to serve as general editor of a series entitled "The Wars of the United States." He had blocked out two volumes for the Indians Wars, one of which had been assigned to the Reverend Francis Paul Prucha, a noted Jesuit scholar who taught at Marquette University. Would I be interested in taking on the other?

Since 1941 the standard history of the frontier army had been Fairfax Downey's *Indian Fighting Army*. I thought it a poor book and believed I could do better. For some time, in fact, I had considered attempting exactly what Lou Morton now offered, but I felt I had not reached a level of experience that equipped me for so large an undertaking. Yet if I did not accept, someone else would write the book that would supplant Downey as the standard authority. On July 25, 1963, I signed the contract forwarded by Macmillan senior editor Peter Ritner and in due course received my first advance against royalties, $1,500.

In October 1963 the Western History Association met at the Hotel Utah in Salt Lake City. One morning I breakfasted with Alfred Knopf, the legendary New York publisher who also served on the secretary of the interior's Advisory Board on National Parks, Historic Sites, Buildings and Monuments. With Bernard DeVoto and other staunch conservationists on the board, he had fought in some of Connie Wirth's most venomous battles against dam builders and others who threatened the national parks. Alfred's beefy face was red with anger as he showed me a copy of the *New York Times*. It reported a conference of park superintendents convened at Yosemite who listened in shock and anger as Assistant Secretary of the Interior John Carver compared their "mystic, quasi-religious" esprit de corps to that of the Hitler Youth movement. Knopf stormed out of the dining room to fire off telegrams of protest.

At the Yosemite conference, Wirth had announced his forthcoming retirement. But the Carver speech dramatized the rift that had opened between Wirth's National Park Service and Stewart Udall's Interior Department. In truth, Wirth had resisted Secretary Udall's policies and plans, principally in opposing the creation of the Bureau of Outdoor Recreation. He had outlived his time.

By February 1964 Udall had an enthusiastically responsive director in George B. Hartzog, Jr.

The change in top leadership seemed to pose no threat to me. Behind the adobe wall, I worked on plans for the proposed new historical areas and looked to the interests of history in all the parks of the Southwest Region. I enjoyed the confidence of my coworkers and a relationship with the new regional director, Daniel B. Beard, much more sympathetic than had dogged me through the years of Tom Allen's directorate. I had the job I wanted for the rest of my career. I also had a growing reputation in historical circles outside the National Park Service. And now I had a contract with Macmillan for a major research and writing task that would occupy such spare time as my Park Service responsibilities allowed.

One sunny day late in 1963 I drove to Fort Union with Franklin J. Smith, a learned anthropologist who served as regional museum curator and was a personal friend as well. Amid the piñon hills west of Las Vegas, Frank suddenly blurted out: "You will be the next chief historian of the National Park Service." Such a preposterous thought had never entered my mind. If Herb Kahler should retire, a cadre of senior staff historians stood ready to compete for his position, and if none of them won, at least three other regions had well-regarded senior historians who had been in the business decades longer than I. Besides, I had the job I wanted. Even so, Frank's sudden declaration led me to wonder whether I could function in the Washington bureaucracy as well as I had handled history in the Southwest.

Early in 1964, while still director designate, George Hartzog visited Santa Fe. Dan Beard hosted a cocktail party at his home. Lucille and I attended, and I met our new leader. A hefty man with thinning hair, he impressed me as intense, energetic, self-assured, and very articulate. I do not think I impressed him at all or gave him any reason to remember me.

In the spring of 1964 Herb Kahler summoned me to Washington for some mysterious assignment in his office. There he informed me that he had decided to retire and that he had put forward my name as his successor. This was not wholly unexpected.

Since the talk with Frank Smith, I had considered all the senior historians whose service entitled them to a claim on the position. They all represented the first generation of Park Service historians, spawned by the Historic Sites Act of 1935. I think Herb understood that Hartzog's advent, reflecting the bold new initiatives of the Interior Department under Secretary Udall, represented the end of one era and the beginning of another; that neither he nor any of the first generation of historians could cope with the challenges and changes the history arm of the Service would confront; and that the time had come for new blood.

Hartzog respected Kahler's judgment. I doubt that he thought much beyond Herb's recommendation before giving me the nod. I still had to run a summer-long gauntlet, however, erected by none other than Assistant Secretary Carver. In his mind the name *Utley* rang alarm bells, although he did not know why. Finally, in August 1964, Herb persuaded Carver that fairness demanded that he either let the papers go forward or state what he had against me. He could not recall and bowed to Herb.

I later learned what he could not remember. At the 1961 Santa Fe conference, Carver stood in for Secretary Udall in delivering the banquet speech. It was openly political, comparing President Kennedy's New Frontier to Frederick Jackson Turner's frontier thesis. I was one of the editors of the book containing some of the scholarly papers presented at that conference. Carver bitterly resented the exclusion of his speech from the volume, and he held me responsible. Carver's bad memory lifted me over the adobe wall and set me on a course for which, at age thirty-four, I was entirely unprepared.

In September 1964 Lucille, Don, Phil, and I moved into a home in McLean, Virginia, purchased for the exorbitant sum of $29,000. I established myself behind Herb Kahler's desk in the Interior building and prepared to supervise a staff only one of whom was younger than my father.

CHAPTER 9

DIRECTOR GEORGE B. HARTZOG, JR., always introduced me as "his" chief historian, and so he regarded me. The title, however, actually rested on Dr. Charles W. Porter III, the staff historian for the colonial period. A short, thin man with a neatly combed thatch of gray hair, faultlessly tailored as befitted his scholarly persona and distinguished Virginia ancestry, Charlie held the best claim to the title. As salve to his self-esteem and bridge to a new leadership, he had been given the title but nothing more.

My title was Chief, Division of History Studies—a misnomer because we studied nothing. We did what the division had always done: We watched over preservation, research, and interpretation in the historical parks. We supervised the National Survey of Historic Sites and Buildings. And we staffed all issues involving history that came before the Washington office. A prestigious national panel of scientists, however, had severely faulted the Park Service for its research failings in the natural sciences, and we found ourselves brigaded with archeology and natural science under an assistant director for "resource studies." *Research* was a word no canny bureaucrat then used in the presence of the keepers of the purse strings; thus the substitution of *studies*.

Hartzog never quite understood that history and archeology, especially research in those disciplines, differed radically from natural science. He thought all three disciplines were busily building show-piece research programs for the Park Service. A lot of tension arose as we in history and archeology continued to do what we had always done.

Not only in the role of my division did I get off to a bad start. At my first meeting of the secretary's advisory board, held in October 1964 in Gatlinburg, Tennessee, I painfully discovered that undiplomatic candor could get one into serious trouble. The issue was the significance and park potential of the Washita Battlefield in Oklahoma, where General Custer won a signal victory over the Cheyennes in 1868. Here was a subject I knew much better than Frank Masland, a mustachioed, distinguished-looking carpet mogul from Pennsylvania and long a power on the board. When he gave his opinion that the Washita was a terrible massacre of women and children, I stood to say that, to put it bluntly, Frank Masland did not know what he was talking about. That of course was a dumb thing to do. Masland rushed out, studied the report, and returned to inform the board that he had been unjustly maligned and wished the record to show his strenuous objection.

Back in Washington, word came down from Hartzog for Utley to get straight with Masland. Utley did, with a letter of abject apology. Frank responded graciously, and we remained good friends for the next three decades, until the end of his long life.

Worse yet was my part in one of Secretary Udall's highest priorities, the Pennsylvania Avenue Plan. During the inauguration parade in 1961, President Kennedy had remarked on the seedy appearance of the north side of the nation's "ceremonial way." The result was the Pennsylvania Avenue Plan, drawn up by one of the country's leading architects, Nathaniel Owings. The plan called for creating a Pennsylvania Avenue National Historic Site, tearing down most of the old buildings, and replacing them with a grand monumental setting for parades and ceremonies.

Udall and Owings were said to have spread a big map on the floor of the secretary's ornate sixth-floor office and on their knees drawn the boundaries of the historic site to meet the plan's needs. Then they discovered that the Historic Sites Act of 1935 required a study of national significance and action by the secretary's advisory

board. The department's solicitor summoned me to the sixth
floor and explained the background. I had the temerity to declare
that the purpose of the Historic Sites Act was to preserve old buildings,
not tear them down, and that ordinarily a study preceded, not
followed, the drawing of boundaries.

Presumably from the solicitor, down the chain of command through
the assistant secretary to Hartzog came the ominous message:
Utley is resisting what the secretary wants. Utley quit resisting.
Prodded by a nasty special assistant to Udall named Bill Posen, I
assembled a task force of historians, saturated the Udall-Owings
boundaries with history, and produced a fascinating study of who
had lived where and what had happened where on Pennsylvania
Avenue even though little remained to illustrate the who and the
what. The study demonstrated that a lot of significant history
happened in the area and that a scattering of individually significant buildings remained, such as the White House, the Patent
Office, the Pension Building, and the Old Post Office. Absent was
any discussion of the integrity of the district as a whole, but no
one noticed that, as the advisory board granted Secretary Udall
the needed compliance with the Historic Sites Act.

Thus began years of contention between preservationists and
backers of the monumental design. As the controversy began to
focus on the proposed demolition of the Willard Hotel, the
Owings plan lost much of its grandiosity and eventually dissolved
in a host of compromises. In those years I took satisfaction in the
belief that I had been right all along. But, still bruised by the Masland episode, I carefully refrained from saying so to Nat Owings.
Udall appointed him to the advisory board, where he promoted
many dubious undertakings. But we became friends, and when I
could support him in good conscience, I did.

By late 1965 I was sure that Hartzog fervently wished that he
had left me behind the adobe wall. The chill I felt in his office,
when I gained entry at all, left little doubt that I sat far from the
inner circle.

The research issue, however, seemed to offer a chance to counter
the chill. In December 1964 I was attending the convention of the
American Historical Association at the Sheraton Park Hotel when

I was informed that Hartzog wanted to see me at once. In his peremptory and sometimes intimidating manner, he grilled me about the Service's historical research program. I informed him lamely that we had one sporadically ongoing project in my division and, like the natural sciences division, a huge stack of paper that supposedly represented the servicewide historical research program.

The paper represented little more than a wish list, I asserted as the impulse to candor began to gain control. It recorded a few projects already underway in the parks and regions and described a host of desirable projects that field personnel set to paper simply because Washington had called for the paper. It was a pointless, expensive waste and ought not to be pursued in a vain effort to force history and natural science together in the same system. In truth, the Service had no historical research "program," only erratic efforts in the parks as money and personnel became available. I had no authority over regional directors or park super-intendents and no money to dole out for research. Under such circumstances, I could hardly be held accountable for a service-wide program.

Ever the quick thinker, Hartzog responded at once: "Then go back to your office and design a program that you *can* be held accountable for." Fair enough. I went back to my office and set to work creating my own empire. Charlie Porter and the other staff historians, still immobilized by their heritage, could only shake their heads at my audacity. I identified about fifteen people scattered around the Service who devoted full time to historical research. I wanted those positions and the money that supported them, I told Hartzog. I would move the incumbents to Washing-ton and build a true division of history studies and establish a program for which I would stand accountable. If any incumbent refused to move, I still got the position and the money.

Hartzog approved. Regional directors, superintendents, and incumbents howled in protest; but few dared his wrath, already legend throughout the service. So large a staff could not fit into the Interior building, and by early 1966 we were installed in leased space in Roslyn, on the Virginia side of Key Bridge, busily turning out studies responsive to park needs and of generally high quality.

The National Survey, which I also succeeded in centralizing under my direct control, shared the office space.

As we geared up for the new look, the old look began to dissolve. One by one, the old generation retired. They had a hard enough time just giving up offices in the Interior building, much less coping with the frightening new directions of their young new chief. So far as I could tell, however, none ever attempted to undermine me, and all gave me loyal and constructive support. They are all gone now, but I honor their memory and what they accomplished in the generation following the Historic Sites Act.

By the time we moved to Roslyn, only Rogers Young remained of the old generation. I put him in charge of the research historians. He and Horace Sheely, chief of the National Survey, reported directly to me. Horace was a dithering mother hen whose hand had to be held constantly. For Rogers Young, the job demanded too much of his nervous temperament and fragile health, and in the summer of 1966 his doctor commanded him to retire at once.

One of the old generation I had not inherited was Roy Appleman. In the reorganization aimed at strengthening research, he had been shunted to Bill Everhart's Division of Interpretation, where he was unhappy and not particularly valued by Bill. One day I caught Hartzog in an elevator and told him I wanted Roy to take Rogers Young's place. Hartzog resisted and stalled for two floors. As he exited the elevator, I asked him if I could tell Everhart that the director had approved Appleman's transfer. As the elevator doors closed, Hartzog gave a noncommittal wave of his hand. I rushed to Everhart and told him Hartzog had let me have Roy.

And so, by an ironic twist of fate, my new branch chief and deputy turned out to be my old friend and mentor. Under Roy's firm hand the historical research program flourished, and the research historians bonded in a camaraderie rare in the federal bureaucracy. One of them was Ed Bearss, who had fiercely resisted the transfer to Washington but who later became chief historian. Ed still remembers this time as "the glory years."

Even with Charlie Porter's retirement, I did not inherit the title of chief historian, although that was what I was in everyone's

perception, including mine and Hartzog's. But the director held back.
I had not fully won his confidence, and a movement was building
that seemed likely to fix a new face on the units of the Park Service
that dealt with history, archeology, and historic architecture.

This was the historic preservation movement. It emphasized not
the buildings associated with great people or the places of great
events—the stock-in-trade of the Park Service since the Historic
Sites Act. Rather it aimed at adaptive use of worthy old buildings
and whole districts of buildings. Its proponents pointed to the
devastation wrought on cities and rural landscapes by urban
renewal, interstate highways, massive dams and power lines, and
other public and private undertakings in a society obsessed with
development. "When you get there, there's no there there," wrote
one of overdevelopment's most effective critics.

The National Trust for Historic Preservation, a private nonprofit
organization, and the U.S. Conference of Mayors took the lead in
promoting a national historic preservation program. Lady Bird
Johnson lent critical support. The Johnson administration readily
incorporated it into the "Great Society."

George Hartzog determined to capture the program for the
Park Service, even though other agencies, and their partisans in
Congress, also had designs on it. Ronnie Lee had retired as regional
director in Philadelphia, and Hartzog made him a special assistant.
To advise him on how to shape a program and execute it if Congress enacted legislation, the director formed a committee consisting
of Lee, Dr. J. O. Brew, and Dr. Ernest Allen Connally. Joe Brew,
director of the Peabody Museum at Harvard, was a member of the
consulting committee to the National Survey, and I had worked
with him for several years. Ernest Connally, professor of the history
of architecture at the University of Illinois, enjoyed a distinguished
reputation in preservation circles, but I had never met him.

In many ways, George Hartzog resembled Lyndon Johnson—
dynamic, brimming with energy, tireless, overflowing with projects
and purposes, politically astute, quick thinking, articulate, urbane
and crude, open and devious, kind and brutal, caring and ruthless,
gentle and hot tempered. Above all, like Johnson, Hartzog master-
fully manipulated the reins of power on both ends of Pennsylvania

Avenue. His achievements as director of the National Park Service fall little short of awesome.

In my judgment, no single person deserves more credit for the National Historic Preservation Act of 1966 than George Hartzog. Others played indispensable roles, but George guided it through the labyrinth of the executive branch and Congress. It emerged securely under the control of the National Park Service.

Of the two years of maneuvering that culminated on October 16, 1966, I retained little memory of participating—in fact, believed I had been deliberately bypassed. So much for the quirks of memory. In the early 1980s, at Cornell University, James A. Glass, undertaking a doctoral dissertation on the origins of the national historic preservation program, turned up ample documentary evidence to correct my memory. My division provided the only reliable source of staff work. I think Ronnie Lee had not wholly approved of my elevation to Herb Kahler's position. But we worked well together as the Lee-Brew-Connally committee sought to steer Hartzog in professionally sound directions. Under Ronnie's guidance, I drafted many of the provisions that found their way into the final legislation. In a 1991 ceremony in San Francisco, I was one of half a dozen honored as prime movers in the passage of the National Historic Preservation Act.

Even so, I was chagrined to learn that the coveted title of chief historian, and the GS-15 grade that had also been withheld, still might not fall to me. Hartzog conceived himself as somehow in competition with Dillon Ripley and the Smithsonian Institution. Most of the Smithsonian's top leaders had doctorates. George thought that the organization he intended to put in place in response to the new law should be similarly crowned with the Ph.D. Lee, Brew, Connally, and Kahler all argued that my publication record, coupled with my acceptance as peer by the scholarly world, was the equivalent of a Ph.D.

I did not get home the night the family was to decorate the Christmas tree in December 1966. Instead I was dining at the Lawyers Club with Hartzog, Lee, Kahler, and Connally, who had been persuaded to give up teaching to head the Park Service's new Office of Archeology and Historic Preservation. At last, Hartzog said, I would be promoted to GS-15 and given the title of chief historian. Moreover, since Connally could not take up his duties until July 1967, I would be acting chief of the new office. And finally, I would assemble and head a task force to prepare standards, guidelines, and procedures for carrying out the law. I missed decorating the tree, but I brought home a prized Christmas present that portended, once again, a job for which I was woefully unprepared.

Ernest Allen Connally brought valuable new perspectives and insights to the National Park Service. Handsome in form, face, and wavy gray-flecked hair, he dressed himself in expensive good taste and pulled on fashionably small cigars. He commanded deep knowledge of art and architectural history and drew on a large vocabulary to express himself clearly and wittily. He enjoyed large stature in historic preservation circles in the United States and Europe. George Hartzog had lured him away from academia with the prospect of creating an American "monuments service" comparable to those in France and Italy. The National Historic Preservation Act would provide the charter.

Through the first six months of 1967, until Connally could free himself from the University of Illinois, he and I spent hours on the telephone as he sought, through me, to organize the Office of Archeology and Historic Preservation and devise guidelines and procedures for carrying out the new law. A learned scholar in the fullest sense, he had experienced little of the intricacies of the federal bureaucracy. Much of that I could supply in translating his objectives into results.

The law called for a National Register of Historic Places. It would be the nation's list of places worthy of preservation—not just the nationally significant places the Park Service had dealt with in the landmark program but places of state and local significance as well. So we established a National Register division and brought Dr. William J. Murtagh from the National Trust for Historic Preservation to head it. Like Connally, Bill Murtagh had an international reputation. On my suggestion, we gave Bill a title with a European flavor: Keeper of the National Register.

The law authorized a grants-in-aid program to the states to help care for registered properties. So we set up a grants division with Dr. Sydney Bradford, a career National Park Service historian, as chief. A huge chasm separated authorization from appropriation, but eventually money in meaningful amounts began to emerge from the congressional appropriations process.

The law provided for an Advisory Council on Historic Preservation, with members appointed by the president, to advise the president and Congress on all issues of historic preservation and to set in place a system for protecting registered properties from harm by federal or federally assisted undertakings. Robert R. Garvey, Jr., executive director of the National Trust, moved to the Park Service as executive staff for the Council. Although closely allied with Connally's office, Garvey reported directly to George Hartzog.

When Connally finally appeared in July 1967, he took charge of an Office of Archeology and Historic Preservation (OAHP) consisting of five divisions: the two new units in addition to my Division of History, Dr. John Corbett's Division of Archeology, and Joseph Watterson's Division of Historic Architecture. History and Architecture consisted of "inhouse" and "outhouse" branches. The former dealt with the National Park System, the latter with state and local governments and other elements of the public sector. I had Appleman's cadre of research historians supporting the national parks and Horace Sheely's National Survey and National Landmarks program. Watterson had Henry Judd's historical architects, who, Connally intended, would oversee Park Service restoration projects through the entire sequence from study to completion of construction. For "outhouse," Watterson had the Historic American Building Survey (HABS) and the Historic American Engineering Record (HAER).

The archeologists could not muster much enthusiasm for joining the new team. John Corbett and his deputy, Zorro Bradley, dealt through field units with the exceedingly well-funded archeological salvage program for recovering cultural remains imperiled by dams, highways, and pipelines. They also kept watch on the many units of the park system set aside for prehistoric significance. Corbett and Bradley enjoyed powerful support from some of the most prestigious figures in their profession, who believed that they should not be merged with history and architecture but given their own separate organization, program, and funding. Not for years did they cease lobbying for this measure.

By the autumn of 1967, OAHP had been brought together in a new home large enough to accommodate all, together with Garvey's Advisory Council office, under one roof. The "801 Building"—801 Nineteenth—stood on the corner of Nineteenth Street and Pennsylvania Avenue, a few blocks' walk from the Interior building and far more convenient to the seat of power than the building across the Potomac in Roslyn. In the 1920s the 801 Building had housed Herbert Hoover's Department of Commerce, but it had been sufficiently upgraded to serve us well.

During the first months of 1967, my task force on procedures and guidelines had crafted an approach to our new responsibilities. We modeled it on the successful grants program of the Bureau of Outdoor Recreation. Secretary Udall signed a letter I drafted to each state governor inviting the designation of a "state liaison officer" (later state historic preservation officer, or SHPO) to work with OAHP to develop survey, grants, and protective systems in each state. In essence, we would formulate standards and guidelines, and with federal funding the states would administer the programs.

I learned much from Ernest Connally—not merely knowledge but concepts of preservation that went far beyond anything the Park Service had dealt with in the past. I soaked it up and became an effective voice for his ideas and objectives. I also came to admire and respect his professional excellence while treasuring his friendship. He learned from me, too, how to get things done in the bureaucracy. Many a bureaucratic battle we fought, not only with our own people but with other federal departments and with all the state bureaucracies. We put on a "road show," traveling to major cities in each region to explain the new program and seek help in making it work. These years of the late 1960s were trying yet exciting, during which OAHP (except for the archeologists) worked hard and bonded in a sense of national purpose.

I also tried to help Ernest relate to the old-line Park Service. I had once worn the gray and the green and, in Santa Fe and

Washington, had been nurtured in Service traditions. The powers who sat in offices on the director's corridor on the Interior building's third floor regarded me as one of their own. Try as he might, however, Connally could never gain admission to the inner circle. He was too much the scholarly dandy, too lacking in Park Service roots, too glibly articulate, too self-assured, and often too devastatingly witty in argumentation. Connally's peers on the second echelon of the Park Service undermined him whenever possible and even, I have always suspected, planted in Hartzog himself the feeling that too much power had been gathered in OAHP.

As one result, Ernest's concept of ensuring professional control over park restorations from beginning to end never materialized. Hank Judd's branch never acquired the personnel to make this possible. As another result, in one of Hartzog's endless succession of reorganizations, I lost my research historians. Henceforth, all professional studies and all construction work in the parks, including treatment of historic buildings, would be handled by two "service centers," later consolidated as one in Denver. OAHP retained all its "outhouse" responsibilities, but for the parks themselves, we merely formulated policies and standards and tried to ensure that the field adhered to them. When my research branch collapsed, Roy Appleman retired. I replaced him with an outsider, my old friend Russ Mortensen, then teaching at the University of Utah.

In truth, Ernest Connally had been promised more than George Hartzog could or would deliver. He had been enticed from academia with the vision of an American monuments office, but he had not been allowed to build one. He endured constant frustration and I think a sense of betrayal. One day he exploded to me: "I had hoped to create a monuments office at least as good as Mexico's; now I doubt that I can even match Bulgaria's."

Not only bureaucratic obstacles impeded progress. Congress had authorized appropriations for grants-in-aid, but the appropriations committees had shown little disposition to allow more than token funds. Only substantial grants could motivate the states to take the new program seriously. We mobilized the state historic preservation officers and other preservationists with clout on Capitol Hill, but in the first years the money hardly swelled beyond a trickle.

In part we were merely suffering the fate of all of Lyndon Johnson's Great Society programs. The war in Vietnam devastated the Great Society and tormented the entire country. We watched the capital city rocked by demonstrations and violence, especially after the assassinations of 1968. Martin Luther King, Jr.'s murder found our "road show" in Savannah, Georgia. Chief Archeologist John Corbett and I had a fine seafood dinner and went to the movies to see *Bonnie and Clyde.* We emerged to find the streets deserted and, at the hotel, learned of King's death. With Washington burning and under military occupation, I had a difficult time getting back home.

Still a militarist in the 1960s, a veteran proud of my army service, I favored the war in Vietnam. I bought the conventional wisdom of the falling dominoes. I remember how Roy Appleman and I rejoiced when the Seventh Cavalry, Custer's old outfit, won a signal victory in November 1965 at Ia Drang, in the Vietnamese highlands.

In December 1967 I had a sobering experience that remains vivid in my mind. Lucille and the boys picked me up at the 801 Building, and we went to the Ellipse to watch President Johnson light the national Christmas tree. Don, now ten, sat on my shoulders to see above the crowd. The marine band played "Hail to the Chief," and the president whom I held in high respect ascended the platform. From his perch, Don declared: "There's the man who is killing our soldiers in Vietnam." I was shocked. I berated him for using such words on this or any other president. But I think my son planted in his father the first doubts about the wisdom of that war. Like so many others who backed the war, in time the doubts evolved into unqualified opposition.

CHAPTER 10

WHILE LEARNING THE WAYS of the Washington bureaucrat, I had also worked hard on the book on the frontier army for Macmillan's Wars of the United States series. Paul Prucha and I had settled on the Mexican War of 1846–48 as a rough dividing line between his book and mine. I tapped the rich resources of the Interior Department library, which included the old Indian Office library. I could not only check books out of the library but also obtain others on interlibrary loan from the Library of Congress.

I strove to ensure that no one could ever accuse me of writing my book on government time. Unlike universities, which encourage and subsidize faculty members to research and write books, the government pays employees to do their jobs, not engage in private undertakings. Since I hoped to earn royalties from the Macmillan book, I took great pains to avoid even a hint of conflict of interest. Such a hint, of course, arose from my use of the department's library, but I thought this not unreasonable since the public also could consult the library's holdings. To the puzzlement of my academic friends, therefore, the book took shape in my home study during weekends and periods of annual leave.

As I wrote, the subject loomed as much too large for a single volume—a common perception among historians, who dread leaving anything out. I proposed two volumes instead of one. The series

editor, Lou Morton, peremptorily vetoed the idea; it would destroy
the symmetry of the series. In Macmillan's executive editor, however, I found an ally. Peter Ritner had unveiled the Wars of the
United States series with great fanfare, yet only one volume had
been published, Russell Weigley's *History of the United States Army*.
None other appeared forthcoming for several years. Peter seized
on my proposal as a way to maintain momentum. He overruled
Lou Morton. Macmillan's fall list of 1967 carried *Frontiersmen in
Blue: The United States Army and the Indian, 1848-1865*. The second
volume would deal with the decades after the Civil War.

The publication date for *Frontiersmen in Blue* coincided with the
annual convention of the Western History Association, held that
year at the Palace Hotel in San Francisco. I had remained active
in WHA since election to the governing council at Denver in 1962,
participating in all the controversies and debates involved in
setting a new association on course. The most contentious centered
on a quarterly publication. The founders had worked to build an
organization that, unlike other professional societies, brought academics and laypeople together. Accordingly, rather than the usual
scholarly journal, we wanted a magazine with popular appeal. In
Salt Lake City in 1963 we had created such a magazine, with my
old friend A. Russell Mortensen, now teaching at the University of
Utah, as editor. The first issue of *The American West*, a slick-paper,
amply illustrated quarterly in magazine format, appeared late in 1964.

As my three-year term on the council drew to a close, Jack
Carroll vigorously promoted my candidacy for the vice presidency,
which of course would automatically lead to the presidency. He
faced a formidable task, for I hardly typified the distinguished,
Ph.D.-holding professor who usually headed professional associa-
tions. WHA had evolved in this tradition. As president, Ray Billington
had been followed by my old professor at Indiana, Oscar Winther;
the Rev. John Francis Bannon of St. Louis University had succeeded
Oscar; then came Robert G. Athearn of the University of Colorado.
But Carroll argued that WHA was different. We reached out to
the Westerner corrals and others outside academia, and therefore

the leadership must not be exclusively academic. He prevailed. At El Paso in 1966 W. Eugene Hollon of the University of Oklahoma took office as president and I as vice president. Within hours of his inauguration, Gene and his wife, Bette, took flight for a year's sabbatical in Spain, leaving me as acting president.

Gene Hollon got back to the United States in time to preside over the San Francisco meeting in October 1967. My own inauguration as president occurred there. Peter Ritner flew out to promote *Frontiersmen in Blue* and talk about its successor volume. Lucille accompanied me, for the first time. It was all a grand experience, highly gratifying to the ego. I made a good president too, for I brought bureaucratic skills to a number of knotty issues, including legal problems, that might have eluded professorial talents.

From the beginning, the most divisive issue had been the publication. Russ Mortensen had done a fine job of launching *The American West*, but the academics felt it not scholarly enough to meet their needs. Besides, it encountered financial troubles at the University of Utah. A professional publisher with a bankroll came to the rescue. Almost no one liked George Pfeiffer III, but he kept the magazine afloat. The editorial offices moved from Salt Lake City to Berkeley, California, and Wallace Stegner allowed his name to appear on the masthead as editor in chief. The real editors, however, were Roger Olmstead, T. H. Watkins, and J. S. Holliday. In format and content, they continued the formula set by Russ Mortensen. But the shift stirred rancor, hard feelings, and controversies that were to swirl around the conspicuously nonacademic George Pfeiffer for years to come.

The new leadership of *The American West* intensified the demand for a journal more conventional in content, format, and scholarly apparatus. Sometime late in 1967, while in Tucson on Park Service business, I huddled with Jack Carroll in my motel room to find a solution. We framed a prospectus inviting universities all over the West to submit proposals for the sponsorship of a scholarly journal. We described conditions of financial support, office space, and editorial direction, and we set deadlines that would allow me to announce the new venture as my presidency climaxed at Tucson in October 1968.

We anticipated a bidding war among universities for the prestige of providing a home for WHA's new scholarly journal. What we could not anticipate was the Tet offensive in Vietnam early in 1968. That calamity imperiled federal grants to educational institutions and all but paralyzed university financial officers. Our invitation elicited not a single response. By September I was resigned to confessing failure. At that critical moment, however, Professor S. George Ellsworth persuaded the administration at Utah State University in Logan to undertake the sponsorship. At Tucson I announced the establishment of the *Western Historical Quarterly*, with George Ellsworth as editor. George created exactly what the scholarly wing of WHA wanted. Successors—Charles Peterson, Clyde Milner, and Anne Butler—continued in the Ellsworth tradition, and more than thirty-five volumes later *WHQ* is still a bright ornament to WHA and Utah State University.

Aside from *WHQ*, Tucson in 1968 provided an even greater ego boost than San Francisco. My program chairman, Donald Cutter of the University of New Mexico, had decided that our association should avoid the deadly scholarly presentations that typified presidential addresses in other professional organizations. WHA would have a presidential luncheon at which the president would serve light fare. I spoke of the vicissitudes of army life in the Arizona desert during the Apache wars, a subject that lent itself to humor aplenty. The audience loved it, and it set just the precedent Cutter hoped. Not many years passed, however, before the precedent collapsed under increasingly heavy fare.

At the banquet, Lucille and I sat next to our featured speaker, Barry Goldwater. He had resigned his Senate seat in 1964 to run for president and now was scarcely three weeks away from regaining it in the election of 1968. He titled his address "The West That Was," but he inserted two full paragraphs complimenting me for my work on Fort Bowie and Hubbell Trading Post. He also took a humorous shot at Stewart Udall (a fellow Arizonan) for replacing the buffalo on the Interior Department seal with a pair of stylized cupped hands. They seemed to say, the senator declared, "You're in good hands with Secretary Udall."

I liked and respected Barry Goldwater, even though I stood at the opposite pole of the political spectrum. Occasionally he came to the meetings of the Potomac corral of Westerners, which I had rejoined on returning to Washington in 1964. When President Nixon embarked on a purge of the upper ranks of the civil service following his reelection in 1972, Senator Goldwater sent word to the Interior Department to "leave Utley alone."

Even less than Barry Goldwater, most of the Park Service disliked the cupped hands on the Interior Department seal. The idea, in fact, had originated in the Park Service itself as one of the many new directions George Hartzog initiated to give a distinctive stamp to his administration. The design experts persuaded Secretary Udall that the buffalo hardly represented the nationwide responsibilities of his department. Worse yet in the eyes of Park Service traditionalists, the same people persuaded Hartzog that the cupped hands should replace the eagle on the park ranger's badge and that the arrowhead shield, with its snow-capped mountain, ponderosa pine, and buffalo did not symbolize the nationwide responsibilities of the National Park Service. Out went the arrowhead, to be replaced by a couple of interlocking triangles with three spheres in the center. I have forgotten the precise symbolism, but I think the spheres stood for cannonballs and conveyed that the park system was about more than western mountains and pine trees.

While all the Service's interpretive programs sported bold new initiatives, none was more visible than design. In publications, museums, films, wayside exhibits, and all other visible expressions of Hartzog's Park Service, graphic artists sought and often gained the applause of the New York arbiters of acceptable modern design. In time the buffalo would return to the department's seal and appear for the first time on the park ranger's badge, the arrowhead would displace the twisted wickets and cannonballs, and interpretive design would aim more at the traveling public than the New York experts. At the height of the elitist orientation, however, I had my own encounter with the new look in design.

Most of the parks sold official "handbooks"—guidebooks that explained what the park stood for and what the visitor should experience. I had written the handbooks for Fort Union, Fort Davis, and Golden Spike. Shortly after moving to Washington, I was asked to find time to write a new handbook for Custer Battlefield. The old handbook, a joint effort of Major and Evelyn Luce, had become a period piece, both in content and design.

Vince Gleason, chief of publications, stood in the forefront of the new-age designers. A short, ruddy-faced man with a volatile temper, a tendency to shout when crossed, and an unshakable faith in his own opinions, Vince had given service publications a new face. Mostly it was an overdue and appealing face, one that would endure. But some of Vince's ideas seemed wrongheaded to me, especially the quest for the design fraternity's approval rather than the park visitor's.

Vince and I had many arguments, some heated and noisy. But I respected much of what he had accomplished, and I think we both regarded the other as a friend. He assured me that the Custer handbook would receive special design treatment. He even traveled to Montana to persuade the nonprofit Custer Battlefield cooperating association to put up $8,000 to pay for a truly handsome package in which to display my prose. I'm sure the crusty old ranchers who made up the association's board visualized an abundance of colorful Remington and Russell artwork.

I snatched a few moments here and there to write the text and finally finished it in 1968. Vince meanwhile spent the association's money—for a design that neither I nor the association's board could have pictured in our wildest imagination. He contracted Leonard Baskin, one of the nation's leading exponents of modern art, to render a series of impressionistic water colors and drawings of the major players, military and Indian, in the Battle of the Little Bighorn.

I was stunned when I saw the mock-up, with a brooding Custer on the cover and equally bizarre portraits scattered throughout. Especially offensive was a full-length view of the naked Custer, dead and mutilated, stretched out on the battlefield. As a final indignity, an essay on "The Art and the Artist," by the distinguished director of the Amon Carter Museum, Mitchell Wilder, lauded Baskin for capturing the very heart of each of his subjects. "Examine Baskin's drawings—Indians and officers," wrote Wilder. "All are asking 'Why?'" Pure nonsense. Neither Baskin nor Wilder had any but a superficial acquaintance with the officers and Indians, yet both presumed to reach deep into each and convey their character and emotions.

Of course I was furious with Vince, and I knew the park association's board members, who had paid the bill, would be even more furious. They had been betrayed, and I felt the same way. Personally, I have never cared for impressionistic art, but the issue here, I felt, transcended personal taste. I strongly believed that literature designed for the park visitor, as aid to touring and understanding the park, should contain only literal illustrations—photographs, for example, and realistic artwork. Vince well knew that I expected the Custer handbook to feature literal illustrations—I provided them, and he included some in an appendix—but he kept the Baskin scheme hidden until it was too late to back out. Anyway, he had never had the slightest doubt about the wisdom of his course, and the Baskin renderings elated him.

Confronted with a fait accompli, I had but one recourse. Take my name off the title page, I demanded; I did not want it associated with the design. Especially did I not want my friendship with the Custer family jeopardized by what I knew would prove deeply offensive to them. The drawing of the naked and mutilated Custer alone, I knew, would infuriate them.

This would have been the simplest resolution of the dispute, one that I still wish had been adopted. But my name already had some value for a title page, and besides, everyone in Washington, the region, and the park knew I had written the text. To separate me from the handbook would embarrass even so self-assured a person as Vince Gleason. We had a seemingly unbreakable impasse, serious because the park urgently needed the new publication.

Then one evening, as the family ate dinner, the wall telephone above the table rang. "Hello, my friend. How's the little woman?" — always the ominous prelude when the caller was George Hartzog. Like Lyndon Johnson, Hartzog had a talent, by joshing cajolery tinged with an overtone of coercion, for getting his own way. I caved in—on one condition: removal of the drawing of the naked, mutilated Custer.

The Custer Battlefield handbook appeared in 1969, with my name on the title page as author. Readers were left to puzzle over why page nineteen was blank, lacking even a page number. It represented all I had salvaged in the standoff.

In the end, however, Vince Gleason reveled in total victory. The Baskin design won instant acclaim from the arbiters of design. The shoulder-length drawing of Custer on the cover quickly decorated the cover of *American Heritage,* with a portfolio of other portraits inside the magazine. They have been printed time and again ever since, partly because they are in the public domain and thus free to the user, but partly also because they resonated with some kind of responsive chord in the public. To the modern generation, Baskin's brooding portrayal is probably the best known of all the hundreds of representations, photographic and artistic alike, of George Armstrong Custer.

Predictably, the board members of the Custer Battlefield Historical and Museum Association erupted in angry but futile protest. Custer purists, even then nurturing an infant organization called the Little Big Horn Associates, also united in a outcry drowned by the applause of the critics. Now several thousand strong, the associates still nurse a grievance against the Park Service for inflicting Baskin on the world.

Even my tiny sense of satisfaction at having substituted a blank page for the most offending of the drawings evaporated. Not for years did I discover that Vince had quietly slipped the drawing into the second printing and kept it there through the life of the publication. Owners of the brochure whose copy contains a blank page nineteen hold a "rare book" indeed.

I wrote the Custer Battlefield handbook not as a part of my job but at the expense of other elements of my job—in other words, voluntarily. One might suppose Vince and I had come to a parting of ways. Almost at once, however, he asked me if I could find time to write a handbook for Fort Bowie, newly authorized for addition to the park system. I said I would try, if he would promise that every single aspect of design would be literal. He promised. When the mock-up was ready, he called me to his office. There, propped up on a bookcase behind his desk, stood the brochure, its cover sporting an Indian portrait by Leonard Baskin. I still have the copy he thus mutilated. When *A Clash of Cultures: Fort Bowie and the Chiricahua Apaches* appeared in 1976, the cover bore a drawing by Frederic Remington of a file of cavalrymen, and every one of the dozens of illustrations inside met the literal test.

In the mid-1980s, after I had left federal service, the superintendent of Custer Battlefield decided that the time had come for an update of the old 1969 handbook. Still head of publications, Vince Gleason proposed that I write it under contract with the Park Service. After much half-humorous banter about Baskin, I consented on explicit condition that the illustrative content be literal. Published in 1988, *Custer Battlefield: Official National Park Handbook* was crammed with the literal—photographs, original and historic artwork, and a set of dramatic color photographs of the battlefield today. But there on page seven, occupying the entire page, was Baskin's Custer. "The 'foreboding air' that seems to hang over Baskin's drawings," stated the caption, "has been called a reflection of 'man's mortality, brutality, and futility' in the face of tragedy no one seemed to comprehend." That sort of interpretation is pompous nonsense, but I can appreciate the relish Vince surely felt at having the last word on Baskin.

The squabble over Baskin coincided with the beginnings of what became the red power movement. In 1968 Vine Deloria, Jr., published *Custer Died for Your Sins.* I recall scanning an excerpt in *Playboy* magazine in my office at the 801 Building and reflecting on how historically farcical it was to fix on Custer as the personification of all the "sins" white people inflicted on Indians. But like Baskin, Deloria captured a public mood that escaped me. The book proved wildly popular, and soon, as the Indian protest movement gathered momentum, bumper stickers proliferated with the slogan "Custer died for your sins."

Vine Deloria gave new life to George Armstrong Custer, in a persona the unflattering reverse of Errol Flynn's portrayal. Amid the swirling public interest kicked up by Deloria, the editor of the *New York Times Magazine* wondered who in fact was the "real" General Custer. He asked Wallace Stegner to write an article answering the question. I had known and worked with Stegner when he chaired Secretary Udall's advisory board; in fact, he presided the day I insulted Frank Masland. Stegner recommended that I write the article.

Here was a wonderful opportunity for an ambitious writer—publication in the *New York Times Magazine*. The editor offered me a handsome honorarium if the article was accepted, a modest consolation prize if rejected. I got the consolation prize, but I sold the article anyway. "Custer: Hero or Butcher?" appeared in the February 1971 issue of *American History Illustrated*. Though not the *New York Times*, the magazine injected my appraisal as a note of historical sanity in a world made wildly unhistorical by Deloria and the mood of the times. "Custer: Hero or Butcher?" has been included in several anthologies designed for college reading.

After excursions into southwestern military and Indian history and my preoccupation with the bureaucratic bustle of Washington, Leonard Baskin and Vine Deloria brought George Armstrong Custer back into my life in a big way.

CHAPTER 11

BY THE LATE 1960s I had won George Hartzog's confidence. I disliked some of his initiatives, such as design, but in my own field I could support him loyally and enthusiastically. In turn, I think he concluded that I had learned enough about Washington's ways to be trusted with relationships with the Interior Department hierarchy, members of Congress, and even on occasion the White House. Also, I proved adept at conceiving justifications and courses of action for accomplishing what he wanted accomplished. Never, however, did he pressure me to compromise my professional convictions. Always, he demanded honest professional advice, and always he got it. If something unprofessional had to be done for political reasons, he would do it and not ask for professional support. For that I shall always be grateful. Despite the turmoil of his entire span of leadership, despite what I regarded as many ill-conceived notions, I came to admire and respect George Hartzog and functioned as a loyal member of his team. I look back on him as the greatest director in the history of the Park Service.

George pioneered in urban recreation, in serving inner-city dwellers, and in opening the Park Service ranks to women and minorities. But his premier achievement was an unprecedented expansion of the National Park System. With the backing of Secretary Udall and President Johnson, Hartzog maneuvered through Congress legislation that added nearly fifty units to the system. Many of these were historical parks or monuments, and I became deeply involved in legislative affairs. I testified in House and Senate subcommittee hearings on Fort Bowie, Golden Spike, Pecos, Hubbell Trading Post, and others.

Two memories of the Hubbell hearings remain with me. As usual, before riding to the Hill for the House hearing, a number of staff people gathered in George's office for discussions. Present was Edward B. Danson, the museum director who had first proposed Hubbell for the park system and now was an influential member of Udall's advisory board. George asked me how we would interpret the post. I said we planned to exhibit the various rooms of the house and trading post as they were in Don Lorenzo's day, stocking the shelves of the trading room with turn-of-the-century merchandise.

George erupted: "I am not going to have another dead and embalmed historical area. We are going to keep it as an active trading post." I protested that the Navajos would never display themselves in the trading ritual to a gawking public, that trade would wither to nothing, and he would wind up with a lifeless if not a dead park. He remained adamant, and surprisingly, Ned Danson spoke up in his support. We went to the Hill, and George's testimony committed the Park Service to a living trading post.

Hartzog's gamble paid off handsomely. With an experienced trader behind the massive wooden counters, the Navajos continued to bring their silver and blankets to Hubbell Trading Post to exchange for groceries and other merchandise. More than three decades later, it was still a highly successful operation, living testimony to my flawed judgment.

My other memory is of the Senate hearings on Hubbell. Senator Clinton P. Anderson of New Mexico questioned the Park Service witnesses closely. Turning to me, he said, "Now, Mr. Utley, tell me just who were the artists of the Taos School that you say are so well represented in the Hubbell collections?" I answered with the list included in my study. "Well, Mr. Utley," he replied with scarcely concealed scorn, "my recollection of the Taos School is this," and he proceeded to rattle off name after name. In this, of course, Clinton Anderson was far more expert than I, for he had known most of them as friends. I could only mumble "Yes, sir," and sit in humiliation. I later learned from Senator Goldwater, however, that Anderson's animus toward the Hubbell proposal arose from a conviction that Don Lorenzo Hubbell had once bested him in the sale of a Navajo blanket.

My most spectacular defeat sprang from trying to stand firm against the Polish American community. To American Poles a specially revered hero was Thaddeus Kosciusko, the Polish general who fought for the colonists in the American Revolution, then returned to Poland to champion independence. Revisiting America in 1797, he passed a winter in a Philadelphia boardinghouse. Edward Pizak, a Philadelphia Polish American who had made a fortune as head of Mother Paul's frozen fish firm, mobilized ethnic Poles all across the nation in a crusade to establish the "Kosciusko House" as a national historic site.

Kosciusko's ephemeral connection to this structure, two decades after his important contributions to American history and distant from where they had occurred, left no base on which to erect even a thin case for historical significance. As Hartzog commented, this building was a monument not to Kosciusko but to his landlady.

We underestimated the enormous political power of Polish Americans when led by a determined and wealthy dynamo who was a political power himself. A huge volume of mail from Polish Americans and from members of Congress with Polish constituencies inundated the Park Service. Much of it centered on me, for Ed Pizak had met with me and come away incensed at my resolve that the "Kosciusko House" lacked national significance. Only prejudice against Poles, advocates suggested, could have blinded me to what to them was incontestable.

Senators and congressmen rushed to cosponsor legislation to meet Pizak's demands. In committee hearings, we resisted. At a Senate hearing, I spotted a huge manila folder labeled "Utley's statements"—one small reminder that Pizak's minions came prepared. Hartzog testified with his usual brilliant performance, although he could not pronounce Kosciusko's name; wherever it appeared in his witness statement, we crossed it out and substituted "the general." Busloads of Poles filling every seat and lining the walls, however, spoke more eloquently to committee members than Hartzog.

Our reasoned arguments about historical significance fell easy prey to Ed Pizak's steamroller. Congress can hardly be faulted for heeding thousands of patriotic Polish Americans rather than the dissent of a handful of bureaucrats. The Thaddeus Kosciusko National Historic Site is now administered as part of Independence National Historical Park.

A continuing exasperation, dating from years before I came to Washington, sprang from the stubby, hyperactive Kansas congressman who sat as ranking minority member of our House legislative subcommittee. Joe Skubitz prided himself on his knowledge of Kansas history, and he worked tirelessly to add Fort Scott, Kansas, to the park system. Fort Scott had played a marginal role on the Indian frontier and as a military post in the Civil War. Many of its buildings were wrecks, while others had been converted to modern uses, and all had been absorbed within the town of Fort Scott. To no avail the Park Service had tried to persuade Skubitz that Fort Scott lacked national significance and integrity. Then a Kansas professor told Skubitz that some of the first black Civil War regiments had been organized at Fort Scott and that this gave it national significance. Hoping to make the problem go away, the advisory board let the fort become a National Historic Landmark. That of course played right into Skubitz's hands, for it was the biggest hurdle he had to surmount. When I reached Washington, one of the earliest assignments to fall to me was to try to keep Joe Skubitz pacified.

Joe was an open, generous, and friendly soul, and we got along well. He grumbled that the Park Service had no historians expert in western history. That obviously included me, since I could not appreciate the towering significance of Fort Scott. Little by little we gave in, finally agreeing to back a proposal to channel federal funds into Fort Scott even though it was not in the park system.

Joe had no trouble getting that through his own House subcommittee, but the Senate entertained some skepticism. With Assistant Director Ted Swem and our legislative chief, Frank Harrison, I appeared before the Senate subcommittee, chaired by Senator

Alan Bible of Nevada. In the course of the testimony, both Ted Swem and Frank Harrison had to admit they had never visited Fort Scott. "Well, Mr. Utley," Senator Bible declared, turning a withering scowl on me, "as chief historian you surely have been to Fort Scott." "No, Mr. Chairman," I admitted, "neither have I." Bible exploded: "The least the Park Service can do when coming in here with an expensive proposition like this is to send witnesses who have visited the place." Before we had even got back to our offices, Bible had called Hartzog and forcefully delivered the same admonition.

That afternoon, a Friday, I ran into Chief Archeologist John Corbett in the hall. He told me he had to testify Monday morning on the Alibates Flint Quarry legislation. "Well, I'm sure glad you've been there," I said, describing our scalding that morning. "But I haven't," replied Corbett. "You better get there," I warned. John flew to Amarillo, Texas, on Saturday morning, visited the site, and flew back Sunday. Monday morning, Senator Bible's first question was whether any of the witnesses had actually visited the site.

While we stalled Joe Skubitz on Fort Scott, he came up with another wild idea—the Cherokee Strip Living History Museum at Arkansas (Ar-kán-sas) City. Hartzog sent me to look at it and to appear before local historical groups to tell them what an outstanding authority on Kansas history they had in their congressman. The museum turned out to be a Quonset hut packed with old things people had brought in for display.

Stall as we might, Joe Skubitz did not waver. He got federal funding for Fort Scott, to be funneled through the National Park Service to the city and spent under Park Service oversight. That proved such a misapplication of funds that we finally surrendered and supported legislation to establish the Fort Scott National Historic Site. If the federal government had to pay for Fort Scott, the Park Service might as well manage it and see to the proper expenditure of the appropriations.

Joe even got his Quonset hut. He slipped a rider onto legislation dealing with other matters and made the Park Service responsible for the Cherokee Strip Living History Museum. There we kept as low a profile as possible, assigning administration to a local entity under a cooperative agreement. At last, after Joe's retirement, the Service managed to divest itself of that responsibility.

I remember Joe Skubitz fondly, for his genial disposition, his innocence in all things historical, his persistence, and perhaps above all his ability to overcome bureaucratic obstruction.

Most of us in the Park Service lamented the end of the Johnson years. War, assassination, protest, social upheaval, and burning cities kept the nation in constant turmoil. More and more the public reviled Lyndon Johnson, and posterity has only begun to be kind to him. But LBJ had been good for the National Park Service, in backing expansion of the park system, in launching the National Historic Preservation Program as part of the Great Society, and in seeking more generous funding for the Service. The career Service enjoyed high morale, for Johnson, unlike other presidents, did not hold federal bureaucrats up to public scorn. He listened to them and even promoted some to high rank.

The First Lady also helped our cause immensely. Lady Bird Johnson's beautification program nicely complemented Secretary Udall's environmental initiatives, and she lent her presence to campaigns for new parks, such as Redwoods. With Udall she rafted the Rio Grande in Big Bend National Park and the Snake River in Grand Teton National Park. She brought her prestige to the movement for the National Historic Preservation Act. Later, after the president had appointed the first members of the Advisory Council on Historic Preservation, she hosted a White House reception for them and other historic preservationists. Lucille and I attended. In many important ways, the Park Service benefited from the magic this gracious and kindly woman worked on her husband, the government, and the people from 1963 to 1969.

The Johnson years also gave us an interior secretary to surpass even FDR's Harold Ickes. A Kennedy holdover, Stewart Udall never fit comfortably with Lyndon Johnson. But his success in arousing the public to dangers to the environment and, with White House backing, in getting landmark environmental laws enacted by Congress made him one of the Johnson administration's brightest stars. Pleased, LBJ turned Udall loose, while Lady Bird entered ardently into his ventures. Udall personally selected George Hartzog to head the Park Service when Connie Wirth proved too independent. The two shared common values and goals. They worked well together. And cannily, Hartzog always made certain that Udall got as much public credit as possible for Park Service achievements.

We lost a great secretary of the interior when Stewart Udall returned to Phoenix to practice law. But he gave us a fine parting gift by appointing Lady Bird Johnson to the secretary's advisory board. The members elected her chair of the history committee. She took her responsibilities very seriously, and I worked closely with her. She, I, and her Secret Service guard would lunch at the Madison Hotel and carefully go over the substance of her report to the full board on prospective National Historic Landmarks.

George Hartzog survived the transition from LBJ to Richard Nixon, but we all greeted our new secretary with trepidation. Oilman and Alaska governor Walter J. Hickel seemed on all issues at opposite poles from Stewart Udall. Hartzog quickly cemented his relationship by drafting a directive to himself from Hickel outlining the secretary's expectations of the Park Service; no other Interior bureau chief had even approached Hickel. When he won the applause of environmentalists by denying an offshore drilling permit near California's sensitive coast, our fears vanished. Then in 1970 the blunt secretary addressed a letter to the president lamenting Vice President Spiro Agnew's attacks on American youth for their antiwar demonstrations, and that sealed his fate in the cabinet.

Hickel's successor was Rogers C. B. Morton, a big, bluff, friendly man who proved, within the constraints of Republican ideology, a fine secretary. As a congressman from Maryland's Eastern Shore, he had sat on the Park Service's legislative subcommittee, and so knew our business. His wife was a historic preservationist, and he took a personal interest in our historical programs, both internal and external. As with Hickel, Hartzog swiftly put his relationship with Morton on a solid footing.

Early in 1972 Hartzog elevated Ernest Connally to a new position labeled Associate Director for Professional Services. That left me,

once more, as acting chief (now director) of the Office of Archeology and Historic Preservation (OAHP). Who would succeed Ernest
became a matter of much speculation. Once more, my lack of the
"terminal degree" disturbed Hartzog. Connally convened a panel
of some of the country's foremost historians, archeologists,
historical architects, and state historic preservation officers. At a
Cosmos Club luncheon the group united in declaring me the best
choice for the position. They all wrote letters to Hartzog urging
the appointment. Russ Mortensen, who had replaced Roy Appleman in 1969, moved up to chief historian.

In gaining the approval of Connally's search committee, I had
to convince archeologists and historical architects that I understood their disciplines and would represent them as well as history.
As director of OAHP, however, my preoccupations focused less on
these disciplines than on the new National Register of Historic
Places and especially the new grants-in-aid program. That meant
conferring frequently with state historic preservation officers (SHPOs),
developing procedures for surveying state historic places and
expanding the National Register, setting priorities for the grants-
in-aid program, and working with Bob Garvey and the Advisory
Council on Historic Preservation to apply the protective provisions
of law to federal and federally assisted undertakings.

As OAHP director, I had much more power and prestige, a
reputation for interdisciplinary competence and fairness, more
challenge and the accompanying stress, but in the end a less satis-
fying job. Some of the SHPOs were prima donnas, incompetents,
or just plain nasty. Other federal departments—especially Defense,
Transportation, and Housing and Urban Development—cooperated
grudgingly or not at all in putting the new law into operation.
Interior's bureaus were scarcely more responsive, and to my chagrin
Park Service officials could not quite accept the new law as applying
to them as well as the rest of the government. After all, the Park
Service had long been the federal agency expert in historic
preservation. Even Hartzog seemed stunned when an outraged
superintendent of Yellowstone National Park called to report that
the Wyoming SHPO had just arrived to carry out his survey
responsibilities in this corner of his state.

Within the Park Service, the old-line veterans had yet to accept Connally as a peer, even though he now operated at the associate director level. Worse yet, many of the people newly added to OAHP came from backgrounds similar to Connally's—academic, scholarly, and lacking understanding or sympathy for the traditional Park Service. They looked down on the gray and the green, and not surprisingly the gray and the green regarded them, often correctly, as a bunch of snobs.

In 1970 the Park Service relinquished its lease on the 801 Building and moved OAHP to a newly constructed building at Eleventh and L streets, not a very desirable location on the very edge of a slum neighborhood. I did not move to this building but rather occupied an office adjoining Connally's in the main Interior building. What I lost in distance from subordinates I gained by sitting near the center of power. At least weekly, Ernest and I went to the L Street Building to "show the flag."

As Richard Nixon approached his overwhelming defeat of George McGovern in the 1972 presidential election, the Park Service celebrated the centennial of Yellowstone National Park. For George Hartzog, it was a high point of his administration. The First Lady, Pat Nixon, and Secretary Morton were among the dignitaries that gathered at Madison Junction on a cold October night to pay homage to the founders of the first national park.

I was not there, but I derived a perverse satisfaction from the ceremony. For several years I had called Horace M. Albright a friend and, with conservationists everywhere, venerated him as an icon from the early days of the National Park Service. With Stephen Mather, Albright had cofounded the Service in 1916, and he had followed Mather as director in 1929–33. A retired borax executive, he used his many political connections to benefit the Park Service, and he continued to exert great influence on the Service itself.

One of the issues I had dealt with for several years was the validity of the "campfire story." For decades the world traced the origins of Yellowstone National Park to a scene enacted around a campfire at Madison Junction in 1869, when a party of early explorers debated the future of the thermal wonders they had marveled at that day. They agreed that these were treasures that ought to belong to the American people and be guarded against commercial exploitation. Congress responded to this idealistic notion by creating the first national park.

By the 1960s the park's engineer-turned-historian Aubrey Haines had cast enough doubt on the validity of this story that the reenactments that park interpreters periodically staged at Madison Junction had been discontinued. By my time, Aubrey's research had left virtually no doubt that the campfire story was a myth. It was a cherished myth, however, one to which Park Service traditionalists clung fiercely. I firmly supported Aubrey, but ultimately his heresy drove him into premature retirement.

Horace Albright vehemently defended the truth of the campfire story, and as planning for the centennial got underway, he insisted that a reenactment be included among the festivities at Madison Junction. This confronted Hartzog with a dilemma, for I told him he could not let Horace have his way without perpetuating as history what had clearly been shown to be legend. One day George called me to his office and declared: "Utley, we are going to have a campfire at Madison Junction, and we are going to have it for the same damn reason they had it in 1869—to keep warm."

And need it they did. The temperature that night plunged below freezing, and snow fell on the assembled dignitaries and their audience. Secretary Morton labored through a long speech as the First Lady and everyone else shivered. Doubtless all wished they could crowd around that campfire.

The Yellowstone centennial turned out to be George Hartzog's last hurrah. Early in December 1972, with Nixon decisively elected to another four years in the White House, we were stunned by the news that Hartzog had been fired. The president himself had ordered Secretary Morton to dismiss him. Morton had lunched with Nixon and pleaded for Hartzog's retention, to no avail. In his book, *Battling for the National Parks,* George tells how unknowingly he offended the president's pal Bebe Rebozo by a decision affecting a concession his brother-in-law held at Biscayne National Monument, Florida. George later related to me that Rebozo had told

Nixon he wanted only one favor as the second term got underway: "Get that son of a bitch Hartzog."

Nixon did, and he compounded the insult by naming one of
his advance men as the first director in history not to be drawn
from within the Park Service. In what must have been a painful
ceremony for Rogers Morton, Nixon aides Bob Haldeman and
John Erlichman both stood by as the secretary administered the
oath of office to Ronald H. Walker.

CHAPTER 12

RON WALKER HAD SERVED ably, even brilliantly, as advance man for President Nixon's visits to China and Russia, but he exhibited no shadow of qualification to direct the National Park Service. He had bought into a popular belief that managers, whether corporate or governmental, were interchangeable; learn to manage, and one could manage anything. Even had that been true, his background revealed very little managerial experience. Thirty-five years old, he brought with him from the White House a squad of equally youthful acolytes. While Ron himself seemed affable and open to aid and counsel, the palace guard sought to insulate him from the corrupting infection of a career service believed to be teeming with anti-Nixon liberals. Moreover, as one of his young retainers declared, in the Walker administration the advice of no one over thirty-five would be trusted. Already I was forty-three.

What Richard Nixon and his cronies never learned was that career civil servants, whatever their politics, have an abiding interest in the success of their politically appointed chief. We wanted Ron Walker to look good and to succeed, simply because it was essential to the well-being of our service and our own careers. Gradually he came to grant us a guarded trust and to rely on our support.

But Ron simply did not know enough about the parks and the Park Service to provide leadership. His congressional relations, and his testimony in congressional hearings, were an almost unbroken sequence of disasters. He fell easily for fads, such as sending his regional directors to Disneyland to learn interpretation from the experts. In another, he turned over Yosemite National Park to Hollywood for a television series about park rangers. Happily, the pilot episode bombed with the public, but even so Ron appointed an assistant director in charge of relations with Music Corporation of America.

As these ventures reveal, Ron Walker came to the Park Service unfettered by habits and traditions that guided the career people. That created an environment in which new ideas could be surfaced and in which sentiments could be voiced that Hartzog would have regarded as disloyal if not treasonous.

As early as 1969, when Hartzog moved some key units out of OAHP, Ernest Connally and I had concluded that an American "monuments office" could never be built within the National Park Service. Superintendents and regional directors would never accept any system that ensured uniform application of professional policies and standards. The external programs of grants-in-aid, the National Register, National Landmarks, Historic American Buildings Survey, and Historic American Engineering Record would always have to compete for dollars with sewer systems at Yellowstone and parking lots at Yosemite. Confronted with such choices in the annual budget cycle, any Park Service director favors the parks.

Against this background, Ernest and I concluded that the only hope for a monuments office lay in a separate agency, one that combined the historical parks and the external programs under its own director. The Advisory Council on Historic Preservation's Bob Garvey shared our conclusion. We could talk this way only in the privacy of our offices. Had even the talk, much less any action, reached George Hartzog, we would have been instantly crushed. So Connally, Garvey, and I contented ourselves with feeding one another's discontent.

Meantime, we had launched an initiative that I thought would benefit the historical parks. That is where my heart and mind had always pointed. I knew that many were being mismanaged by superintendents who flouted the policies and standards and did as they pleased without any hindrance from regional directors. A cynical declaration that a practice or proposed project conformed to policy gained equally cynical approval in regional offices. I wanted the Washington office to have a stronger capability of focusing on the care of the park system's cultural resources.

Connally agreed with my proposal to make OAHP exclusively the domain of external programs—those dealing with historic preservation outside the National Park System. Those concerned only with the parks would be consolidated in a new assistant directorate. This concept had already been advanced under Hartzog. We laid it before Ron Walker and gained his approval. Although it would mean a step down in power and prestige, I wanted to go with the parks. By the end of 1973, I was assistant director of the National Park Service for park historic preservation. Russ Mortensen took over OAHP.

My organization, created from existing units in OAHP, consisted of the divisions of history, archeology, and historic architecture. Harry Pfanz, who had taken Roy Appleman's old post when Russ moved up, became chief historian. Hank Judd, who knew more than anyone in the Service about taking apart and putting together a building, became chief historical architect. And in Doug Scovill I finally found an archeologist willing to work in an interdisciplinary team and bring the rest of the archeologists into line.

I took great satisfaction in my new job. Ron Walker responded well to my plea for a mandate to spotlight management's failure to live up to the Service's policies and standards. My staff drew up a three-page "horrors list" of management blunders that had damaged or destroyed irreplaceable historic features at parks throughout the system. With the director's backing and the undeniable validity of the horrors list, I gained the attention of regional directors and superintendents and held constructive meetings all across the nation. I soon discovered, however, that Walker had given similar mandates to other high officials, that not all were compatible, and that when two clashed, the director was not there to mediate. In the end, my efforts bore fruit in shaping the attitudes of some of the younger generation who would rise to key positions in the 1980s and 1990s. But I discerned little immediate change in the imperious way in which superintendents and regional directors did as they pleased without regard for official Service policy.

I also raised my voice against what I regarded as the perversion of historical interpretation into mere entertainment. The biggest target was "living history," which had spread wildly through the Park Service as one of Hartzog's initiatives. Ironically, George always traced the birth of living history to his decision to keep Hubbell Trading Post as an active, living enterprise. That experiment succeeded wonderfully.

But soon, under the prodding of aggressive lieutenants seeking to put the Hartzog stamp on interpretation, every superintendent joined in the stampede to costume their interpreters and "make history come alive." Relevance to the main park themes fell casualty to the drive. Interpretation exists to give meaning to the historic resources and values that justify preservation for public benefit. Yet living history took on a life of its own, swelling into productions that entertained but threw little light on park features and sometimes even competed with them. Thus a costumed lady dipped candles on the Saratoga Battlefield, thousands of dollars supported a "living historical farm" on the Gettysburg Battlefield, and mules turned a sorghum grinder on the Lookout Mountain Battlefield. Interpreters, I charged in voice and print, used historic landscapes and structures merely as stage sets for what was entertainment rather than interpretation.

My blunt rhetoric stirred anger in the ranks of interpreters and superintendents alike. They replied that the public loved to watch cannons fired by men (and even women) in Union blue and Confederate gray, eagerly bought loaves of tasty bread baked in adobe ovens at Pecos National Monument, and played the game of trying to penetrate with modern allusions the 1865 persona of a paroled Confederate soldier at Appomattox Court House. My critics were right: park visitors delighted in living history, just as they delighted in the pseudohistorical productions of Disneyland. In a popular slogan of the 1970s, "the medium is the message." The more thoughtful interpreters agreed with me but made scant headway against the mania sweeping the Park Service. Only shrinking appropriations rather than a distinction between interpretation and entertainment finally reined in the more egregious productions. Costumed demonstrations that were relevant to the principal park themes finally replaced the excesses of earlier years.

Much of my success in articulating issues and gaining a hearing, if not action, sprang from a trio of exceptionally able young historians in Harry Pfanz's history division. These were Barry Mackintosh and Dave Clary; and when Dave went off to the Omaha office, Marcella Sherfy took his place. Their fine minds and verbal skills, combined with their unswerving commitment to fundamental park values, not only kept me honest but put clear and compelling words in my mouth.

Throughout all these bureaucratic adventures, my domestic life developed along not uncommon lines. Lucille enjoyed being the chief historian's wife, and we entered wholeheartedly into the social life of the Park Service. Because of my position, we entertained often with large cocktail parties and smaller dinner gatherings. Lucille was a good cook and a good hostess.

But our worlds gradually drifted apart. I immersed myself in policies, programs, and bureaucratic machinations so complex that I shrank from explaining them. She wanted to know about this world, but I did not let her in. I traveled a great deal, and when home, spent most of my free time writing history. The second of the frontier army volumes—*Frontier Regulars*—was due at Macmillan in 1973. More and more, her world consisted of Don and Phil. She resisted repeated entreaties to take a trip now and then as a couple rather than a family. She went to the Western History Association meetings of 1967 and 1968, during my presidency, but would not leave the boys for any other trip.

At forty-three, without knowing it, I was a midlife crisis waiting to happen. It blew in June 1973 at Utah State University in Logan. I gave the keynote address at a weeklong writers' conference, then remained as part of the "faculty" through the week. One of the participants was Melody Webb Grauman, wife of a brilliant physician practicing in Soldotna, Alaska. With slim figure, straight brown hair falling far down her back, and a beautiful face, she caught my eye almost at once. She had a master's degree in history, wanted to write history, and talked and behaved with a candor and honesty that startled a polished bureaucrat adept at role-playing. She was twenty-seven, sixteen years my junior. Throughout the week, repeated eye contact testified to mutual attraction.

Logan plunged me into three years of turmoil to put my life back in shape. When I traveled to Alaska that summer, what had been assumed at Logan became explicit. The Western History Association meeting in Fort Worth in October provided another opportunity to get together, which we followed up with an Arizona trip that included Fort Bowie. Ever the embodiment of blunt expression, Melody broke off the affair abruptly because I could not bring myself to dismantle my family so suddenly.

Repairing a marriage that had come unglued proved impossible. Early in November 1975 I moved a few possessions out of the McLean house and into a one-bedroom apartment in Arlington.

Meantime, with the consent of her husband, David, Melody had readmitted me to her life. For one thing, he had little interest in history or historic sites and was pleased to have a surrogate for a pursuit in which she took such pleasure. Her ambition was to be a historian, not a housewife. She had no interest in teaching, but my speech at the Utah State writers' conference opened to her the world of the National Park Service and the role its historians played. Both personally and professionally, we fit well. For the next four years, Melody and I saw each other several times a year—always at the Western History Association and frequently during other of my travels.

Alaska beckoned officially as well as personally. In 1971 Congress had enacted the Alaska Native Claims Settlement Act, and the Park Service fell heir to the task of helping Native corporations select places of historical or cultural value for transfer to their custody. Establishing a means to carry that undertaking forward took me often to Alaska.

My midlife crisis had hardly ended, for much remained to be worked out between a middle-aged bureaucrat, product of the America of the 1950s, and a liberated child of the 1960s. But we worked hard at it, sometimes with seemingly little hope of success.

And while I finally gained a divorce late in 1977, she remained married to David.

The relationship with Melody produced one ironic result. In Santa Fe Lucille and I had been friends and neighbors of Zorro and Natalie Bradley. Big, soft-spoken, and easygoing, Zorro belied his namesake but was one of the Southwest Region's leading archeologists. By the time I got to Washington, Zorro was already there, lieutenant to Chief Archeologist John Corbett. Both resisted bringing their personnel and programs into Ernest Connally's new interdisciplinary office. Not until 1971 could Corbett be pressed into retirement. Zorro might have inherited his mantle had he been willing to join the team. The price of unwillingness was exile to a make-work position at the University of Alaska in Fairbanks. Ignored by an old-line regional director in Seattle, John Rutter, Zorro built a splendidly successful professional presence and program for the Park Service at the university. Although I had been instrumental in his exile, we repaired our friendship, and I became his staunch supporter in Washington as the Native claims legislation more and more involved the Service, and Zorro, in Alaskan affairs.

By now, Melody and David had relocated to Fairbanks. Soldotna, haven of fundamentalist Christians and right-wing extremists, had proved so obnoxious that Melody served notice on a reluctant David that if he would not leave, she would. David gave in, and by early 1974 he had reestablished his practice in Fairbanks, where Melody had a university library in which to pursue her avocation.

Meantime, Zorro and I had been working to set up an organization at the university, funded by the Park Service, to help the Native corporations identify historic and cultural properties they wished to take custody of under the Alaska Native Claims Settlement Act. I told Melody to introduce herself to Zorro. She did. They hit it off at once, but he had no job for her. She spent the summer of 1974 on the North Slope as an archeologist for the Alaska Pipeline, then under construction.

By the end of 1974 Zorro had a job. He had succeeded in establishing another Park Service position at the university. He hired Melody to take charge of assembling a cadre of more than a dozen anthropologists and historians to work with the Natives, identify cultural properties, and describe and evaluate them in terms persuasive enough to overcome the resistance of the three agencies from whose domain they would be taken—the Bureau of Land Management, the Fish and Wildlife Service, and the Forest Service. Although only a temporary appointment, Melody had her first job with the National Park Service.

On August 8, 1974, I spent the day at a meeting of the Advisory Council on Historic Preservation, where I argued Interior's position in a long-running clash between a highway and a cultural landscape in Hawaii. Back at Interior early in the evening, I dropped by the office of Deputy Director Russ Dickenson. Russ and I had come to Washington together in 1964, he to work in new-area studies after a solid career as ranger and superintendent. Able, thoughtful, relaxed, not easily stampeded, he had demonstrated rare diplomatic and managerial skills overseeing the political minefield of National Capital Parks. Now he tried to provide direction and stability for Ron Walker.

After I had briefed Russ on the happenings at the Advisory Council, we talked about the big news of the day. The "smoking gun" had been found at the White House. President Nixon would address the nation on television that night. There seemed no doubt that he would bring the long, sordid scandal of Watergate to a dramatic end by announcing his resignation from the presidency. In the midst of our conversation, Ron Walker shuffled in, his shoulders stooped, his face drawn, his hands clutching a bottle wrapped in a brown bag. He threw himself into a chair, looked at us with tears in his eyes, and said, "How do I explain to my kids what they are going to see on TV tonight?" It was a touchingly sad scene. Ron, I mused at the time, sat there as the personification of so many of the tragedies of Richard Nixon's creation.

Ironically, Ernest Connally had dined with Ron only the night before. Ernest and I had agreed that we had established good enough rapport with Ron to float the idea of a separate monuments office within the Department of the Interior. During this twice-postponed meeting, Ernest explained the concept and its rationale. How much of it Ron understood, especially the removal of all the historical and archeological parks from the National Park System, may be wondered. Nevertheless, he gave his approval to explore the notion unofficially with Secretary Morton. Ernest did so and met with a favorable response.

August 1974, however, was hardly the time to put much faith in Ron Walker's ability to sponsor a bold new measure. With the Nixon presidency ended, Walker's days as director were patently numbered. Also, he had grown embittered toward the administration, if not the president, as he had poured out to Connally in their dinner meeting. Heavy-handed antics as a presidential advance man had Walker in court for violating the civil rights of antiwar demonstrators. He had spent nearly $20,000 of his own money in attorney fees, he said, with no end in sight. The coffers of CREEP—the Committee to Reelect the President—still brimmed with donations from Republican fat cats; this money had helped other Nixon stalwarts with their legal fees, but not Walker. He felt betrayed.

In retrospect, Connally and I were foolish to think that Ron Walker could carry so radical a measure to fruition. Cut loose from his White House moorings, he had lost his clout within Interior. We thought Secretary Morton's approving reaction encouraging, but he probably had more pressing battles to fight.

The mortal blow came swiftly when Assistant Secretary Nathaniel Reed got wind of the plan. A shrewd, smart, and able Floridian with impeccable environmental and Republican credentials, Nat dominated and even micromanaged the Park Service as Walker grew weaker. Ernest and I were fortunate to emerge from this adventure with our careers intact.

Some of the same obstacles to the professional conduct of the Park Service's historic preservation responsibilities still exist. But I no longer believe a separate American monuments agency to be the answer. I applaud Nat Reed for squashing the seed before it could germinate.

On September 11, 1974, Ron Walker called a staff meeting of associate and assistant directors. He said he had not given enough time to his family in recent years, and so this morning he had handed his resignation to Secretary Morton, effective January 1, 1975. He thanked us profusely and emotionally for our support. Ernest Connally, ever the skilled impromptu speaker, delivered a felicitous pledge of the staff's continued support during the rest of Walker's tenure. As we filed out, he stood at the door and movingly thanked each of us.

CHAPTER 13

By the end of 1974, when Ron Walker's directorship expired, Secretary Morton had already selected a successor. Unlike Ron, Gary Everhardt came out of the career ranks: civil engineer in several regional offices capped by assistant superintendent of Yellowstone and superintendent of Grand Teton. Apparently Everhardt was the choice of Assistant Secretary Nat Reed, who urged the appointment on Morton. Except for the leadership Russ Dickenson could exert as deputy director, Reed had been running the Park Service anyway while Walker grew weaker. Some of us worried that Everhardt would not stand up to Reed as forcefully as Dickenson had.

Had he been a Texan, Gary Everhardt would have been labeled a good ol' boy. Forty years of age, beefy, balding, with a cherubic face always on the verge of a smile or a hearty laugh, he took on his new responsibilities thoughtfully and confidently. Anger rarely disturbed his good humor. Equanimity rarely yielded to any provocation. He drawled and smiled his way through congressional hearings with a low-key affability that earned him many friends and supporters in both House and Senate.

Gary came to Washington with little background and less interest in historic preservation. He came, however, seemingly determined to learn. He proved a good listener, and he asked question after question until he understood an issue. Ernest Connally and I found him receptive to our pleas for greater emphasis on historic preservation. He even gave sympathetic attention to our proposal to move OAHP out of the Park Service to separate status within the Interior Department. He finally decided to reject that idea, but he never reconciled the budgetary demands of the external programs with the needs of the parks. Grants-in-aid to the states for historic preservation could not excite his sympathies like upgrading failing sewer systems at Yellowstone National Park—a dilemma our organizational scheme for OAHP would have spared him.

I had ample opportunity to present my concerns to the new director, stressing the need for upgrading historic preservation in the parks and for sensitizing line managers to their stewardship for cultural as well as natural and scenic resources. Reflecting the conviction of many in the Service, I argued that preservation of the resources that justified a park's national status must take precedence over development and, indeed, all else. The Service had always given lip service to this creed, but the pressures for buildings, roads, trails, utilities, and visitor services had cultivated a management mindset that undermined it in practice.

Everhardt not only professed to agree with such a basic reordering of priorities but in turn promoted it in meetings with regional directors and other officials. He even embraced and gave wide publicity to the "horrors list" we had drawn up to impress Walker with Park Service failings. With Everhardt's backing, I continued my "road show" travels to espouse the proper care of the historical parks and the historic features of the other parks.

Gary established a "missions and priorities" task force, headed by the able director of the Southwest Region, Joe Rumberg, and bringing together several of the Service's best thinkers. It included my old friend Bill Brown, now in Alaska and increasingly an articulate philosophical spokesman for the principled approach to all issues. Also seated with us was Robert G. Stanton, a rising African American destined two decades later for the directorship. I won a seat on the "Rumberg Task Force" and drafted much of the proposed new statements of mission and priorities that we submitted to the director. The report embodied the "preservation first" philosophy.

Alas, like most task force reports in government, this one encountered the resistence of entrenched bureaucrats who could talk about change better than they could cope with it. As Regional Director John Rutter stressed to one of his colleagues, they had to close ranks to prevent Utley from shoving this historic preservation "nonsense" down their throats. They did. Of the nine regional directors, only two, Rumberg and San Francisco–based Howard Chapman, supported such a drastic new approach. Everhardt shrank from taking issue with this consensus.

The summer of 1975 was not a happy time, especially with my domestic crisis at home worsening. Everhardt's failure to live up to the promise of the task force on which so much labor had been expended was discouraging. My long-time foe John Rutter, still entrenched in the Seattle regional office, threatened to demolish all Zorro Bradley and I had tried to build in Alaska. In June the able and supportive Rogers Morton left to become secretary of commerce. His successor, former Wyoming governor Stan Hathaway, suffered such rough confirmation hearings in the Senate that he wound up in Bethesda Naval Hospital with a bout of depression and in late July submitted his resignation. As the next secretary, President Gerald Ford named former North Dakota congressman Tom Kleppe, a mediocrity who ensured the continued domination of the Park Service by Assistant Secretary Nat Reed.

Fall brought somewhat brighter prospects. John Rutter retired, to be replaced by my old friend Deputy Director Russ Dickenson. The new deputy would be Mount Rainier superintendent Bill Briggle, another old friend, who bore the reputation of merciless hatchet man but with whom I had always enjoyed a warm relationship. Suddenly the dark clouds lifted from Alaska, although not from the corridors of the Interior Department, where the other land-managing agencies continued to battle against turning over any of their domain to the Alaska Natives. Above all, however, I suddenly discovered a new and admirable courage in Gary Everhardt.

It arose from a long-simmering controversy over Valley Forge State Park in Pennsylvania, scene of the terrible winter camp of George Washington's embattled army in 1777–78. With the Bicentennial extravaganza approaching in 1976, Valley Forge had been proposed for addition to the National Park System, and congressional hearings had been set for September 29. No historian could plausibly argue against the national significance of Valley Forge—as a historical episode, as a historic site, or as a focus of the Bicentennial celebration. Yet both the Office of Management and Budget and the Interior Department itself had decreed otherwise and instructed Gary to testify against the legislation.

On September 11 Gary summoned Chief Historian Harry Pfanz and me for a briefing. For two hours we discussed the history, the site, and the proposal. Gary then declared that the National Park Service should express its professional opinion on such issues and let the politicians worry about the political constraints. For his part he would not make the Park Service look foolish by testifying that Valley Forge did not belong in the park system.

Four days later a park planner and I joined Gary in a U.S. Park Police helicopter for a flight to Valley Forge. After landing for a meeting with Regional Director Chet Brooks and his staff, we conducted an aerial inspection of the entire park. When we returned to Washington, Gary was more convinced than ever that he could not oppose this legislation.

As the date of the hearing approached, we learned that Gary had been replaced as the department's witness by Doug Wheeler, Nat Reed's deputy, and that Doug would testify against the legislation. On the morning of the hearing, we assembled in Nat Reed's office for prehearing briefings. Somehow, over the weekend, the scenario had been rewritten. Now Nat would testify instead of Doug, and he would testify in favor of the legislation. I sat at the witness table with Reed and Everhardt, scribbling answers to questions they slipped to me on scraps of paper. Both performed splendidly, and of course Valley Forge duly joined the National Park System in time for the Bicentennial.

I do not know what happened over that weekend. I believe, however, that Gary simply dug in and—come what may—refused to be part of such a transparent charade. I think that he not only persuaded Nat Reed of the political fallout from a negative report but found in Nat a sympathetic ear and a voice prepared to take on the Office of Management and Budget. For all his mischievous interference in park operations, Nat Reed was an informed, principled, and courageous functionary. And for me, Gary Everhardt had won back some of the respect the summer's setbacks had cost him.

He quickly lost it. As the autumn of 1975 fell over Washington, Gary grew increasingly cool toward both Connally and me. When we met with him, his mind seemed elsewhere, his attention span short and easily diverted by the telephone or other interruptions. The cordiality of earlier months, and the apparent agreement with our thinking, evaporated.

I can account for this shifting attitude only by pointing to the reaction in the field to my evangelizing and, a related cause, the stubborn refusal of line management to understand that the National Historic Preservation Act of 1966 applied to the Park Service the same as to all other federal agencies. That act, fortified by an executive order issued by President Nixon in 1971, required that all significant historic and archeological features under our jurisdiction be identified, entered in the National Register of Historic Places, and guarded by the protective measures established by law. Protection was not absolute. It merely mandated that managers "take into account" the effect of any undertaking on registered properties by following certain consultative procedures involving the state historic preservation officers and the Advisory Council on Historic Preservation.

Superintendents, regional directors, and even the director could not or would not understand the law and its implementing regulations, no matter how often and clearly explained. Superintendents had lost the freedom they once enjoyed to knock down old buildings they regarded as eyesores or wanted replaced with a new development. Now they had to find some means to preserve or to justify demolition with an overriding need. They resented this outside interference in long-standing prerogatives, and many saw me as the culprit. Their exasperation must have percolated up the chain of command and reshaped Gary Everhardt's attitude toward me.

The issue exploded early in November 1975, with Yosemite and Grand Canyon the focal points. All of Yosemite Valley had been nominated for the National Register because of the subsurface archeological remains of early Indian inhabitants. Neither

Superintendent Les Arnberger nor Gary would understand that this meant only that any development that would disturb archeological artifacts, such as a planned sewer line, would have to be preceded by archeological survey and recovery. The concept that registration carried no other burden for the superintendent simply eluded them.

Far more serious was Grand Canyon. Everhardt wanted the master plan revised to remove all development from the south rim of the canyon, but he discovered that the old power plant and a row of old residences had been nominated for the National Register. At a meeting called on November 14 to prepare for legislative hearings, Gary used an entire morning to attack me. His face red, his temper flashing beyond anything I had ever witnessed in him, he barked: "You historians have drawn lines around worthless old buildings of no significance that will cause me problems." Why should historians or architects make such determinations? he wanted to know. Especially in big parks like Grand Canyon, he could not understand why natural values should not override historical values.

I stood my ground. Over and over I described the law and its regulations. Natural values could in fact override the historical, I explained, if it could be shown that the two were in irresolvable conflict. I knew that politically he could never clear the south rim of Grand Canyon, for that would have included El Tovar Hotel and Bright Angel Lodge. I declared that if he could remove everything from the south rim, natural values would indeed prevail, and I was sure I could get the Advisory Council to agree to the demolition of the registered buildings. But any plan that called for tearing down *only* the historic buildings would be sure to run into trouble with the Council.

At lunch a friend who had been present informed me that Gary refused to accept my explanation of the law and the regulations, that he was sure that I was "trying to put one over on him." That afternoon, confirming what I had been told, Gary summoned one of the staff of the environmental compliance office to brief him on National Register procedures. Since this man knew the process, I can only assume that he told Gary I had not misled him. But never after did Gary exhibit any understanding of the subject, nor make any effort to understand it.

That Friday was probably the low point of my Park Service career. Monday morning's meeting in preparation for congressional hearings found Gary his serene, friendly self of old. Nothing was said about Friday's blowup or about Grand Canyon. But I knew the rupture could not be healed. The director and I had irreconcilable differences that would severely affect our relationship and my ability to do my job as I thought it ought to be done.

This perception drew reinforcement from other events. For several months one of the Park Service's never ending studies of organization had been underway. Neither Connally nor I had been consulted. Only the top line managers tinkered with the realignment. I was not surprised, however, when Everhardt and Associate Director John Cook called a staff meeting on November 21 to announce the new order. Among other changes, my three divisions would be consolidated into one, I would lose my title of assistant director, and my division would be moved from under Ernest Connally and placed in the operations hierarchy, under the same Bob Stanton I had worked with on the Rumberg task force.

I tried to put the best possible face on this sweeping change. As part of operations, I might be able to accomplish more than I had while standing to one side as a professional services unit. But nothing could conceal from me, my staff, a growing loyal following throughout the Park Service, and of course my detractors that I and what I stood for had been downgraded and would not enjoy the profile or influence that had flourished since the advent of Ron Walker.

My only hope was that this reorganization, like many that had preceded it, would falter, collapse, or evolve differently than first announced. All reorganizations take a long time to accomplish, and this proved no exception. For almost a year, through 1976, I retained my title of assistant director, my three divisions, and a faint hope that somehow what I had built could be salvaged.

Vastly aggravating the setbacks at the office, in September 1975 my home life tipped into its final collapse. All the wrenching emotions of the breakup of a marriage and a family with two teenage boys dogged the professional descent, which in turn made the domestic turmoil all the more painful. Less than two weeks before the Grand Canyon blowup, I rented a pickup truck, and Don and Phil helped me move a few pieces of furniture and the books and other contents of my study into an Arlington apartment.

CHAPTER 14

THE EARLY 1970S REAWAKENED public interest in Custer—a new Custer. Against the backdrop of the antiwar demonstrations and the rising activism of the red power movement, Vine Deloria's *Custer Died for Your Sins* (1968) provided a symbol for white misdeeds with instant name recognition. My article, "Custer: Hero or Butcher?" did nothing to counter the popular symbolism. Nor did another, "The Enduring Custer Legend," which appeared in *American History Illustrated* in the centennial month of June 1976.

In 1971 Dee Brown's *Bury My Heart at Wounded Knee* gave new rationale to the red power drive and further spotlighted Custer as a scapegoat. A polemic masquerading as history, Brown's book swept the nation, ultimately gaining press runs in the millions and earning its author dollars in the millions. Although bad history, *Bury My Heart at Wounded Knee* turned out to be, over the span of a generation, the single most powerful influence on public attitudes toward Indians.

Then came Dustin Hoffman's vivid portrayal in the motion picture *Little Big Man*. Although a transparent metaphor for Vietnam, it was set in the Old West. Blood-lusting cavalry rampaged through Indian villages gleefully slaughtering women and children. A mad George Armstrong Custer staggered around the Little Bighorn battlefield emitting maniacal rantings.

Indians seized the Bureau of Indian Affairs headquarters, across the street from my office in Interior. They threw out the employees, trashed the building, and forted up. SWAT teams outfitted in the hall outside my office. Among the police ringing the BIA building were the horse-mounted officers of the U.S. Park Police, an arm of the National Park Service. One morning Dave Clary came into my office and remarked, "There's a switch for you. The Indians are barricaded inside the fort and the cavalry are circling outside."

In 1973 came Second Wounded Knee. On South Dakota's Pine Ridge Reservation, Sioux activists gunned down two FBI agents and launched a tense standoff that lasted for weeks. Summoning images of the slaughter of Big Foot's Sioux at Wounded Knee in 1891, the clash vividly symbolized the history the militants sought to rewrite.

In the midst of all this national turmoil, early in 1974 Macmillan published the second of my histories of the army in the West, *Frontier Regulars: The United States Army and the Indian, 1866–1891.* Custer, of course, played a prominent role, not as hero or villain, and assuredly not as depicted by Vine Deloria, Dee Brown, or *Little Big Man.* With the military widely execrated because of Vietnam, and with Indian grievances drawing more and more sympathy, this was hardly a propitious time to publish a book about the frontier army. Stephen Ambrose gave it a splendid review in the *Washington Post,* and the Military Book Club published its own edition. Even so, it did not fare as well as it would have in less tumultuous times. One scholarly reviewer, an Indian woman, castigated me in fierce terms not only for failing to blanket the blue-clad butchers of Indians with unqualified opprobrium but for daring to write a serious book about them at all. Nonetheless, both *Frontiersmen in Blue* and *Frontier Regulars* are still in print and considered the standard authorities on the subject.

Although Vietnam finally drew to its tragic finale in 1975, it left enough residue of social unrest to worry the National Park Service about the approaching centennial of the Battle of the Little Big-horn. The park had made commendable strides in bringing more balance to the interpretive presentations, telling the story in both military and Indian dimensions and virtually eliminating the heroic cast of my years on Custer Hill. But in the activist climate of the early 1970s, no amount of "balance" could satisfy demands welling up from the writings of Vine Deloria and Dee Brown and the noisy theatrics of the American Indian Movement (AIM). One of my more moderate Indian friends, a Sioux woman on the Fort Belknap Reservation in Montana, quipped that AIM stood for "assholes in moccasins."

The zealots cared for the historical record only as it could be twisted to fortify their campaigns. Custer Battlefield had become the battleground in a new war, a war of symbolic possession. Who owned this symbol, and all it could be made to yield in terms of tangible public atonement for centuries of white oppression? Russell Means and his fellow agitators in AIM valued the battlefield not for the story it told but as a publicity tool to dramatize their social, political, and economic objectives.

From within as well as from without the Park Service a rising chorus called for renaming Custer Battlefield National Monument. Few battlefields bore the name of either the victor or the vanquished, ran the argument, so why should Custer be enshrined in the designation of this battlefield? Proponents of the name change wanted to substitute "Little Bighorn" for "Custer."

I took no part in this debate. In truth, I did not care very deeply about the issue. On one hand, the name reflected the intent of the officials who set aside the park shortly after the battle and thus took on historical importance in itself. Moreover, I had enough experience in tampering with established nomenclature to know that it always set off a controversy. On the other hand, "Little Bighorn" described the battlefield as well as "Custer," and I felt little would be lost if the advocates won. As I foresaw, tampering with this nomenclature grew into another of the battles in the war over symbolism.

Nor did I take much part in the debates in and out of the Park Service over what kind of ceremony should mark the centennial of the Little Bighorn in June 1976. Planning began in 1970 under the auspices of the Custer Battlefield Historical and Museum Association, the park's nonprofit cooperating organization. The same people whom Vince Gleason had betrayed by spending their money on the Baskin drawings in my park handbook now prepared for an elaborate celebration that would rival the fiftieth anniversary extravaganza of 1926. They hoped to draw one hundred thousand spectators. A dramatic attraction would be a "Custer Reride," as many as four hundred cavalry reenactors staging the final day of Custer's approach to the Little Bighorn.

At the same time, Russell Means and his AIM cohorts excited national publicity with plans to stage their own ceremony at the battlefield, a ceremony that implicitly courted violence. Means even vowed to set fire to the museum displaying Custer's uniforms and other personal memorabilia. Park officials took the possibility seriously enough to move much of Custer's belongings to safe storage at the museum laboratory in Harpers Ferry, West Virginia.

An AIM demonstration that would disrupt the formal program and raise the danger of violence alarmed Park Service officials. If the alarm stirred any action in the Washington office, I never knew of it. Rather the regional office in Denver seems to have resolved to allow Russell Means as small a stage for national publicity as possible. In 1974 a new superintendent and new park historian took station at the battlefield. The "historian," Rich Rambur, came out of the ranger ranks and had police experience. As executive secretary of the association, he soon dominated its affairs, alienated its officers, and by 1975 had succeeded in having the centennial committee abolished.

Rich Rambur was smart, able, and effective, more so than the new superintendent. Despite the fury of the association members and others incensed at Rambur's heavy-handed tactics, he later went on to a distinguished career as superintendent of several parks. I always liked him and never asked him about the centennial planning. But I believe he came to the battlefield with the regional director's mandate to mark the centennial as inconspicuously as possible.

Perhaps that is why I was invited to deliver the principal address.

No one ever told me the motive for moving the main ceremony from June 25 to June 24—I suppose some misguided hope of throwing Russell Means off stride. The day was cold and cloudy, with occasional falls of light rain. Instead of one hundred thousand spectators, about seven hundred gathered. As I rode up the hill with the public information officer from the regional office, she told me that security would be heavy but inconspicuous. "Low profile," she muttered as we drove through the gate and took in the array of ranger cars with light bars on the roof, a heavily armed SWAT team of rangers assembled from parks throughout the region, a contingent of the Montana Highway Patrol, and even some U.S. Park Policemen from Washington with attack dogs on leashes. Only the FBI agents remained "low profile."

A speaker's platform and rows of folding chairs had been set up next to the road between the museum and the national cemetery. A handsomely uniformed army band flanked the gathering audience. Before the program even began, the band had hardly struck up "Garryowen," Custer's rollicking battle song, when the sound of thumping Indian drums drifted from beyond the national cemetery. The Indians, it seems, had gathered almost as stealthily on this battleground as they had a century earlier.

Around the corner of the cemetery and up the road toward us marched 250 Indians, chanting, singing, and pounding drums. Russell Means led. Behind him, two Indians dragged an American flag, upside down, over the pavement—a signal, it was later explained, of distress.

Park superintendent Dick Hart, an affable, easygoing man with a white beard, now performed probably the signal contribution of his career. He advanced to confront Russell Means and emerged with a truce if not a treaty. Means would be given his time at the microphone, after which he and his little army would withdraw to the monument and stage their own ceremony while ours got underway below.

Of the tirade Russell Means delivered I have little memory. It was typical of the bluster that characterized most of his speeches. It included what had become an article of faith with AIM and its supporters: Custer had led an invasion of the Sioux homeland with the intention of killing as many Indians as he could and seizing territory that belonged to the Sioux. The Sioux fought back to protect their families and homeland. Conveniently omitted, if ever even understood, was that the Sioux Custer attacked were intruders on Crow tribal ranges, that in fact the battle occurred within the reservation set apart for the Crows in the Treaty of 1868.

Ironically, my speech featured an appeal to avoid corrupting history and this battlefield for the purposes that Russell Means and his demonstrators were at that very moment inflicting the corruption. I don't know how many in the audience carefully followed my plea, for Means had left his palace guard behind. As I spoke, about a dozen beefy Indians in red berets ringed the seated assemblage and stood with folded arms and scowling visages.

If they were listening, I doubt that they caught the message in my concluding paragraph:

> In the spirit of reconciliation we should dedicate ourselves in this bicentennial and centennial year to righting the wrongs of the past. But in reaching for that goal, let us not infuse this battlefield with a modern meaning untrue to the past. Let us not bend it artificially to serve contemporary needs and ends, however laudable. Let us accept it and understand it on its own terms, not ours. As we shall want posterity to look back on us, so we ourselves must look back at those who have preceded us.

That was a cry lost in the wilderness. It also betrayed a bit of my own naïveté. Fifteen years later Edward T. Linenthal, in *Sacred Ground: Americans and Their Battlefields*, thoughtfully explored the ways in which Americans had exploited the "sacred ground" of their battlefields to promote modern purposes. Of my words about bending the past to serve contemporary needs and ends, he wrote: "Of course, for a century patriotic orthodoxy at the battlefield had done precisely that: it had helped shape a culturally constructed—hence an 'artificial'—interpretation of the battle." And as Linenthal rightly observed, "Utley's caution about twisting history for political purposes certainly meant little to protesters who saw this as *their* opportunity to overturn symbolic domination by winning the symbolic battle of the Little Bighorn."

The day's adventures did not end with my speech. In the audience were two old friends. I had first met Colonel George

Armstrong Custer III, Brice's son, as a newly commissioned second lieutenant at the battlefield on June 25, 1950. I had first met Larry Frost, the Monroe podiatrist, in 1948 and visited in his home in 1950. Since then Larry had published a couple of well-received books on Custer and had become an exalted idol of the Little Big Horn Associates.

Colonel Custer had brought with him a floral wreath with ribbons emblazoned to the memory of the brothers George, Tom, and Boston; the nephew Henry Reed, and the brother-in-law Lieutenant James Calhoun. He wanted to lay the wreath on the monument. That would have been an invitation made to order for Russell Means—television cameras recording another confrontation between a braided Sioux and a George Custer. The arbiters of security ruled against any such rite so long as Means and his crowd remained on the battlefield.

Late in the afternoon, after Means and nearly everyone else had left, I went out from the museum building, linked arms with Colonel Custer, and marched up the hill to the monument. Larry Frost fell in behind, together with George's son Kip, a college student with blonde curls and brushy mustache that made him almost a mirror image of his famous forebear. At the monument, as Larry, Kip, and I stood by, Custer solemnly placed the wreath at the base and saluted.

The next day, the true anniversary, featured an anticlimactic program that drew few people and left nothing memorable in the record. No Indian protesters showed up. The main attraction was the "Custer Reride"—a dozen, rather than four hundred, blue-clad horsemen tracing Custer's route from the Rosebud divide to the battlefield. Since the Park Service had barred them from the formal program and they could not bring horses into the park without a special permit, the ride ended at the park boundary rather than on Custer Hill.

The centennial observance left many people angry. They felt the Park Service had allowed itself to be intimidated by an Indian rabble. They contrasted the Indian costumes of Means's demonstrators with the absence of any military presence beyond the army band. They deplored the proscription from the scene of anyone dressed in the cavalry uniform of Custer's time and the ban on the "reride" that stopped the reenactors at the park boundary. They were outraged by the treatment accorded Colonel Custer: that he did not sit on the podium, that he was not even recognized as a distinguished presence in the audience, and that he was then barred from the wreath laying until everyone had left. Above all, they denounced the desecration of the American flag by Indians dragging it over the pavement. Some even believed that the firepower of the park rangers should have been deployed to halt such a sacrilege.

These resentments took tangible form in a flood of mail addressed to the president, members of Congress, the secretary of the interior, and the director of the National Park Service. No matter to whom addressed, the letters all found their way to my inbox. The writers, many of them friends or acquaintances, never knew who replied because someone else signed, but the answers came out of my office.

I find it hard to fault Park Service officials for their caution. AIM had shown at Second Wounded Knee and elsewhere the inclination to stir serious trouble and even violence when television cameras stood by. The Little Bighorn centennial offered an irresistible stage on which to score symbolic points by disrupting the official program, even if it involved violence. Had men uniformed in historic cavalry garb been on the scene, had Superintendent Dick Hart not yielded the podium for a time to Means, had Colonel Custer laid his wreath while the demonstrators remained nearby, Means might well have seized the chance at disruptive grandstanding while the cameras rolled.

At the same time, I think it petty and reprehensible that Colonel Custer was not at least named as one of the dignitaries in the audience, if not indeed seated on the platform. And I think the reride squad of a dozen horsemen could have been allowed to end their trip at the monument. The reride took place on June 25, after nearly everyone, including Russell Means and the national media, had gone home. The risk of trouble would have been all but nonexistent.

Finally, of lasting damage, the schism opened by Rich Rambur between the Park Service and the Custer Battlefield Historical and

Museum Association left wounds that never healed. At least two of the longtime powers in the association, men of local respectability and influence, flatly refused to attend the observance. The sores would fester for more than a dozen years before breaking forth again.

The 1976 centennial pleased hardly anyone. It was a big battle in the war for symbolic possession of Custer Battlefield, but not the final battle. Others lay in the future. Custer Battlefield had not seen the last of me—nor, less constructively, of Russell Means.

My coworkers gathered at the Decatur House on Lafayette Square to mark my retirement from federal service, February 25, 1980. Left to right standing: Ed Bearss, Jack McDermott, Bob Garvey, me, Ernest Connally, Jerry Rogers. Sitting: Ben Levy, Russ Keune, and Ross Holland. *Courtesy Advisory Council on Historic Preservation.*

Melody Webb and I were married in Santa Fe in November 1980. We settled in a solar, pueblo-style home in Eldorado, a subdivision east of the city. *Courtesy of the author.*

We devoted six years to the Eldorado Volunteer Fire Department, in which Melody rose to assistant chief and I to lieutenant. Here we are with Chief John Liebson and our antique engine. Later we got a big new engine and state-of-the-art protective gear. *Photograph by Larry Murphy, author's collection.*

With friends at the Custer Battlefield in 1983. Left to right: Paul Hutton, Larry Frost, me, and Paul Hedren. This view overlooks the site of Major Reno's skirmish line. Custer Hill is on the skyline behind Hutton. *Courtesy Paul A. Hutton.*

At the Western History Association in Salt Lake City in 1983, some friends staged a tribute to me and presented a drawing of me as Custer. Left to right: Jerry Greene, Paul Hutton, Paul Hedren, me, and Ed Bearss. *Courtesy Western History Association.*

In 1985 the Western History Association, meeting in Sacramento, honored all former presidents at a special table. *Courtesy of the author.*

In March 1989 my biography of Custer, *Cavalier in Buckskin*, won a Wrangler Award at the National Cowboy Hall of Fame and Western Heritage Center in Oklahoma City. Director George Bauer of the University of Oklahoma Press shared the podium, with Paul Hutton looking on. *Courtesy National Cowboy and Western Heritage Museum.*

In April 1990 the Lyndon B. Johnson National Historical Park celebrated its twentieth birthday. All four people in this picture played important parts in my life. Left to right: former Park Service director George B. Hartzog, Jr.; park superintendent Melody Webb; Lady Bird Johnson; and Regional Director John Cook. *Courtesy of the author.*

In September 1992 we moved into Quarters No. 1 at Beaver Creek in Grand Teton National Park. We lived there for four years while Melody served as the park's assistant superintendent. *Courtesy of the author.*

The Grand Tetons provided a splendid setting in which to write my mountain man book, *A Life Wild and Perilous. Courtesy of the author.*

I served on the board of directors of Eastern National Park and Monument Association from 1978 to 1997. Here, in New Orleans in January 1993, I relinquished the chairman's gavel for the second time. Former NPS director Russ Dickenson and Monticello executive director Dan Jordan are to my right, Eastern National president George Minnucci to my left. *Courtesy Eastern National.*

At the TA Ranch in Wyoming, September 1997. Here the Johnson County War of 1892 reached its bullet-ridden climax. *Courtesy of the author.*

14th Inaugural Gala   April 3, 2001
Southwestern University   Georgetown, Texas

After we settled in Georgetown, Texas, Southwestern University anointed us "Affiliated Scholars," with faculty privileges. We have enjoyed the relationship. Here in April 2001 we help celebrate the Fourteenth Inaugural Gala. *Courtesy Southwestern University.*

I owe a huge debt of gratitude to my agent, Carl D. Brandt. In 1989 he introduced me to the world of trade publishing and has ever since contributed wise counsel to strengthening my books for the general reader. We periodically join for a long lunch at an Italian restaurant near his Broadway office in Manhattan. *Courtesy of the author.*

At the Little Bighorn Battle-field on the 125th anniversary of the battle, I inscribed an entire stock of 150 copies of a new Custer book. Sharing the table are Paul Hedren and Jerry Greene. *Courtesy of the author.*

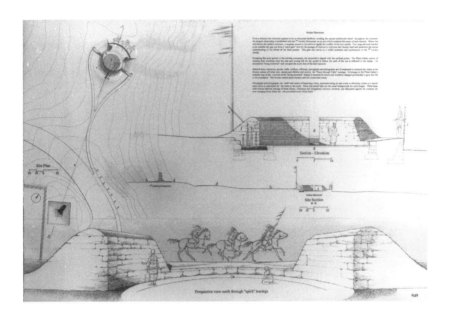

The winning design for the long-awaited Indian memorial at the Little Bighorn Battlefield, selected from many entries in 1997. The memorial based on this design was dedicated on June 25, 2003. *Little Bighorn Battlefield National Monument.*

In April 2001 we moved into a home newly built especially for the needs of a pair of historians. Our study overlooks Lake Georgetown. *Courtesy of the author.*

CHAPTER 15

ROBERT R. GARVEY, JR., long the executive head of the National Trust for Historic Preservation, joined the National Park Service in 1967 to provide executive staff for the presidentially appointed Advisory Council on Historic Preservation. This panel of professional preservationists, civic leaders, politicians, and federal agency heads had been authorized by the National Historic Preservation Act of 1966.

Bob Garvey was a tall man with a brushy mustache and reading glasses perched precariously on the tip of his nose. He had piloted a navy torpedo bomber against the Japanese during the war, and he kept his upper body fit and well proportioned with vigorous outdoor activity. He keenly felt the lack of a string of academic degrees such as hung on most preservationists, but he lacked nothing in intellectual power and bureaucratic savvy. He rivaled even George Hartzog in plotting, as if on a chess board, the intricate bureaucratic and political moves that would lead to a desired outcome.

One such outcome climaxed in the summer of 1976, just as the Park Service was shrinking my stature, influence, and staff. With the backing of the powerful senator Henry "Scoop" Jackson, Garvey won independence from the Park Service. So long as a prisoner of the Park Service, the Advisory Council could never attain credibility as a watchdog over the entire federal government, especially since the Service itself was one of the worst offenders against the law's requirements. In 1976, therefore, Congress set up the Advisory Council as an independent agency, reporting directly to the president, and provided the funding to enable it to function as the framers of the Historic Preservation Act had intended.

Bob Garvey and I got along well. We liked each other, respected each other's abilities, and shared similar convictions about historic preservation and the policies, programs, and organization needed to advance it. As his legislation seemed increasingly likely to become law, he began to sound me out about the possibility of leaving the Park Service to work with him. At a luncheon in September 1976, he made the offer official. I would be deputy executive director, second only to him, and run the Council staff while he tended to the Council's welfare on Capitol Hill and elsewhere. The post would elevate me to GS-16 and ultimately to the newly created Senior Executive Service. I stalled for several weeks as my situation in the Park Service continued to deteriorate, then accepted.

I moved into the Council's K Street offices in February 1977. Leaving the National Park Service was very hard on me. Some thought I had sold out for the higher grade. That had nothing to do with it. I left because tempted by the prospect of working with Garvey to make the most of the new law. But I left too because I had lost the confidence of Director Gary Everhardt, because we stood poles apart on how the historical responsibilities of the Service ought to be met, because I could not loyally support him, and because he had put me off in an organizational corner where I felt I could not function. The kind of work I had been doing in support of the parks appealed to me more than the "process" and "new preservation" of the Advisory Council. But I knew Garvey and I would make an effective team, and the challenges and stimulation of breaking new ground seemed preferable to continued frustration in the Park Service.

As it turned out, I was not happy in my new job. It was process rather than substance. I oversaw the process of goading federal agencies into obeying the law by "taking into account" the effect of their "undertakings" on historic properties. If they successfully negotiated a series of procedural hoops, they had "taken into account." Many of these "Section 106" cases involved multimillion dollar projects with huge economic and political consequences. Rarely were we without a Section 106 crisis that brought on us storms of denunciation and resistance from powerful interests. Rarely did we have a case, however, in which a reasonable compromise could not be found to accommodate both the undertaking and the threatened cultural property. Even so, whether dull or exciting, the Section 106 process never provided the gratification I had felt in park work.

For years, with both Ernest Connally and Bob Garvey, I had believed that historic preservation, whether in the parks or the nation at large, could never be properly served without major reorganization. That conviction drove the move Ernest and I had made to take the Office of Archeology and Historic Preservation and the historical parks out of the Park Service and into a separate "monuments office" such as George Hartzog had recruited Connally to create.

My first year at the Council, the first year of Jimmy Carter's presidency, coincided with two major initiatives aimed at addressing this issue. They not only saved me from drowning in process but afforded exciting challenges as well. I worked with two master tacticians—Garvey and our general counsel, Ken Tapman, a brilliant, driven, mercurial attorney endowed with one of the quickest and most focused minds I have ever observed. No longer held down by layers of unsympathetic supervision, we could operate with a freedom that allowed us to bring major influence to bear.

The first initiative surfaced in February 1977, when Congressman John Seiberling introduced a bill to create a single federal historic preservation agency by merging the Office of Archeology and Historic Preservation into the Advisory Council. The language was largely the product of a sub rosa collaboration between Seiberling aide Loretta Newman (formerly of the Park Service) and Ken Tapman, but its timeliness sprang from a swarm of state historic preservation officers angry at Gary Everhardt for his action the previous year in cutting $10 million from the federal grants-in-aid program to pay for sewers in national parks. As the bill spread

consternation through the Park Service, Garvey, Tapman, and I
met at Colonial Williamsburg with a panel of sympathetic Council
members and in May got the full Council to endorse a paper
supporting the concepts in the Seiberling bill.

No sooner had the Council adopted this paper than the second
initiative sprang up. On May 23 President Carter sent his environmental message to the Hill. He disclosed that he had instructed
the secretary of the interior to develop, within 120 days, a "National
Heritage Program" that combined natural and cultural preservation—the very antithesis of the Seiberling legislation and the Council
paper. As governor, Carter had installed such a program in Georgia
and made it work. What he did not know was that, without his
personal oversight, it was now widely regarded as a failure.

Launched with great fanfare, the National Heritage Task Force
drew participants from all interested federal and state agencies
and private groups—in fact, virtually anyone who wanted to take
part. It labored all summer and effectively muted support of the
Seiberling bill. Garvey, Tapman, and I decided that the Council
had to take a leading role.

We felt guardedly optimistic because Carter had appointed a
first-rate interior secretary. Former governor of Idaho, Cecil Andrus
was destined to achieve an enviable environmental record during
his four years as secretary. Unfortunately, he entrusted task force
oversight to Paul Pritchard, who had worked with Carter in Georgia
and now served as deputy director of the Bureau of Outdoor Recreation. Pritchard's bureaucratic ineptitude, ignorance of historic preservation, and disorderly mind created constant confusion and frustration.

Tapman, John Fowler, Ellen Ramsey, and I worked nearly full-
time all summer to steer the heritage program in the right direction. We could freely speak our minds while representatives of the
big agencies had turf their superiors expected them to protect.
We decisively influenced the content of every paper touching our
interests. At its meeting in October 1977, the full Council endorsed
the report of the task force. We thought we had organizations and
programs that might work well.

But something went fatally wrong in the secretary's office. Ignoring
the task force report almost entirely, Andrus's staff framed the

wrong issues for the president's consideration. At the Council, we prepared comprehensive and persuasive comments, but they stirred no response either at Interior or the Office of Management and Budget. By the time President Carter acted on his "options" document in December, the options bore little relation to the work of the task force.

The principal outcome of the year's labor was organizational. Secretary Andrus restyled the Bureau of Outdoor Recreation the "Heritage Conservation and Recreation Service" (HCRS) and moved the Office of Archeology and Historic Preservation out of a shocked Park Service into the new agency. Chris Delaporte, a hard-charging Oklahoman who had campaigned for the Park Service directorate, took over HCRS, with Paul Pritchard his deputy. They lacked the knowledge and experience to make it work. "Hookers," Capitol staffers derisively labeled it, and others translated HCRS as "Who Cares?" With the advent of the Reagan administration in 1981, Interior Secretary James Watt abolished HCRS and moved historic preservation back to the Park Service.

The sorry performance of HCRS did not change sentiments I set to paper at the end of 1977, sentiments that I still hold: "I guess this year's activities simply reinforce the experience of a couple of decades of government service that mighty labors are likely to bring forth nothing but disappointment. I have served on many task forces and can recall none that justified expectations. Also, I guess it should be plain now that in our traditions and practices natural and cultural programs are not separable, and instead of trying so hard and futilely to run off somewhere with the cultural, the effort would be more productively devoted to making them compatible."

In my spare time, especially now that I lived alone, I continued to pursue outside interests. In 1974, with *Frontier Regulars* in print, General Custer had again shaken his golden locks in my face. The Beinecke Library at Yale University contained the diaries and letters of Albert and Jennie Barnitz. As an officer of the Ohio Volunteers, Albert had served worshipfully under Custer in the Civil War and in 1866 had applied for a regular army commission. The War Department made him a troop commander in the Seventh Cavalry. Captain Barnitz took a near-fatal wound at the Battle of the Washita in 1868 and left the army on a medical discharge. But the diaries and letters of these two sparkling, literate, observant people presented an intimate and human account of life in Custer's Seventh Cavalry for the years 1867–70. Archie Hanna, director of the Western Americana Collection at the Beinecke, asked me to put these documents into shape for publication by Yale University Press, which in 1963 had issued my *Last Days of the Sioux Nation* and in 1964 my editing of Richard Henry Pratt's memoirs, *Battlefield and Classroom.*

Albert and Jennie proved the most engaging historical characters I had ever known. Working on their diaries and letters was pure delight. With very little assistance from me, their own words brought them to life on the printed page. No more vivid glimpse of the people and the life of those who served in the Seventh Cavalry during its formative years is to be found, even in the charming writings of Elizabeth Custer. Yale University Press published *Life in Custer's Cavalry* in 1977, and the University of Nebraska Press reprinted it in paperback in 1987. It has found an enduring place in Custer scholarship both as a captivating read and as a basic historical source.

As Albert and Jennie neared completion, another project fell to me—*The American Heritage History of the Indian Wars.* I did not feel qualified to take on the wars before 1846, so editor Stephen Sears agreed to a joint authorship, with the Smithsonian's Wilcomb Washburn covering the early wars. This would be a large-format, lavishly illustrated coffee-table book with authoritative narrative text. Sears wanted a topical organization, while I argued for the chronological. Sears won. Near the end of 1976, however, with my text all but completed, Ezra Bowen replaced Steve Sears. Bowen insisted on chronological organization but could make no change in the deadline. I had to produce, or suffer my narrative to be worked over by someone else. For a few weeks early in 1977, between the Park Service and the Advisory Council, I labored nonstop to rewrite my entire manuscript. The book appeared in the fall of 1977 and won critical acclaim. Subsequently, Houghton

Mifflin published a text-only paperback edition, titled simply *Indian Wars*, that continues to sell well. A new edition appeared in 2002.

As a highlight of this project, American Heritage put up $1,500 for me to visit many of the western battlefields treated in the text. In September 1976, after delivering the annual Harmon Memorial Lecture at the U.S. Air Force Academy in Colorado Springs, I met Melody in Denver, and together we set forth on a ten-day drive around mountains and plains. It was a grand tour that enriched our relationship. We ended back in Denver for the Western History Association convention.

Since 1969 I had served on the board of advisors to the National Historical Society. The chairman was Bell Wiley, the distinguished Civil War historian who had pronounced me fit for the Joint Chiefs of Staff in 1954. In June 1977 the society met at the St. Francis Hotel in San Francisco. Ray Billington, still the dean of western historians, came up from the Huntington Library to give the banquet address. The next day he and his wife, Mabel, accompanied the group in a tour of Muir Woods National Monument. Ray, Mabel, and I strolled leisurely beneath the giant redwoods and at length sat on a bench. There Ray alluded to the Histories of the American Frontier Series, of which he had been general editor for fifteen years. Despite numerous volumes, the series had yet to include one on the Indian frontier. First Robert G. Athearn, then Francis Paul Prucha had committed and then backed out. Would I be interested? As Ray put it, this would be a distillation of my many years of study and reflection on the Indian frontier. I gave Ray no answer then, but soon accepted. Ensconced in a more comfortable and spacious condominium in the Fairlington section of Arlington, I set to work in earnest.

By the mid-1970s my professional career had developed along two paths. I had a foot firmly planted in each of two worlds rarely bridged by historians. I had gained distinction as a historian and bureaucrat in a field that would soon be labeled "public history." I had also compiled a publication record and a conspicuous presence on college campuses, mainly through the Western History Association, that gave me credibility with academics.

This unusual combination gained me honors that further enhanced my standing in the latter world. In 1974 Purdue University awarded me an honorary doctor of letters degree. The University of New Mexico followed in 1976 and Indiana University in 1983.

In 1977, furthermore, Indiana University called me to Bloomington to receive the Distinguished Alumni Service Award. I was met at the Indianapolis airport and driven to Bloomington by a young doctoral candidate in history, Paul Andrew Hutton. Paul also returned me to the airport. Thus began a friendship and a mutually rewarding professional relationship that has endured to this day.

The record and the honors, however, were not enough to win full admission to academia. In 1977 an endowed professorship at the University of Oregon opened with the retirement of Earl Pomeroy. Unhappy at the Council, I applied. Ray Billington weighed in heavily in my behalf, as he told me in San Francisco in June. I had been his first choice, he said, and he had urged the selection committee for once to put aside the conventions of the academic guild and drop the usual requirement of the "terminal degree." The appointment went instead to Ray's second choice, Richard Maxwell Brown. I have long been grateful not only to Ray Billington for his confidence in me but also to that selection committee for choosing the better candidate for the job and for leaving me free to take advantage of the wonderful opportunity that lay only two years in my future.

For all the faults of the Park Service, I still missed it, as I did for my remaining years at the Advisory Council. In May 1977 Gary Everhardt had been nudged out of the directorate and made superintendent of Blue Ridge Parkway, where he would rule ably for years to come. Young William J. Whalen, who headed all the parks in the San Francisco Bay area, took his place. Whalen seemed sympathetic to historic preservation, and Ernest Connally sounded me out about returning. Before long, however, Whalen revealed himself as entirely unfit for the post, and Connally moved to HCRS.

My old, now shrunken organization still existed at the Park Service. After consulting me, Gary Everhardt had named Ross Holland as my successor. Ross was the best selection that could have been made, and in time he regained the title and organization that I had lost. With Ross in place, of course, the prospects of my rejoining the Park Service were remote at best.

By 1979 I did not want to go there or anywhere else in the government. Fast-breaking developments opened new and unexpected possibilities. With luck and a willingness to gamble, I might realize two long-cherished dreams: to unite with Melody and to write history full-time.

CHAPTER 16

STAFF PERSONNEL FOR CONGRESSIONAL committees and subcommittees wield enormous power. They do the research and put the words to paper that, if embraced (or even noticed) by their chairpersons, shape legislation. Every federal agency has both friends and foes among these people. The Advisory Council, for example, benefited greatly from the friendship of Loretta Newman, who worked for the chairman of our House legislative subcommittee, Congressman John Seiberling of Ohio.

The Council's special foe was Fred Mohrman, the crotchety staff director of our appropriations subcommittee, chaired by Congressman Sidney Yates of Illinois. Mohrman disliked the Council, believed that it should never have been created, and detested Bob Garvey. Each year, Fred embedded in our appropriations bill or its accompanying report one or more hurtful jabs at either our money or our people. Often we succeeded in getting these eliminated in our Senate subcommittee, where we enjoyed a friend in Senator Ernest Hollings of South Carolina. The Council's chairman, Richard Jenrette, a wealthy Wall Street investment banker, was a South Carolinian close to Hollings. As often, however, we simply had to live with Fred's nasty little surprises.

Late in July 1979 I returned from a lengthy trip to Hawaii and Guam, where I successfully battled a Corps of Engineers plan to build a boat harbor on the Agat Invasion Beach, which had just been included in the newly created War in the Pacific National Historical Park. At the office, I learned of Fred Mohrman's gift-of-the-year: elimination of funding for several Council positions, including that of deputy director.

If Fred prevailed, we could still circumvent him by simply giving me a different title. But the moment I learned of his latest artifice, I concluded that, with Garvey's help, it might be transformed into a truly welcome gift to me. If Garvey, bowing to the House, abolished the position of deputy director, I could take early retirement from the government. I would be fifty years old in October and by February 1980, with accumulated sick leave, could count thirty years' service. Of those years a "high three" in the Senior Executive Service (SES) would form the basis for my annuity. I would have to accept a 10 percent reduction in the annuity, 2 percent for each year below the base retirement age of fifty-five; but that seemed little enough price to pay for the freedom to write full-time. Besides, in the absence of some radical move, the legislated ceiling on executive pay, crushing alimony obligations, and annual inflation rates ranging between 10 and 15 percent forecast nothing but poverty.

As an act of pure friendship, Bob Garvey agreed to give up my SES position if we failed to thwart Morhman. We thought we could get Senator Hollings to remove the offensive provision in the House-Senate conference, but Syd Yates, miffed at something we had done, stood firm. Even then, weeks of uncertainty followed as I labored through the intricacies of the retirement process. Not until near the end of the year could I be assured of my freedom. For his generous sacrifice of his own self-interest, Bob Garvey carried my undying gratitude to his grave in 1997.

Early in October 1979 I participated in a historical conference in Montana, then flew to Albuquerque and met Melody. She had taken a four-month leave of absence from the Park Service in Alaska to begin work on a Ph.D. in history at the University of New Mexico. As we drove around Santa Fe and northern New Mexico, we fantasized that here was an ideal "neutral ground." She did not want to live in Washington, and I did not want to move to Alaska.

These musings had been prompted by a vacancy in my old job of regional historian of the Southwest Region. Knowing that an applicant had already been secretly selected, we agreed that Melody should apply simply to get her mobility on the record and shed her image in Alaska as a "dilettante housewife." Teaming up in Santa Fe, however, seemed no more than an unrealizable dream.

From Albuquerque we occupied a compartment on Amtrak's Southwest Limited to Los Angeles and San Diego, where we attended the Western History Association's annual convention. Afterward we visited with Evelyn Luce, the major's widow, now seventy-two. She and Melody got along famously.

I had no sooner returned to Washington than I learned that the preferred applicant for the regional historian's position had turned it down, and it had promptly been offered to Melody. Suddenly the dream seemed realizable after all, although my retirement remained uncertain. After two days of agonizing, she accepted.

In mid-January 1980 I met Melody in Seattle. We picked up her old Mercedes at the ferry wharf and headed for Santa Fe, racing a crippling snow storm all the way. There we scouted the housing market for several days, without much promise. Leaving her to continue the search, I returned to Washington to grapple with some lingering problems at the Council. Melody reported to her new chief, Richard Sellars, and assumed the title I had relinquished in 1964.

On February 25, 1980, the Council staff and many of my friends from the Park Service, including George Hartzog, gathered at Decatur House on Lafayette Square to mark my retirement. A week later the movers came and emptied my condominium, which I had sold for a good markup. In my old and unpredictable Dodge Dart, I drove west. Melody met me in Little Rock. We paused in Eureka Springs, Arkansas, where my parents had retired. They took to Melody at once.

In Santa Fe two problems loomed. First was housing. Melody had rented a tract house in a subdivision while negotiating to purchase a house on the outskirts of the city. That fell through, leaving me each day to pursue my profession in a tiny house set in a neighborhood swarming with children, dogs, and cats and littered with every manner of battered vehicle. I was happy when Melody was home, unhappy when she was not. Finally, in May, we found a passive-solar house in Eldorado, a development thirteen miles southeast of Santa Fe. Surrounded by piñon and juniper, commanding sweeping views of mountains on all sides, it offered every amenity except ample space. We crowded in, however, delighted with the adobe walls, the tile floors, and the expanse of glass opening on splendid scenery.

The other problem was marital status. Regional Director Lorraine Mintzmyer suggested rather forcefully that living in sin did not accord with the Park Service's image of its employees. She was right, of course, although that image would be liberalized in time. I too was anxious to get married. But Melody needed time to arrange an amicable divorce from David, which she accomplished in October. David has since remarried, and we all remain close friends to this day. In a low-profile ratification of the existing situation, on November 12, 1980, a local magistrate presided over the nuptial vows in his office in the Santa Fe County Courthouse.

That first year in Santa Fe justified the seven years we had worked at our relationship. We were supremely happy personally and professionally. As I wrote in my journal at the end of 1980, I felt like a man who had been falling into an abyss, only to be rescued and dragged onto a cliff ledge that turned out to be a utopia. It still is.

Time to write did not develop as amply as expected. For one thing, I was now a "house husband." Melody brought home the paycheck, while I took care of most of the household chores. This was especially vital as Melody pursued her doctoral studies at the University of New Mexico while also holding down her new job in the regional office. By the end of 1983 she had completed all require-ments and received the degree. The University of New Mexico Press published her award-winning dissertation as *The Last Frontier: A History of the Yukon Basin of Canada and Alaska.* The University of Nebraska Press and the University of British Columbia Press jointly reissued it as a paperback in 1993, with the title *Yukon: The Last Frontier.*

Another demand on my time arose because we needed money. Bob Garvey came through. Under contract to the Advisory Coun-cil, I developed a two-day training course in historic preservation law and procedure. The Council and the Office of Management and Budget offered it jointly and contracted with me to teach it. Federal and state officials charged with compliance responsibilities made up most of the classes, although private groups also sent representatives. Every few months I presented the course in such cities as Washington, Boston, Chicago, Denver, San Francisco, Portland, Seattle, Anchorage, and even Cedar City, Utah. After three years I found these travels too burdensome and bowed out. Council staff took over the responsibility.

Thanks to Melody, a community commitment developed almost as soon as we moved into our Eldorado home. The local newsletter appealed for residents to join the Eldorado Volunteer Fire Department. Melody announced to me that she intended to respond. Stunned, I declared that the last activity I had ever thought of pursuing was firefighting, but that if she joined, so would I. We did.

Chief John Liebson was a professional firefighter. He knew all there was to know about fighting fires but not much about how to motivate people. He drove us mercilessly in weekly training sessions. Our 1947 pumper had a top speed of forty-five miles an hour, and most of the volunteers were white-collar professionals short on mechanical know-how. Many of them were Park Service. Within two years, however, we had raised the money to buy a huge pumper-tanker combination and modern turnout gear. We had also learned much from Chief Liebson. We installed red flashers and sirens in our private vehicles, and when the pager sounded day or night we raced to the scene. Auto accidents and house and grass fires kept us busy. Shared training and dangers drew us together in a rare camaraderie. The fire department and its people became a major part of our lives. Ultimately Melody rose to assistant chief and I to first lieutenant.

In a sense, I had married back into the National Park Service. I enjoyed renewing old acquaintances and vicariously, though Melody, observing issues come and go. In a way, though, I found this frustrating—often incensed over wrongheadedness but powerless to do anything about it.

In other ways I connected with the Park Service. In 1978, shortly after joining the Advisory Council, I was elected to a seat on the board of directors of the Eastern National Park and Monument Association. This nonprofit organization operated bookstores in many of the eastern parks and plowed the profits back into the parks. I arrived as the association reached a low of mismanagement and fiscal irregularity. Bankrupt, with $100,000 in obsolete inventory, Eastern National verged on collapse. A rescue team appeared in the persons of the distinguished preservationist Fred Rath as executive secretary and an astute and canny businessman, George Minnucci, as business manager. The board met at least once a year. Although I intended to relinquish my seat in a year or two, I was destined to work with both Fred and George for many years as Eastern National not only climbed out of the pit but soared high above it.

I found still another Park Service tie in the early 1980s at the Harpers Ferry Training Center in West Virginia. Melody's chief, Dick Sellars, periodically offered a historic preservation course for park managers. As a concluding feature of a week's training, George Hartzog and I staged a dog and pony show. George would reminisce in his magnetic style about the issues and fights of his director-ship, and I would follow with a recitation of some of the radical notions I had espoused a decade earlier. George's performance always drew plenty of hearty laughter, mine plenty of heated argument.

We applauded in the spring of 1980 when the Park Service gained a new director. Secretary Andrus finally disposed of Bill Whalen and, in an unprecedented selection formula, called in all the regional directors and instructed them to agree on Whalen's replacement. They chose my old friend Russ Dickenson, who had been regional director in Seattle since the collapse of Ron Walker's administration. With the advent of the Reagan administration in 1981, we did not expect Russ, an Andrus appointee, to survive. But he did, at the request of the new secretary of the interior, James Watt, the only Interior bureau chief save one held over.

Jim Watt's three-year reign kept the Interior Department in constant trouble and turmoil. He brought a right-wing philosophy and a highly political in-your-face style to the management of the public lands. Russ Dickenson accomplished the amazing feat of steering a tortuous course through the endless political minefield the secretary created. Probably no one else in the Park Service could have served Watt while at the same time retaining the respect and affection of the career service *and* preserving its integrity. For cushioning the Park Service from the wild antics of Jim Watt, Russ Dickenson ranks high among the Service's directors.

My commitment to Ray Billington still hung over me, but I had made little progress on the Indian volume for his Histories of the American Frontier Series. In fact, I had embraced the notion that I could write fiction. Charles Eastman, the Indian doctor who ministered to the casualties of Wounded Knee, a man caught tragically between two cultures, would be the protagonist. But Ray called in my commitment to him by arranging a two-month fellowship at the Huntington Library, and in February 1981 I set out for San Marino, California.

At the Huntington I returned to Ray's Indian volume while also enjoying the leisurely life other scholars pursued amid the beauties of the Huntington gardens. Long lunches and garden walks with Billington, Rodman Paul, Wilbur Jacobs, Martin Ridge, Harwood Hinton, Andrew Rolle, and other noted westernists afforded pleasure. I told Ray about my Eastman project, only to be discouraged. I had demonstrated that I could write history, he said, and I should stick with that. At the same time, he reviewed and commented favorably on the first three chapters of my Indian volume, handing the manuscript back to me at lunch on March 6. That night a heart attack struck him dead.

Ray Billington's unexpected death shocked and saddened the world of history. For three decades he had reigned as the leading historian of the American West. Everyone who knew him loved him, for his wit, sagacity, intellect, generosity, and warm fellowship. Unlike many academics, he befriended grassroots historians and buffs and even ushered some past the stern, disapproving guardians of the Huntington's treasures.

After Ray's death, I grew bored at the Huntington. I had plumbed about all it offered for the volume in the Billington series and even researched Eastman materials for my historical novel. Back home, Melody had passed ("with distinction") the comprehensive exam for her doctorate. She flew out to Los Angeles. I cut two weeks off my stay at the Huntington, and we drove a circuitous scenic route back to Santa Fe.

Without giving up on fiction, I set to work to finish the volume in the Billington series. The completed manuscript went to the University of New Mexico Press in September 1982, and *The Indian Frontier of the American West, 1846–1890* appeared early in 1984. It was what Ray had wanted: a synthesis of Indian-white relations from the Mexican War to the passing of the frontier in 1890. Comprehensive, well illustrated and mapped, it was an alternate selection of the History Book Club and at once found extensive classroom use in college courses. It still holds its own in academia and still earns a modest annual royalty. The University of New Mexico Press published a revised and updated edition in 2003.

With *Indian Frontier* in press, in late 1982 I turned back to the Eastman project, which I now called a "docudrama." By that I meant a dramatic story with well-developed characters rooted in documentary evidence and as true to history as possible. Yet it would be a novel, with dialogue contrived to represent what plausibly might have been said by the characters. By the end of 1983, I had drafted five chapters.

At the Western History Association convention in Salt Lake City in October 1983, I had a long talk about Eastman with Chester and Joan Kerr. Chester had been director of Yale University Press when it published *Last Days of the Sioux Nation.* Now he was president of a newly revived New York house of distinguished lineage, Ticknor and Field. Joan worked there, too. I told them that Ray Billington had discouraged me from turning from what we knew I could do well to a genre in which I probably could not excel. Chester invited me to send him the five chapters, and he would pass them around among his editors for a reaction.

In suspenseful anticipation, I waited for almost three months. Finally, late in January 1984, just as I received my first copies of *Indian Frontier,* the response came. The language was gentle but the meaning clear: "Ray Billington was right."

Eastman went to the back of a bottom filing drawer, where he remains to this day. Never since have I had the slightest desire to attempt fiction. The truth is that Ray Billington was indeed right.

CHAPTER 17

THE LITTLE BIG HORN Associates boasted no more vocal, stubborn, or dedicated member than John M. Carroll (not John Alexander Carroll, of earlier note). A short, rotund, gregarious bachelor with bald pate and neat white beard, he had committed his life almost exclusively to the worshipful memory of George Armstrong Custer. He spewed out mountains of published writings about Custer and dealt in the sale and exchange of Custeriana. Every room of his modest frame house in a rundown section of College Station, Texas, overflowed with paper, pictures, artifacts, and even toys associated with Custer. As his overnight guest once, I slept in a bedroom with an entire corner devoted to a carefully composed shrine consisting of pictures, sabers, insignia, and other Custer memorabilia. Carroll had been one of the founders of the Little Big Horn Associates (LBHA), and he remained prominent in their top leadership and in their affections until the day of his death in 1991.

John Carroll anointed himself keeper of the flame, ever ready to embark on a noisy crusade against any perceived danger to the memory of Custer and his troopers as gallant American heroes. Joined by some like-minded members of the LBHA, he launched a series of assaults on the National Park Service as it began, in the 1970s, to shift the interpretation at Custer Battlefield to a stance more friendly to the Indian side of the story. The Park Service's handling of the 1976 centennial, in which Russell Means was allowed to posture while Colonel George A. Custer III was kept under wraps, drew heavy fire. Especially galling was a quotation from the Sioux holy man Black Elk attached in large metal letters to the outside wall next to the entrance to the visitor center: "Know the Power of Peace." The sentiment seemed out of place on a battlefield and could be interpreted as pandering to Indian activists while implicitly slandering the soldier dead.

When Carroll threw his wordy protests at members of Congress, government officials, and patriotic organizations such as the American Legion, he typed on the letterhead of the LBHA. His campaigns commanded wide support among members, but they did not carry the official sanction of the leadership. To the distress of some of the more moderate officers, however, the LBHA found itself dragged into the controversies stirred up by Carroll.

As I settled into my new life in Santa Fe in the early 1980s, I found myself caught between two fires. Most LBHA members, including Carroll, held me in high regard, even though I had attended only one meeting. And I retained credibility in the Park Service as an authority on Custer and the battlefield. Copies of Carroll's letters and those generated by his letters fell by the ream on my desk, while Park Service officials telephoned for my counsel on how to respond to the latest barrage.

Central to the altercation were two people and two issues. The people were Superintendent James V. Court, who took over in 1978, and the park historian, Neil C. Mangum. The issues were "balance" in interpretation and the method of selecting books for sale in the visitor center. Critics felt that Court and Mangum allowed the seasonal interpreters, in their oral presentations, to exalt the Indians and denigrate the soldiers—a charge not without merit. From the exaltation of the military in my years at the battlefield, the interpretive pendulum had swung toward not only an exaltation of the Indians but also a denigration of the military.

The book issue exploded when Mangum turned down *Custer Legends*, by Lawrence Frost, as excessively biased toward Custer, as indeed it was. But my old friend Larry Frost, the Monroe podiatrist, had not only written much hagiography about Custer but attained stature in the LBHA equal to John Carroll's.

Carroll demanded the ouster of Court and Mangum. Somehow (possibly through William P. Clements, Texas's first Republican governor since Reconstruction), Carroll caught the attention of G. Ray Arnett, Jim Watt's assistant Interior secretary with oversight of the Park Service. Arnett promised to fly out to Montana and investigate the matter personally. He would be there in late June 1983, within days of the LBHA's annual convention in Billings. Someone in Washington asked me to prepare a background paper for Arnett, which I did. And I had already promised to go to Billings to deliver the banquet address to the LBHA.

My address, "Custer: Hero or Butcher?" (a warmed-over version of the 1971 article in *American History Illustrated*), drew a prolonged standing ovation. Indeed, for the entire three days, I seemed to be the celebrity of the moment, called on constantly to autograph books and program pamphlets. But behind the scenes I spoke some blunt words to both sides of the dispute.

I had no sooner arrived than I cornered John Carroll in his hotel room and served notice that, if he persisted in his campaign to remove Court and Mangum, I would publicly oppose him. He denied that he had sought such an outcome but backed down when Court joined the conversation and confronted him with the evidence. John suffered further embarrassment when evidence also showed that he had represented the entire board of directors as supporting his ouster drive. The board formally censured him for that.

But to Carroll and other members of the board, I also conceded that the battlefield had a problem with interpretive balance and that I would back their call on the Park Service to scrutinize the interpretive program. Later, at a dinner meeting with a defensive Court and Mangum, I repeated my concerns about balance— principally the failure to control the tendency of their interpreters to editorialize. I also told them that they would have to revamp the book selection process, and I urged that, however badly biased *Custer Legends* was, they should let pragmatism overcome their scruples and accept the book for sale.

The upshot of all the talking was that the board of directors adopted sensible resolutions for addressing the dispute, and Court made the appropriate peace-seeking gestures. He even promised to adopt *Custer Legends* for sale at the battlefield. The meeting with Arnett, involving Carroll and two other board members as well as Court and his chief, Regional Director Lorraine Mintzmyer, seemed to satisfy everyone while also allowing Arnett a graceful exit from a mess in which he doubtless had no other stake than the political. I found myself credited on both sides as the mediator who had brought the conflict to a reasonable resolution.

I had not. The newly broadened selection committee promptly rejected *Custer Legends* as too biased. The outside group chosen to look into balance came up with little that was constructive and nothing that appeased the LBHA. Relations between LBHA and Jim Court continued to be cool at best, hostile at worst. And John Carroll continued to write lengthy, abusive, and demanding letters to a long list of addressees.

The 1976 centennial had given me a glimpse of the heat the battle for symbolic possession of Custer Battlefield could generate. My entanglement in the continuing quarrel between the LBHA and the battlefield staff provided new insights. Other adventures on the symbolic battlefield lay in the future.

Meanwhile, I had my own quarrel with Jim Court and his Park Service superiors. Some superintendents continued to do as they pleased without much regard for Service policy, and regional directors still hesitated to curb their independence. Jim Court was a strong man with his own agenda and some skill at enlisting media support when it ran afoul of either policy or higher authority. He ruled the park for eight years, 1978–86, and overall I judge him as among the few effective superintendents. But on one issue we clashed publicly.

In August 1983 a wind-driven fire swept over much of the Custer Battlefield, reducing the dry prairie grass and sagebrush to ash-covered roots. Court and his friend, archeologist Richard A. Fox, agreed that the exposed ground offered ideal conditions for an archeological project, and they persuaded the Custer Battlefield Historical and Museum Association to put up the money. Never mind that Service policy mandated that archeological remains not be disturbed unless threatened with destruction, that Park Service archeologists had not been brought into the planning and the regional director's sanction had not been obtained, or that Montana's state historic preservation officer had not been consulted as required by the regulations of the Advisory Council on Historic Preservation.

For two summers, 1984 and 1985, the project moved forward. Eager volunteers from all over the nation, and even foreign countries, converged to provide the labor. Publicity in all the media focused national attention on the battle ridge. The Park Service brought in one of its ablest archeologists, Douglas D. Scott, to provide legitimacy for what could not be shut down without a public outcry. As the second summer loomed, the Advisory Council branded the project a violation of federal law and demanded compliance. Volunteer workers already on the scene stirred up their congressional delegations, and the Advisory Council patched together an expedient solution that allowed the work to get underway.

I looked on the enterprise as mostly a fishing expedition: Let's see what treasures we can unearth and what they may tell about the battle. Let's make sure the media are there to keep the world watching for dramatic discoveries. Having presided over the formulation of the very policies now being flouted, I knew that the archeological profession felt strongly that the rapid evolution of technology counseled against removing subsurface remains unless essential to knowledge or to modern development. In other words, don't dig unless a highway or pipeline is going to destroy it anyway. In time such technology as remote sensing may reveal more and more buried secrets without ever turning a trowel of earth.

At a meeting of the editorial board of *Montana The Magazine of Western History* in the fall of 1985, I gave vent to my frustrations. Other board members shared the public's enthusiasm for pushing the project to its limits to find everything that could be found. The magazine's editor, William L. Lang, challenged me to make my case in an essay for the "Historical Commentary" section of the magazine. "On Digging Up Custer Battlefield" appeared in the spring 1986 issue.

Charging the Park Service with violating its own policies as well as federal law, I asked: What has been gained? First, the variety of spent ammunition showed that the Indians had more and better firearms than previously thought. Second, fragments of human bones and other items in meaningful association permitted the speculative reconstruction of dramatic individual scenarios, valuable as human interest vignettes in interpreting the battle to the visitor. Third, plotted on a topographical map, the distribution of empty cartridge cases and spent bullets formed a pattern that suggested firing positions and targets. Troops using the same ammunition to fire ceremonial volleys in the years after the battle complicated this line of inquiry, but it is useful. In fact, it had been underway for forty years.

And what had been lost? Certainly the dignity appropriate to the scene of a great historic event had been lost. "Media hype that translates the recovery of fifty kinds of Indian ammunition into fifty Indian rifles, that postulates a particular spent bullet as the very one that felled Custer, cheapens the monument while also doing a disservice to history and the edification of the public." Another loss was to the credibility of the National Park Service, which could not live up to its own canons and had embarked on a course of predictably rich publicity but highly doubtful, certainly unessential, data yield. And a third loss lay in an archeological record no longer underground but in a Nebraska laboratory, where the data it yielded could never be greater than the capabilities of the technology and specialists of 1985.

The article hardly endeared me to Jim Court or Rich Fox. Bill Lang told me that it prompted more mail than any article in fifteen years. Some appeared in the fall 1986 issue, led off by a wordy rebuttal by Fox. The letters ran heavily against me. Archeologists fumed over the effrontery of a historian intruding on their domain. For professional and buff alike, not surprisingly, the suspense and excitement of digging up Custer Battlefield drowned stuffy arguments about law and policy.

My article appeared as Court and Fox prepared to organize a third summer of digging, this time on the Reno-Benteen Battlefield.

I doubt that my arguments had much effect on Regional Director Mintzmyer, but I do think she felt burned by the ruckus over Court's failure to comply with the regulations of the Advisory Council. I also suspect that the breathless media coverage, stoked by Court and Fox, added to other irritations she felt over the superintendent's freewheeling management style. I can't vouch for the story, but it rings true: She met with Court in her Denver office and told him to abandon his plans for a third summer of digs. Shortly after he left, she received a call from a *New York Times* reporter asking why she had killed the project.

Whether or not Court actually summoned the *Times* to his support, he had alienated his chief. She gave him a "directed transfer" to another superintendency. He refused. By the autumn of 1986, he was out of the Park Service altogether and settled in nearby Hardin, doubtless not as a comforting presence to his successor. But Jim quickly showed how sincerely dedicated he was to the welfare of the battlefield. In 1982 he had founded the Custer Battlefield Land Preservation Committee, a fund-raising enterprise devoted to acquiring key parcels of historic land outside the park boundaries. After his retirement, he gave the committee vigorous leadership. Although never properly appreciated by the Park Service, over the years his efforts scored some notable successes. He stepped down from the leadership of this effort in 2003. He merits the gratitude of all friends of the battlefield.

In a stream of publications, Fox and Scott, and Fox himself, trumpeted the momentous contributions to knowledge of the archeological work of 1985–86. Beyond the three modest findings cited in my article, however, I have yet to discover how our understanding of the battle has been significantly changed. But Fox has emerged as a major authority on the Battle of the Little Bighorn, one who commands a large and loyal following. He tends also to regard his interpretations as beyond challenge, which in the volatile world of Little Bighorn aficionados is a sure invitation to challenge.

CHAPTER 18

ONE JUNE WEEKEND IN 1983, Melody and I watched the movie *Chisum* on television. John Wayne played cowman John Chisum in a badly mangled rendition of New Mexico's Lincoln County War. We decided to use the Independence Day weekend to tour the southern part of the state and visit Lincoln.

We found that the old town retained much of its historic ambiance. Major landmarks of the war still stood, including the Tunstall, Ellis, and Murphy-Dolan stores, the last of which had become the Lincoln County Courthouse by the time of Billy the Kid's dramatic escape in 1881. The Wortley Hotel had burned, but it had been reconstructed in 1960 and now served its original purpose. The Rio Bonita paralleled the single street, and piñon-dappled mountains rose steeply on both sides. Despite its prominence in history and folklore, Lincoln had escaped commercialization.

New Mexico state park personnel staffed the Tunstall Store and the courthouse. Our National Park Service standards pronounced their interpretive efforts abysmal. Far superior were the offerings of the newly formed Lincoln County Heritage Trust, a preservation group fueled by the philanthropy of oilman Robert O. Anderson, whose ranch sprawled along the banks of the Hondo River about twenty miles to the east. The trust operated a museum that presented Lincoln's story in professionally designed exhibits.

We checked into the Wortley for the night. Its quaint rooms, furnished with iron bedstead and Victorian furniture, opened on a long roofed porch with comfortable rocking chairs. The host and hostess were warm, friendly people whose kitchen turned out splendid meals.

As twilight fell, Melody and I sat on the veranda sipping drinks and talking about the Lincoln County War. Its history, I knew, had never been well researched and written. The two standard books were flawed both stylistically and interpretively and made deadly reading. Before we went in to dinner, we had agreed that the Lincoln County War offered a dramatic and significant story, replete with a cast of vivid characters in conflict, that had not been properly told. We thought I ought to consider taking it on. It would represent a refreshing shift of focus after more than thirty years of concentrating on Indians and soldiers.

The next morning, before heading for home, we bought a stack of books at the trust's bookstore. But I had no intent to put them immediately to good use. As *Indian Frontier of the American West* made its way through the publication process in 1983, I turned with renewed determination to my novel about Charles Eastman. When Chester Kerr dashed that purpose in January 1984, however, I lost no time bemoaning an ambition that had overreached talent. I turned at once to the Lincoln County War.

Despite the peripheral participation of cowman John Chisum, the Lincoln County War was not the range war of popular imagination. It was a war for monopoly control of the economy and the federal beef and supply contracts for nearby Fort Stanton and the Mescalero Apache Indian agency. The entrenched Murphy-Dolan crowd faced challenge by an upstart young Englishman, John Tunstall, and his lawyer ally, Scotsman Alexander McSween. When a Murphy-Dolan posse gunned down Tunstall, the war was on. It pitted McSween's "Regulators," including an adolescent destined for immortality as Billy the Kid, against a sheriff and a judge who were tools of Lawrence Murphy and Jimmy Dolan.

The plot unfolded in federal and territorial records, old newspapers, the reminiscences of participants, the personal papers of Governor Lew Wallace, and scattered other sources. I researched in the State Records Center in Santa Fe, the National Archives, the University of New Mexico Library, and elsewhere. Easing the task, a cadre of diligent grassroots historians had collected mountains of firsthand evidence but had lacked the ability to shape it into a coherent narrative. Their papers, at the University of Arizona Library, the J. Evetts Haley Library in Midland, Texas, and the Lincoln County Historical Society, vastly shortened the research trail.

The causes, progress, and outcome of the conflict were complex and difficult to sort out in understandable, readable fashion. But as I labored at a newly acquired and, by later standards, entirely primitive word processor, the story developed in what I considered a sound and engaging narrative. In this book, I convinced myself, I had the key to enhanced reputation and robust royalties. I wanted it published by a New York trade house that would give it national exposure and aggressively promote its sale.

I had never worked with a literary agent. Macmillan, which published my two frontier army books, had come to me. So had Yale, American Heritage, and the University of New Mexico Press for *Indian Frontier*. Throughout 1985 I sought a New York agent. Bill Decker, a veteran New York editor, put me in touch with Al Hart. Steve Ambrose connected me with his agent, John Ware. And Al Josephy brought me a response from his agent, Julian Bach. All three read portions of the manuscript without much enthusiasm. When in New York in April 1986, I met with all three. Hart and I failed to hit it off. Bach, agent for some of the biggest names in authordom, flatly declared the subject too complex and regional for a popular market. Ware and I got along famously, and he seemed ready to take on the book. After reading the first chapters, however, he wrote that he just couldn't get into the story. As a last desperate gambit, I persuaded Ash Green at Knopf to read some of the text. He sent it back as "unsuitable."

Obviously, here was a book for a university press, not a trade press. Nebraska held appeal because it continued to bring my earlier books back to life under the successful Bison Book imprint, for which I was grateful. Oklahoma, Texas, and Arizona also made offers. New Mexico, however, had the advantage of nearness—only seventy miles down the interstate at Albuquerque. New Mexico also offered the most generous royalty formula. I had worked well with David Holtby on *Indian Frontier*, as well as a slim book of four lectures I had delivered at the university, entitled *Four Fighters of Lincoln County.* In September 1986 I signed on with New Mexico.

High Noon in Lincoln: Violence on the Western Frontier appeared on New Mexico's fall 1987 list. Despite a hundred review copies thrown at newspapers all over the nation, not a single paper, not even the Albuquerque and Santa Fe papers, saw fit to notice it. When the scholarly reviewers weighed in a year later, however, they gave it high praise. In March 1988 Melody and I drove to Oklahoma City to receive the Wrangler Award of the National Cowboy Hall of Fame and Western Heritage Center, whose judges had chosen *High Noon* the best nonfiction book of 1987. Even so, it achieved hardly even a modest sales record and fell dramatically short of the royalty sums I had fantasized. Clearly, the New York agents knew the popular market better than I.

While seeing *High Noon* through the publication process, I had worked on another book. Richard Etulain, who taught at the University of New Mexico, had persuaded the University of Oklahoma Press to launch a western biography series. It would consist of brief undocumented biographical treatments of westerners, each work capturing both the person and the large themes personified. Dick asked me to establish the model for all to follow by writing about George Armstrong Custer and the historical themes he embodied.

For the first time, I approached Custer systematically. I went through Elizabeth Custer's papers on microfilm at the Custer Battlefield and in the Marguerite Merington collection at the New York Public Library. Otherwise, my files already contained sources on Custer assembled during a preoccupation with the man and his times that had begun in childhood. I wrote the book in less than a year. It went to press at Oklahoma in the autumn of 1987, about the time *High Noon* came off the press.

Cavalier in Buckskin: George Armstrong Custer and the Western Military Frontier appeared on Oklahoma's fall 1988 list. Again, except for the *Chicago Tribune*, the big newspapers ignored it. But it gained wide approval and was adopted as an alternate selection by both History Book Club and Book of the Month Club. Oklahoma ordered a first print run of 13,500, very high for a university press, and within months went back for a second printing. Royalties for the first year approached $20,000. Again in March 1989 Melody and I went to Oklahoma City to receive a second Wrangler Award for the best nonfiction book of 1988. Although I resented the best-sellerdom of Evan Connell's *Son of the Morning Star*, which captured the public in ways I still fail to comprehend, George Armstrong Custer had been much kinder to my reputation and bank account than the Lincoln County warriors.

Although *High Noon in Lincoln* failed to make me rich and famous, one of the Lincoln County warriors seemed to offer some potential. Despite thousands of books and articles and repeated dramatizations on film, Billy the Kid had never been tackled by a professional historian. With only a little additional research, my notes for *High Noon* might be made to spin off a biography of the legendary outlaw. As *Cavalier in Buckskin* made its way through the publication process, I set to work on the Kid. The project was truly a spin-off—finished in eight months, by the summer of 1988. Here was a book that might attract a trade press, but I had no agent, and the manuscript was finished. The University of Nebraska Press eagerly contracted for it on favorable terms. *Billy the Kid: A Short and Violent Life* appeared on the press's fall 1989 list.

If the world cared little for the other characters in the Lincoln County War, it cared a great deal for Billy the Kid—literally the world, for acclaim came from many nations. The book was a main selection of the History Book Club and gained rave reviews in many papers, although only a brief and condescending notice in the *New York Times*. Nebraska hired a publicist to arrange signings and radio and television appearances. Within three years, the Kid had earned more than $80,000 in royalties, an almost unprecedented sum for a university press book. I. B. Tauris did a London edition, and in 1991 Ediciones Paidós of Barcelona and Buenos Aires published *Billy el Niño: Una vida breve y violenta*. Recorded

Books issued an audio edition. In 1997 Éditions du Rocher of Paris gave the French *Billy the Kid: Une vie courte et violente.*

My excursion into New Mexico outlawry ended in caustic irony. *High Noon in Lincoln,* the book I thought would find a large and appreciative readership, the book in which I had invested three years of research and writing, achieved only moderate success. *Billy the Kid,* tossed off in eight months, soared to sales and accolades beyond anything I had ever written.

By the late 1980s I defined myself as a narrative historian, a genre created a century and a half earlier by Francis Parkman and continued in the twentieth century by Bernard DeVoto and others. Professors wrote largely specialized interpretive monographs for one another. I wrote primarily for the general public, not the academic community, although their work is a vital part of researching narrative history. I strove to create readable prose that moved the reader easily from page to page. I tried to tell stories that illustrated the larger themes and to create characters that were believable people rather than mere faceless names on a page. I paused occasionally to place my own interpretation on what I had written. I adhered to scholarly standards of research and documentation and hoped that the academics would approve even though they were not intended as the principal audience. They have, so far.

I also concluded that if a narrative historian devoted years to a book, it ought to address a subject of wide public appeal. This was more likely to resonate with the public, sell more books, and earn more royalties. I became convinced that above all, people were interested in people. Custer and Billy the Kid dramatized for me that people were even more interested in *particular* people, especially people with wide name recognition. Most Americans had heard of Custer and Billy the Kid, and so had people in almost every other part of the world.

Two biographies had succeeded. Why not a third? And if it consumed several years of my life, why not a name that everyone had heard of? I had spent years following General Custer. The time had come to cross the battle lines at the Little Bighorn and examine one of his opponents. Both Crazy Horse and Sitting Bull held appeal, as well as extensive name recognition. Both already had standard biographies, but I judged them severely flawed—romanticized literary works rather than reliable history. I chose Sitting Bull because he lived the longer, richer, more significant, and ultimately more tragic life. With Billy the Kid in the hands of the publisher, I began to research Sitting Bull late in 1988.

Military History Quarterly, a hardcover, slick-page magazine, debuted in the autumn of 1988. In that first issue, editor Rob Cowley ran an excerpt from *Cavalier in Buckskin* and asked me to prepare additional articles. Since the honoraria were substantial, I agreed to furnish an article on the relationship between generals George Crook and Nelson A. Miles and a biographical article on Geronimo. But Cowley liked the Custer item so well that he thought I ought to be represented by a literary agent. He said an old friend and classmate of his seemed a likely person to handle the kind of work I did. His name was Carl Brandt, and his agency, Brandt and Brandt, claimed a long and distinguished lineage in New York.

Prompted by Cowley, Brandt gracefully took the initiative in a letter of August 22, 1988. Through the winter we corresponded and talked on the phone. I told him about my unhappy experience with New York agents and publishers, whose western horizons, I declared, lay no farther west than the Hudson River. He responded that he worked in New York because his business was there, that he would much rather live where I did, in Santa Fe. He added as further testimony to his western interests that he represented Wallace Stegner and David Lavender.

That was enough for me. I sent him *Cavalier in Buckskin* and a copy of the Billy the Kid manuscript, and I told him about Sitting Bull. He liked what he read, and he liked the idea of a book about Sitting Bull. By early 1989 I was Carl's client.

When Melody and I finally had lunch with Carl Brandt in Manhattan, we discovered a tall, open, kindly man with a mobile face and a presence best described by the single word *gentleman*. It is a word, I have since discovered, that comes first to the mind of others of his friends. Melody and I value him not only as a friend but as a professional infinitely wise in the ways of publishers and publishing. He is a voracious reader whose counsel in the development of a manuscript is invariably cogent. He seems to limit the book proposals he will handle to those that not only promise a profitable market but appeal to his personal interests as well. I am grateful to Rob Cowley for what proved a turning point in my professional life and to Carl Brandt for a treasured professional and personal relationship.

In February 1989, with Sitting Bull now definitely selected for my next project, Carl asked me to draw up a two-page statement of what I hoped to accomplish and why it was important. I had constant diversions through March and April involving travel that took me from my desk. Also, Melody and I had signed on for a three-week tour of Europe to begin in the middle of May. Nevertheless, I found time to compose my thoughts, set them to paper, and mail them to Carl.

After a thirty-two-hour day beginning in Paris, Melody and I got back home on the afternoon of June 7. There, amid all the accumulated mail, was a telegram from Carl Brandt asking me to telephone him as soon as we returned. I did. He said that, on the basis of my short prospectus, Henry Holt and Company stood ready to conclude a contract providing for an advance against royalties of $50,000. I was still innocent enough of the New York publishing world to be stunned that a trade house would offer such a commitment to a book that remained several years in the future.

Carl said that John Macrae, a senior editor at Holt who had his own imprint there, would call shortly to talk about Sitting Bull. Jack and I had a long and mutually assuring conversation by telephone. As Carl later explained, Jack was one of the few New York editors with a genuine commitment to the West. I counted myself exceedingly fortunate that I had wound up with both an agent and an editor who knew that a land and a story lay west of the Hudson River.

Before the end of June I had signed a contract. By early August I had received the first installment of my advance, $15,000. At last, I had surmounted the ramparts of the New York publishing world.

CHAPTER 19

As a graduate student, Paul Hutton had driven me from the Indianapolis airport when I received an award from Indiana University in 1977. We remained in touch as Paul received his degree and went to Utah State University to teach and help edit the *Western Historical Quarterly.* He was one of a handful of protégés who staged a surprise testimonial dinner for me at the Western History Association meeting in Salt Lake City in 1983. Not long afterward, he joined the faculty at the University of New Mexico and became editor of the *New Mexico Historical Review.* And by 1986 he had moved his family to Eldorado and settled into a home only a couple of miles from Melody and me. And so we became neighbors.

From the young graduate student I had met in 1977, Paul had matured into a first-class editor and teacher, widely known for the award-winning book drawn from his doctoral dissertation, *Phil Sheridan and His Army.* Dapper in professorial tweeds, with a sometime mustache and beard, Paul was quick minded, articulate (perhaps even glib), witty, self-assured, and ambitious in ways not always condoned by his more conventional colleagues. We enjoyed a close and bantering relationship, especially after he turned up in Eldorado.

Paul had cut his professional teeth on General Custer. As a member of the Little Big Horn Associates, he had served as the editor of two of their annual anthologies, and Custer, of course, figured prominently in his Sheridan work. Shortly after our first meeting, we both attended the 1978 convention of the LBHA in Monroe, Michigan. I had published *Life in Custer's Cavalry* the previous autumn and had been invited to speak about Captain Albert Barnitz's opinion of Custer. We followed the faithful to all the local landmarks—the handsome equestrian statue of Custer, the Custer home, the church where Libbie and Autie were married in 1864, the cemetery full of Custers, and as a finale, a visit to the farm of Nevin Custer, the only Custer brother left after the Little Bighorn. Here, as a memento, we each received a small plastic vial containing soil from the Custer farm.

John M. Carroll, the ebullient and bellicose monarch of the LBHA, informed me that I would undoubtedly receive the association's book prize for *Cavalier in Buckskin*. He therefore arranged an invitation for me to speak at the awards banquet concluding the annual convention in Manhattan, Kansas, in July 1989. I have always felt an obligation, no matter how costly or inconvenient, to be present in person when an organization chooses me for an award. I therefore agreed to serve as banquet speaker and invited Paul Hutton to join me for the drive to Kansas.

Several hundred members showed up, since the site had been chosen for its proximity to Fort Riley, which played an important part in Custer's early plains experience. My speech went over rather well, I thought; but I could see Paul in the back of the room wince and cover his face when I cast Custer as a human being instead of a spotless hero. He thought, probably rightly, that some of the more worshipful in the audience would take offense.

After speaking, I returned to my seat at the head table as Larry Frost went to the podium to present the book award. I had already sufficiently sized up the dynamics of the award committee to be prepared for what came next. The prize went to a book tracing in detail the movement of the Seventh Cavalry from the South to Dakota Territory in 1873. My countenance registered no surprise, and later I offered congratulations to the winner.

An embarrassed John Carroll (a member of the committee) confessed that the vote had been four to three against me. *Cavalier in Buckskin* had contained some speculations about Custer's sexual dalliances together with a discussion of some questionable financial escapades in which he had become mired. In the minds of four of the committee—including, I am convinced, Larry Frost—those aspects of the book proved heresies sufficient to disqualify it.

It is a long drive from Manhattan, Kansas, to Santa Fe, over mostly uninteresting country. Somewhere amid the desolation of the Cimarron Cutoff of the Santa Fe Trail, Paul suddenly burst out in a fit of laughter. He simply laughed and laughed and laughed. Finally, he explained that, reflecting on the scene in the banquet hall the night before, he was reminded of the memorable concluding scene of the movie *Treasure of Sierra Madre*. Humphrey Bogart and his comrades have worn themselves out in an exhausting pursuit of mountain treasure, only to find that there is none. In a finale heavy with ironic fate, they all burst into uncontrollable laughter over their defeat. It seemed an apt comparison.

Jim Court's successor at the Custer Battlefield found the superintendency even less congenial than had Court. A tall, serious, conscientious ranger, Dennis Ditmanson was fated to have his own painful encounter with Russell Means and his activist friends of the American Indian Movement. Although increasingly irrelevant within the Indian community, Means had continued to garner media attention by using Custer and the battlefield as targets for shamelessly overblown rhetoric and protest. He seized on the battle's anniversary date of June 25, 1988, to dramatize his long-standing demand for an Indian memorial at the battlefield equivalent to the cavalry's memorial.

As in the 1976 ceremony, Means gained the speaker's stand and ranted for half an hour on the iniquities of white Americans and on his own bizarre interpretation of Custer and the Battle of the Little Bighorn. As he spoke, a knot of his followers emerged from the crowd with shovels, removed a square of sod from the mass grave of the soldiers at the base of the monument, and embedded a plaque into Redi-mix concrete. The crude inscription read: "In honor of our Indian Patriots who fought and defeated the U.S.

Calvary. In order to save our women and children from mass-
murder. In doing so, preserving rights to our Homelands, Treaties
and sovereignty. 6/25/1988 G. Magpie Cheyenne."

Desecration of the mass grave of the Seventh Cavalry troopers
made exactly the media splash Means intended. For standing
passively aside while the excavation proceeded and "warriors" "counted
coup" on the monument, Ditmanson drew the wrath of large seg-
ments of the Custer fraternity. But in fairness, what else could he
do? He had not the force to intervene, and even if he had, it
would have provoked violence and given Means an even splashier
media event. The plaque remained in place for three months and
then was installed as an exhibit in the museum, which stoked even
more rage at the timidity of the Park Service and its willingness to
display the symbol of an illegal act committed under the very eyes
of its uniformed personnel.

Ironically, Russell Means's despicable drama, defying both the
law and any measure of propriety, pushed the Park Service into
making good a long-standing commitment to explore the idea of
an Indian memorial at Custer Battlefield. And so, once again, I
was drawn into the war for symbolic possession. Early in May 1989
I found myself the token white on an all-Indian committee that
assembled in a Billings hotel. (Several other whites had been named,
but none appeared.) And who should sit across the table from me
in two days of meetings, one at the battlefield? None other than
Russell Means, who throughout was affable, friendly, and cooperative. I doubt that he remembered me as his competitor for the
speaker's podium in 1976.

Strangely, the Park Service had convened this meeting during
an interregnum between superintendents. With what I imagine
was a sense of relief, Ditmanson had repaired to the quieter superintendency of White Sands in New Mexico. Regional Director
Mintzmyer probably already had his successor in mind but had
made no announcement. The conduct of this critical meeting,
therefore, had been entrusted to a planner on her regional staff,
Mike Snyder.

Mike had his marching orders, which struck me as altogether
too low-key and unrealistic. According to his concept, our committee

would conduct a design competition and solicit private donations to pay for the memorial. I had no intention of engaging in such a charade and doubted that any of the other eight or ten members— surely not Russell Means—possessed the ability to judge design or raise money. I flatly branded the approach as nonsense and argued instead for a grand national competition, paid for by the United States, authorized by an act of Congress, and judged by a panel of nationally recognized design experts. The recently completed Vietnam Memorial in Washington, D.C., would furnish the model.

The committee unanimously bought my argument. I drafted our report, which every member present signed. It specified both process and criteria for sensitively harmonizing the Indian memorial with the existing military memorial. It even identified a site that we believed met the criteria. One of the committee members was Congressman Ben Nighthorse Campbell of Colorado, who was represented at the meeting by a legislative assistant, Kimberly Craven. In Washington she took the lead in drafting legislation and winning the cosponsorship of the Montana congressman whose district included the battlefield. That proved difficult and time-consuming because Representative Ron Marlenee was a conservative Republican who had done much to antagonize Indians and therefore to be antagonized by Indians.

The congressional involvement, however, moved most of the decision making out of the Denver office of the Park Service and laid the groundwork for what I thought could be turned into an undertaking of national interest and significance. As the token white, also, I felt a bit of pride in having led the Indians of the committee into a vision much grander than what the Park Service had conceived.

Congressional offices, of course, are not the best incubators for grandiose visions. With the backing of Russell Means and others of the committee, I had merely launched this project on an exceedingly rocky road.

Western residence seemed to me reason enough to step down from the board of directors of the Eastern National Park and

Monument Association. I had agreed to serve as vice chairman, but declared my intent to leave the board when my term expired in the fall of 1984. Executive Secretary Fred Rath, however, flew to Santa Fe and persuaded me that the chairmanship would fall into the wrong hands if I didn't stand for the post. Thus I wound up as chairman of the board during a critical three-year period. The organization had grown and prospered so impressively that it demanded a thorough corporate overhaul, which it fell my lot to oversee. The reorganization had its traumatic moments, but by 1987 we had a more efficient structure. Fred Rath had retired, and all executive authority had been vested in George Minnucci in the Philadelphia office. With the new title of president, George led Eastern to unprecedented highs of profit and service.

I retired from the board in 1987, after a grand farewell party in Tucson. Only a year later, however, George induced me to put my name on the ballot once more. And so the connection with Eastern continued, with another three-year term as chairman of the board.

By 1989 we had lived in Eldorado for nine years. Melody liked some aspects of her job, but others, chiefly the "process" that had so frustrated me at the Advisory Council, bored her. Santa Fe itself began to lose some of its charm, as California money poured in to change the city's character and heighten ethnic tensions. Our principal attachment to Eldorado remained the volunteer fire department, but in the spring of 1986 the county fire marshal launched a successful campaign to topple Chief John Liebson. The action was so political, personal, and unprofessional that all the officers resigned, and the department had to be rebuilt. For six years the fire department had been an integral part of our lives, and we were immensely saddened to leave it. After that, we were ready to move if the opportunity presented. Melody applied unsuccessfully for several other positions, and we even tried to structure finances that would allow her to resign and join me in writing history full-time.

Now and then Melody had toyed, not too seriously, with switching from history to management. The thought was not very realistic.

Park superintendents almost always came from the ranger ranks. Historians who made the transition entered at a much lower grade than Melody held in the Santa Fe office. Moreover, only one park in the Southwest Region appealed to her management instincts—the Lyndon B. Johnson National Historical Park in Texas.

The only reason we gave much thought to such a shift in Melody's career lay in the persona of the regional director. John Cook had a reputation for doing surprising nontraditional things. He had been the Alaska regional director who backed Melody's leave to get her doctorate in 1979, and he had urged her to apply for the position in Santa Fe she had held since 1980. Now, in what we thought might be a veiled signal, in the spring of 1989 he made her interim superintendent of Chickasaw National Recreation Area in Oklahoma, sent her to a business course at the University of Southern California, and entrusted her with organizing and staging the fiftieth anniversary celebration of the construction of the big adobe office building in Santa Fe. In all three assignments, she excelled.

In that same summer of 1989 the LBJ superintendency fell vacant, and Cook seemed unable to find an acceptable candidate. Knowing that he could make a simple lateral transfer of Melody from her Santa Fe position to the LBJ superintendency, we decided after lengthy discussion that she should express her interest. One Monday morning, she stuck her head in Cook's office and said that, if he were so disposed, she would be interested in the LBJ superintendency. He turned back to his work with hardly any response. He had made it plain, we concluded, that he had no intention of sending a staff person into so important a superintendency.

Shortly afterward, Melody and I flew to Kansas City for a meeting of Eastern National's board of directors. As a sidelight, we were bused to Independence to visit the Harry S Truman National Historic Site. En route we stopped for lunch. As we settled into our chairs around a large table in an upstairs dining room, one of the restaurant staff entered and loudly announced that Melody Webb had a telephone call at the reception desk downstairs. We were all well launched into our meal when she returned, slid in beside me, and whispered that the caller had been John Cook, who had said: "Get yourself back here because you are going to LBJ."

CHAPTER 20

MELODY AND I THOROUGHLY enjoyed our Texas years, 1989 to 1992. Headquartered in Johnson City, the Lyndon B. Johnson National Historical Park lay in the heart of the Texas Hill Country, a scenic land of rocky ridges and hills spotted with groves of live oak and cedar and gashed by the rivers falling from the high plains to the black-soil prairies below. Austin, the state capital, lay forty miles to the east, San Antonio about sixty miles to the south.

We acquired a "ranch" of our own—an eighteen-acre spread four miles south of Dripping Springs. We lived in a big limestone house with porches and a separate apartment that made an ideal study. A barn, goat shed, swimming pool with pool house, and a garden surrounded by a high deer fence afforded special amenities. Live oaks stands teeming with deer covered the entire property, which crowned a ridgetop affording a sweeping view of the land. Appropriately for historians of the West, we leased seventeen of our acres for the grazing of a herd of splendidly endowed long-horn cattle. Melody commuted thirty miles west to Johnson City, while I could reach the University of Texas Library and the Austin airport in a twenty-mile drive to the east.

The Lyndon B. Johnson National Historical Park consisted of two units, one in Johnson City and one thirteen miles west near Stonewall. In Johnson City were the president's boyhood home and the "Johnson Settlement," including the pioneer log cabin of LBJ's grandparents in the trail-driving days of the Texas cattlemen. Near Stonewall was the LBJ Ranch, the "Texas White House" during the presidential years, together with his reconstructed birthplace, his elementary school, and the family cemetery, all bordered by the scenic Pedernales River. Guarded by the Secret Service, Mrs. Johnson lived at the ranch. Tour buses allowed visitors to view the attractions.

Melody hit the ground running and became an instant success as a park superintendent. The staff closed ranks to support her, and she fashioned them into an effective team. She liked them, and they liked her. They welcomed me too, and we enjoyed many tastefully planned social events. Special occasions were the barbeques in the aircraft hanger at the LBJ Ranch.

Melody's tenure featured not only a smoothly functioning staff but numerous accomplishments of lasting consequence. Among the more notable were the acquisition of a new fleet of tour buses to replace the aging relics of an earlier time and the political, financial, and planning groundwork for converting an abandoned hospital into a imposing new visitor center. In the latter, she worked closely with J. J. "Jake" Pickle, protégé of LBJ who occupied his old seat in the House of Representatives for thirty years. We came to treasure Jake and Beryl Pickle as much as the legions of Texans who returned him repeatedly to his congressional seat.

Like all Texans, we quickly grew to adore Lady Bird Johnson. Melody took care to consult with her on every major park decision and to keep her informed of park issues and developments. We enjoyed the small dinner gatherings at the LBJ Ranch, over which she presided with the graciousness for which she was widely admired.

For both of us, the move to Texas contained elements of irony. Melody had marched with the Berkeley antiwar protesters in 1965 and held their negative view of LBJ. Now she was superintendent of his park, an experience that gave her a new and more favorable perspective on Johnson and his presidency. For my part, I had played no small role in the establishment and early development of the park, and in the early 1970s I had worked closely with Mrs. Johnson when she chaired the history committee of the national parks advisory board.

The move to Texas greatly facilitated my research on the Sitting Bull biography. Bill Goetzmann and Ron Tyler got me anointed a "visiting scholar" at the University of Texas, which meant I had faculty privileges at the library, one of the best in the nation for research in history. I spent many days among its treasures. I also traveled to research libraries in Montana, Utah, Colorado, and North and South Dakota as well as to Yale's Beinecke Library, the National Archives and National Anthropological Archives in Washington, D.C., and the Glenbow Museum in Calgary, Alberta. The last afforded a rewarding opportunity to follow Sitting Bull's trail in Canada and visit the places where he dealt with the North-West Mounted Police. Periodic installments of my advance against royalties helped pay for these trips. By the fall of 1990 I had enough notes to begin drafting chapters of the book.

Meantime, Custer Battlefield continued to stoke controversy. In Congress, early in 1990, representatives Campbell and Marlenee managed a precarious cosponsorship of legislation to authorize the Indian memorial. It incorporated most of what the advisory committee had recommended but muddied the proposal with some confusing nomenclature. I corresponded with Campbell's assistant, Kimberly Craven, in an effort to refocus the language and submitted a statement to be placed in the record of subcommittee hearings. The bill died in the second session of the 101st Congress but was introduced again in the first session of the 102nd, in February 1991. Unfortunately, Campbell, who discovered his Indian heritage only when it became fashionable, also filed a bill to change the name of the park from Custer Battlefield to Little Bighorn Battlefield. That long-running dispute at once overshadowed the Indian memorial legislation.

Already, the Park Service had roused its critics to new anger. In July 1989 Regional Director Mintzmyer named Ditmanson's successor as superintendent. She was Barbara Booher, a Ute Indian whose principal qualification for the position was her politically correct ethnicity. She was a realty specialist for the Bureau of Indian Affairs cycled into the Park Service as Mintzmyer's executive assistant and then sent to the battlefield. The appointment garnered much favorable publicity throughout the country, as Mintzmyer intended. It also raised a bright crimson flag in the face of antagonists already furious over the coddling of Russell Means, a flag that Booher did not lower during her tenure.

The antagonists had grown not only more vocal but more numerous. Death removed John Carroll from the fight, but many of the Little Big Horn Associates weighed in with all his zeal. Jerry Russell's Order of Indian Wars, based in Little Rock, Arkansas, also joined the fray. Even the Custer Battlefield Historical and Museum Association began to distance itself from the park and take adversarial positions that belied its role as a "cooperating" association.

Booher's appointment, together with the congressional bills to change the park name and erect an Indian memorial, kept Custer Battlefield in the national spotlight. The Park Service took some vicious blows, but Mintzmyer had read her audience correctly. Most people thought the Indians had got a raw deal, and here was a small gesture of national remorse. Unfortunately, having thrust the neophyte Booher into the front lines, Mintzmyer left her there unsupported to fight the battle virtually alone.

I submitted a statement for the record as the House subcommittee held hearings in the spring of 1991. I thought the legislation contained major flaws and said so, especially the failure to ensure that the memorial would stand as a truly national undertaking, paid for by the United States. Instead, private funds would be solicited. The name change, which the Park Service backed, gave me special problems. I had never been forced to take a position on the issue. I had hoped that it would simply go away. Now, for my testimony, I had to decide. After much agonizing, I declared in favor of the name change.

In a speech to the annual Montana History Conference in Helena on October 25, 1991, I explained my reasoning. I said that, on one hand, the Custer name, like the landscape and the monument and markers, was genuinely historic, part of the battlefield from the beginning. To change it was to tamper with history itself by overriding the action of an earlier generation. This should not be done lightly.

On the other hand, the Indian community had assigned to Custer a symbolism that, although historically invalid, was a reality. Custer's name attached to the monument was genuinely obnoxious to nearly all Indians. I likened the Custer name to the Confederate flag, offensive to blacks when flaunted at sporting events or incorporated into state flags. Neither Custer nor the Confederate flag should be expurgated from the national memory, but their uses should be sharply examined to limit or remove offense to the offended groups. The time had come, therefore, to substitute the more neutral label of Little Bighorn.

My letters and congressional testimony had no discernable effect on the legislation enacted by the House on June 24, 1991, and the Senate on November 24. Despite the strident objections of opponents, hardly any member of Congress could be caught voting against a measure so politically correct. I still stand by my position on the name change, but with uncomfortable ambivalence. I can understand the feelings of the only member of the Senate committee to vote nay, Malcolm Wallop of Wyoming. "As a Nation, we diminish ourselves when we sway with the political winds and bury the lessons of history," he declared. "The Committee is yielding to a misdirected emotional clamor."

Just how intensely opponents of the name change felt I discovered after my speech was published in *Montana The Magazine of Western History*. Hate mail from Custer loyalists savaged me for breaking the faith.

The law directed the secretary of the interior to establish an advisory committee to oversee the design competition. Although tentatively queried about my interest in serving on the committee, I think the Park Service regional staff in Denver was greatly relieved when I said that on this particular issue I had paid my dues. I did turn them toward Paul Hutton, who received a secretarial appointment and, I suspect, caused the Park Service more grief than I might have.

As I had foreseen, the committee fell well short of the expectations written into the 1989 report that underlay the legislation. Its eleven members included the relevant specialists, but they lacked the stature to give the competition national interest and credibility.

Nine of the eleven were Indians, leaving Hutton and one other as token whites. Rather than recruiting a truly distinguished judging panel, moreover, the committee designated seven of its own members as judges—two artists, one historian, one architect, one landscape architect, an Indian tribal judge, and an Indian public relations director. None had the national standing in the design world that I believed essential to so important an alteration of the newly styled Little Bighorn Battlefield National Monument.

Despite constant bickering in the committee, the design competition concluded in 1997 with the selection of a concept submitted by John Collins and Allison Towers of Philadelphia. The secretary of the interior approved the choice. The design featured an earthen circle topped by metal sculptures of warriors on horseback. Texts, graphics, and pictographs adorned the interior walls on three sides to present the role and history of the tribes that fought in the battle. An opening in the wall framed the historic monument on Custer Hill. When unveiled, the concept impressed me with its power and simplicity. I was greatly relieved, although glad not to have been a party to all the dissensions that troubled the committee.

Although a flawed process had produced an exemplary outcome, the memorial still faced formidable obstacles. The same people who fought so staunchly against the name change took up the fight against the site, which had been recommended in our 1989 committee report and written into law. A newsletter, the *Custer/ Little Bighorn Battlefield Advocate*, kept watch on politically correct happenings at the park, provided a forum for attacking the Park Service, and urged readers to sign a petition to the president and Congress labeling a memorial on the chosen site "inherently abhorrent to every notion of honor and good taste."

In addition, Indian groups began squabbling with one another. In particular, the Sioux threatened to oppose the memorial because the winning artists had not been Indian. Moreover, any financial benefits to the local community would fall to the Crows, who had fought with the cavalry at the Little Bighorn. And of course the money remained to be raised from philanthropy, an uncertain prospect at best.

In June 1991 the board of directors of Eastern National Park and Monument Association, of which I was again chair, held its summer meeting at the Lake Hotel in Yellowstone National Park. Melody and I flew to Salt Lake City, then drove to Yellowstone. En route we toured Grand Teton National Park and spent a night at Jackson Lake Lodge. The day was gloriously bright, and from our hotel room we looked out across Jackson Lake to watch the sun dip behind the jagged peaks of the Teton Range. Melody said here at Grand Teton she wanted to end her Park Service career as superintendent.

That seemed a long time in the future. She loved her job at LBJ and had much that she wanted to accomplish before leaving there. In fact, we both thought our hilltop ranch might be our home forever. At the same time, because of her success at LBJ, Melody began to pick up signals from higher management that she should start thinking about moving on. If she didn't apply for desirable vacancies, she might find herself posted to an undesirable one.

In the spring of 1992 the assistant superintendency of Grand Teton fell vacant. We discussed whether Melody should apply, but the competition seemed so great that she did not get around to filling out the forms. Early in April, with the deadline for filing only a few days away, I went to Boston for an Eastern National executive committee meeting and dined with Russ Dickenson, former Park Service director and now a board member. Russ had served as chief ranger at Teton in 1959–61. He told me to get on the telephone and inform Melody that she must apply for that position. No other would give her the range of experiences needed for the superintendency of a large park. Although sick that weekend, Melody duly prepared the application and submitted it on the very day of the deadline.

Weeks and then months passed with no word at all, then word that the position seemed destined for another, then word that forty-two people had applied. We thought Teton unattainable and anyway were happy in Texas.

In the middle of July 1992 Melody and I flew to Seattle for Eastern National's summer board meeting. As our plane descended from the clouds and the sunlit snows on Mount Rainier appeared in our window, I turned to Melody and said, "When we check into the hotel, there will be a note for you to call Jack Neckels," Grand Teton's superintendent. She laughed that one off, but I was right. There was a note at the Hilton's desk. As soon as we got to our room, Melody put in the call. Neckels offered her the post. She accepted.

The next morning, as I opened the board meeting, I asked Melody to tell the members about her telephone call. Her announcement brought a round of applause. No one beamed more brightly than Russ Dickenson.

CHAPTER 21

MIDWAY THROUGH JUNE 1992, almost exactly three years after signing the contract with Henry Holt and Company, I put the finishing touches on my biography of Sitting Bull and mailed copies of the manuscript to Carl Brandt and Jack Macrae. Both responded with fine compliments, and Jack began to work his way through the chapters. Carl and Jack thought little revision would be needed.

Through August we busied ourselves preparing for the move to Grand Teton. The movers were scheduled to come on September 15, and our days were crowded with all the labors of a move, as well as the sale of our home. Also, Melody flew to Grand Teton for two weeks of orientation. Superintendent Jack Neckels wanted her to experience the park during the summer inundation of visitors, who would all be gone by the time we arrived. I flew up for a couple of days to see our new home.

A little more than two weeks before we were to move, Jack Macrae called. The manuscript, he thought, would profit from what he termed "judicious pruning," and he took me through it chapter by chapter to point out examples. The slight revision forecast in June had turned into a major revision by late August. But if I waited until after the move, the publication schedule would slip by six months. I sealed a bargain with Jack. If he would guarantee spring 1993 publication, I would do the judicious pruning before we left Texas.

I did. The manuscript went back on September 10 with the comment "You were right. There was plenty of fat." I reduced the number of chapters from thirty-two to twenty-four and fried out one hundred pages of fat. It was an arduous task, accomplished in thirteen days. Carl and Jack were both impressed, and in truth so was I. Relieved that Sitting Bull would make Holt's spring list, we abandoned our beautiful Hill Country ranch on September 15 and headed for Wyoming.

Jack Neckels rightly believed that either the superintendent or the assistant superintendent should live in the park. He had bought a house in Jackson, so the responsibility fell to Melody. For all the years we had dedicated to the National Park Service, neither of us had ever actually lived in a park. Our home was a big log house erected as the superintendent's residence in 1933 by the Civilian Conservation Corps. It was located in the Beaver Creek area, amid an ensemble of log buildings that had once served as park head-quarters. Two miles north of the present headquarters, the district had been listed in the National Register of Historic Places.

Our home, Quarters No. 1, had been modernized without compromising its architectural integrity. The spacious living room, with viga ceiling and log walls, was dominated by a huge stone fireplace and log mantel. The fireplace itself, however, had been sealed shut and a wood-burning stove substituted as a source of heat. We lamented that change, until the winter snows and subzero temperatures highlighted its prudence. Upstairs our bedroom faced east with a view across the Snake River Valley to the Gros Ventre Mountains. In summer and autumn herds of elk gathered beneath our bedroom window. My study, tiny in comparison with Texas and overwhelmed by my huge horseshoe-shaped desk, faced west. In glorious compensation, however, I looked above my computer screen at the Grand Teton itself, soaring from foothills that began at the very edge of Beaver Creek. We counted ourselves fortunate to live in such a beautiful setting.

For Melody, Grand Teton posed a challenge that often assumed painful dimensions. It is one of the most complex parks in the system, rife with problems without acceptable solution and plagued by the personnel vexations common to every large park. That Neckels had chosen as the manager responsible for park operations a woman historian angered some of the ranger and maintenance force. No woman had ever held the position. The chief ranger quieted some of the more vocal critics by circulating her application papers, and he told her that her Alaskan record, her fire department experiences, and her pilot's license counted for more in their estimation than her Ph.D.

Even so, she had a very rough four years at Grand Teton. Compared to this big, troubled park, LBJ seemed like a managerial holiday. For my part, I reveled in the surroundings and in being a Park Service veteran who was now the spouse of the assistant superintendent. And living in a park, experiencing its afflictions through Melody's eyes, gave me a new perspective on the Service to which I had devoted most of my government career.

The Lance and the Shield: The Life and Times of Sitting Bull appeared in May 1993. It was handsomely designed and printed, the first of my books in which I could find nothing to criticize. Working with Jack Macrae had been a delight. He was gently persistent in urging changes to make the text leaner and faster paced. Nothing he asked did I find objectionable. In particular, a last-minute substitution of a brief prologue for the original opening chapter turned out to be highly effective.

With one exception—a sour commentary by the editor of the *Lakota Times*—the media greeted the book enthusiastically. Celebrity historian Patricia Limerick gave it a fine, full-page review in the *New York Times* Sunday book review section, and in December it made the *Times* list of the hundred most notable books of 1993. Other papers that reviewed it favorably included the *Wall Street Journal, Washington Post, Christian Science Monitor,* and *London Economist.* It was the main selection of the History Book Club for May and an alternate selection of the Book of the Month Club. Holt's first printing was twenty-five thousand copies, and subsequent trips to the press upped that number by ten thousand. History Book

Club did its own edition of twenty-five thousand. Holt sold the paperback rights to Ballantine for an advance of $75,000 and recovered its advance to me of $50,000 in the first month. For both Holt and, a year later, Ballantine, I went on the road for signings at selected bookstores throughout the country. *The Lance and the Shield* won the Spur nonfiction award of the Western Writers of America and the Caughey prize of the Western History Association. Subsequently, Carl Brandt negotiated contracts for an audio edition with Books on Tape and for printed editions in Italy, France, England, Poland, and the Czech Republic.

The Lance and the Shield was clearly my best book to date and may turn out to be the best of my writing career.

As Sitting Bull made his way through the publication process, both Carl and Jack wanted to talk about the next book. I had decided to build on the Sitting Bull research to write a history of the Lakota people and had devoted the first few months of 1993 to gathering sources. But Carl thought public fascination with Indians had peaked (he was wrong on that one), and we explored other topics. First we settled on a book about the bicultural sons of trader William Bent, but that collapsed when I discovered my friend David Haalas of the Colorado Historical Society already hard at work on it. Next we agreed on a biography of Kit Carson, and Carl and Jack began to draw up a contract. Then I found out that another friend, Marc Simmons, had devoted fifteen years to Kit Carson. Although I could have embarked on either project, I did not want to intrude on preserves staked out by David and Marc. Finally I conceived the notion that a "triple biography" of Carson, Jim Bridger, and Tom Fitzpatrick could serve as a vehicle for showing how the Rocky Mountain trappers went on to play major roles in advancing the national boundaries to the Pacific. Jack simply amended the title of the contract to "Kit Carson and Friends," and when signed in the fall of 1993 it carried a hefty advance (for a historian) of $90,000.

The triple-biography concept did not work out. Both Carl and Jack thought it too cumbersome, and as usual they were right. In May 1994 Melody and I flew to New York for my induction as a Fellow of the Society of American Historians and had a long lunch with Carl and Jack. The result was an overhaul of the scheme: to keep the biographical focus but to expand the list of mountain men who would personify both the story of Rocky Mountain trapping and the part trappers played in national expansion.

Jackson Hole and the Tetons afforded an inspiring setting in which to dig into the history of the mountain men. In particular, the area positioned me to explore the complex geography of the northern Rockies, mastery of which was crucial to working out the daunting puzzle of who went where when. While touted as the "crossroads of the fur trade," however, Jackson Hole could hardly be regarded as an ideal center for documentary research. I spent time in libraries of Utah State and Brigham Young universities and in the Colorado Historical Society and Denver Public Library. But my great good fortune was to find someone who had done much of my research for me. Dale Morgan, premier historian of the fur trade in the 1940s and 1950s, had mined the collections of the Missouri Historical Society and transcribed hundreds of items from St. Louis and other newspapers indispensable to my project. I obtained ten reels of microfilm containing all his research data from the Bancroft Library at the University of California at Berkeley. Dale Morgan greatly reduced my travel time and allowed me to do much research at my own desk at the foot of the Grand Teton.

Even before leaving Santa Fe, I had dabbled in television. Several producers sought me out as a talking head in documentaries about Billy the Kid. Todd Robinson's *A.K.A. Billy the Kid,* for instance, finally turned up on the Disney Channel, where it played periodically for several years. I joined with Scott Momaday in helping the Nebraska Educational Television Network prepare a documentary on Indian education for the Public Broadcasting System. Titled *In the White Man's Image,* it aired on PBS early in 1992. Only after the phenomenal success of Ken Burns's production on the Civil War popularized the historical documentary, however, did I become almost continuously involved with television.

The Old West emerged as a favorite for documentary producers in the 1990s. I could talk authoritatively (or at least sound authoritative) about Indians, soldiers, Custer, Sitting Bull, mountain men, and assorted other topics. Television took time from writing and returned almost no dollars, but I thought it might help sell books. I doubt that it did, for I now suspect that only a small overlap joins those who get their history from books and those who get it from television.

Several producers hurried to apply the Ken Burns formula to the West, including Ken Burns himself. His nine-part extravaganza, entitled simply *The West,* took three years to complete. Ken's brother Ric also tackled the subject with *The Way West.* Ric's crew filmed me in his New York apartment in August 1993, and Ken's camera caught my contribution when the Western History Association met in Tulsa two months later. I also reviewed script and rough cuts for Ric Burns. Both series aired on PBS but fell far short of *The Civil War* in popular acclaim.

Backed by Time-Warner, Doug Netter's Rattlesnake Productions of Los Angeles turned out *The Wild West,* a ten-hour documentary that played on the Prime Time Network. I went to Los Angeles several times in 1992 to work with producers John Copeland and Jami Smith. In the spring of 1993 I flew to Detroit with Doug Netter to premier an introductory tape for Lincoln-Mercury executives who had put up some of the money. Netter sold the Time-Warner people on another documentary, about Indians, and in the early months of 1993 they paid me $15,000 to develop a concept, with much more in prospect if it went into production. It didn't, replaced by a documentary about rock-and-roll music.

The series that proved to be the most fun was *How the West Was Lost*—lost, that is, by the Indians. In 1991 two people working with KUSA-TV, the ABC affiliate in Denver, asked me to help develop a pilot that could be used to promote funding of a series by the Discovery Channel. Thus began a warm association with Chris Wheeler and Sonny Hutchison that endures to this day. The pilot, portraying the tragedy of Chief Joseph and the Nez Perces, caught Discovery's attention. Ultimately, we made thirteen one-hour episodes that have aired several times on the Discovery Channel and gained critical acclaim as well as a prestigious prize.

But the series that made my face and voice familiar to thousands of viewers of the Arts and Entertainment Channel (A&E) and its subsequent spin-off, the History Channel, was *The Real*

West. Donna Lusitana of Greystone Productions invited me into this enterprise in 1992 and thus inaugurated a long-term association. Hosted by Kenny Rogers, the first block of thirteen one-hour episodes gained top ratings on A&E during the fall of 1993. Ultimately Greystone produced sixty episodes. I appeared in approximately half. Paul Hutton may have been in more. He and I alone dominated many an hour of screen time as he recounted a story in his inimitable fashion and I then appeared to place it in a larger context and explain its significance.

How the West Was Lost involved numerous trips to Denver, but the others took me to the Los Angeles area. Greystone worked me hard, for little recompense. Aided by a two-hour time lag, I would fly in for a full day's filming. Any producer who wanted me for an episode, whether I knew anything about the topic or not, signed up for an interview. Sometimes I talked into a camera for as long as ten hours, with lunch brought in. The producers then extracted the few passages, rarely more than five to ten seconds each, that matched the visuals and threw the rest of the film away. Once producers caught on to our new home in the mountains, they brought their camera crews to Grand Teton and set up in our living room of log and stone.

Like a powerful magnet, the newly restyled Little Bighorn Battlefield National Monument continued to attract controversy. Interpretation, the Indian memorial, the name change, the agenda of an Indian superintendent—all were legitimate issues that merited serious debate. But a truly bizarre dispute intruded into my life within four months after we had settled into our Grand Teton home. Even now, years later, I find it hard to understand how anyone in the Park Service could have taken it seriously, but they did.

An outfit styled North Shield Ventures, headed by one Lawson Warren, proposed a "partnership" with the National Park Service that held astonishing implications. In January 1993 a Hardin newsman used the Freedom of Information Act to smoke out a secret memorandum of understanding concluded the previous September between North Shield and the Denver regional office. The document stated that if negotiations between the parties produced agreement, Warren would raise $75 million to erect a new visitor center and underwrite various other high-cost projects. North Shield would then hold a thirty-year monopoly to operate the visitor center and conduct all tours and other interpretive activities in the park.

I was astounded, but not so much by the prospect of Disneyland on the Little Bighorn. I predicted that it would collapse of its own weight—too much money for too little promise of gain. Little Bighorn drew a primarily seasonal visitation of several hundred thousand, hardly enough to support so elaborate an operation. My outrage, rather, sprang from the spectacle of Park Service officials taking the proposition seriously, as evidenced by the secret September agreement. Would Regional Director Bob Baker actually cede his authority and responsibility for a unit of the National Park System to a profit-making entity? Would the new Park Service director, Roger Kennedy, let him? Kennedy embraced enough other ruinous measures to suggest the possibility.

I had known Baker for many years. A pleasant, friendly fellow, he had many admirers at parks throughout his region. He had detractors too. He had come out of the old Bureau of Outdoor Recreation and possessed only the thinnest background in national park philosophy and tradition. I telephoned him and told him we had been friends for a long time and I did not want to stab him in the back. So I was notifying him that I intended to stab him in the front. I would fight this idiotic idea openly, not covertly. I then sent hard-hitting letters to the chairmen of the House and Senate subcommittees overseeing the Park Service as well as to other members of Congress. I helped the *Denver Post*, the *Billings Gazette*, and other papers to pry out the story. My interviews with the Associated Press brought national attention to the issue.

On the telephone, Baker had been pleasant enough. As the press turned up the heat, however, he phoned Teton superintendent Jack Neckels and suggested that Melody would be well advised to silence her husband. Neckels laughed that off with the reply that even Melody could not restrain an aroused Bob Utley. Even so, the clear implication that my opposition could imperil Melody's career reflected poorly on Baker.

One of Baker's lieutenants, Mike Snyder, handled the North Shield project. Indeed, he may have been the one who persuaded Baker that it had merit. Throughout 1993 both Baker and Snyder championed the idea and fought off dissent. So did Lawson Warren, who took station in Helena and joined the fray. Snyder kept urging me to let him come to Teton and explain the matter. Several times I told him that nothing he could say would appease me, that my opposition lay not in the details but in the concept of turning a national park over to private enterprise.

I do not recall a conclusive end to the North Shield scheme. It limped along for about two years, occasionally prompting a news item. I assume that, as I had foreseen from the beginning, Warren could not find the financial backing. Even had he come up with the funding, I believe the Park Service or Interior Department would have killed the idea—perhaps, if Director Kennedy had hesitated, with some congressional prodding. In any event, by the end of 1994 the Denver office had a new regional director. John Cook enjoyed high stature in the Park Service as a manager of experience and good judgment. As he remembers it, he leaned on Mike Snyder to lean on Lawson Warren to put up or shut up. Of course he could not put up, as Cook well knew, so he shut up.

CHAPTER 22

By the summer of 1995 we had been at Teton nearly three years, time in Park Service practice to start thinking about the next assignment. A disruptive (and destructive) reorganization scheme launched by Director Roger Kennedy, however, had all but frozen for the indefinite future moves based on competitive selection, and we lived with constant uncertainty. The Kennedy design required a drastic downsizing, and to get rid of enough people it invited anyone as young as fifty to apply for early retirement regardless of years of service. For a variety of reasons, not least her husband's aging, Melody decided to take advantage of this opportunity as I had in other circumstances fifteen years earlier.

Retirement hardly connoted what we intended for our future. Now I could cease being a house husband and devote more time to writing history. And now Melody could share the household tasks and also pick up her writing career. So we needed an appealing setting close to a good library. We had long planned to build a home on land Melody owned in the foothills overlooking Tucson, Arizona, but we worried about the water table and the miles of traffic-clogged streets that would separate us from the University of Arizona library. So we turned back to Texas. We regarded Austin as a center of enlightenment in a state burdened with too many social conservatives and hard-right Republicans. The University of

Texas offered a splendid library of western history, and we loved
the ambience of the Texas Hill Country. Moreover, Texans were
so friendly and welcoming that we decided liberals could live
among them without undue stress. In September 1995 we slipped
away from Teton and flew to Austin to look for a house. Several
disappointing days turned up nothing satisfactory.

Then we drove thirty miles north to Georgetown. We found the
small city appealing. It retained its historic ambience, with a traditional Texas courthouse square lined with businesses restored to
their original appearance. Reflecting the determination of its citizens
not to yield the downtown to suburbanization, their efforts had
won a Main Street award from the National Trust for Historic
Preservation. Georgetown was also home to Southwestern University, the oldest institution of higher education in Texas and a
highly rated liberal arts college. Its attractive campus occupied the
eastern edge of the city. After a single afternoon's search, we bought
a house.

On April 1, 1996, Melody turned fifty. On April 2 she retired.
On April 3 the big moving van labored through the snow to our
cherished log home in Beaver Creek. The farewells of Jack Neckels
and his staff and the leading townspeople of Jackson were sincere
and heartwarming. We left with a strong affection for and fond
memories of the park, the city, and the inhabitants of both.

Our Georgetown home, located in a development named Wood
Ranch, stood on the very edge of the Hill Country. The black-soil
agricultural plains that stretch from the Balcones Escarpment to
the Gulf of Mexico began just across Interstate 35 two miles from
our residence. It was a two-story stone structure set amid live oaks
and resting on a limestone ledge characteristic of the Hill Country.
The developer had created a huge master bedroom upstairs. Spacious
enough to contain our desks and filing and map cabinets, we
made it our study. An adjacent "reading room" and an outside
deck completed an ideal ambience for a pair of historians.

Fortune favored us also because of Southwestern University. Its
library scarcely measured up to the University of Texas, but its
interlibrary loan program made up for much of that shortcoming.
Furthermore, its Special Collections held rich archives of Texana.

As further good fortune, Provost Dale Knoble, a historian, knew who I was and had admired my frontier army books. History professor Bill Jones turned out to be another who recognized me as a kindred soul. Knoble and Jones both took to Melody (we were Mr. Utley and Dr. Webb), and they reached out to cement a relationship between us and the university. It took the form of faculty privileges and, most important, faculty status at the library. Ultimately the relationship was formalized with certificates designating both Melody and me as "affiliated scholars." As the years passed, we came to use the Southwestern library more than the UT library, a thirty-mile drive on the heavily traveled interstate.

In this new environment, I resumed work on what the contract called "Kit Carson and Friends," and Melody began work on a memoir by which she hoped to expose the consequences of use and abuse of the national parks. We kept in touch with the National Park Service through my continuing membership on the board of directors of Eastern National Park and Monument Association. When I finally stepped down in 1997, the board chose Melody to fill an unexpired vacancy. In 2003, after three years as vice chair, they chose her as board chair. For seventeen years she had accompanied me to the board meetings as spouse. After 1997 I went with her as spouse.

We occupied our Wood Ranch home for five years. In 2000 we bought a lot with a beautiful view of Lake Georgetown and built a stone home, all on one floor and all to our particular wants. We moved in April 2001, and here we intend to remain for the indefinite future.

I had finished the research and begun writing the mountain man book before we moved to Texas. I had completed six chapters and had seven to go, with contract target of August 1, 1997. Early in June 1996 Jack Macrae called with a dismaying proposition. He wanted to schedule the book for Holt's spring 1997 list, which meant I would have to finish the seven chapters by October. I declared that impossible, but Melody talked me out of it. She said I could do it. She would take over all chores and leave me to do nothing but write. The completed manuscript, still without a title, went in the mail on September 12.

From the beginning I recognized how essential superior maps would be. To understand the mountain men, the tangled geography in which they worked had to be surpassingly depicted. I suspected that computer technology might have reached a level of sophistication to provide the solution. Ron Tyler, director of the Texas State Historical Association, put me in touch with Ken Foote in the UT Department of Geography. He in turn connected me with one of his doctoral students, Peter Dana. Happily, Peter lived in Georgetown, not a young graduate student but an established middle-aged consultant in geographical information systems.

Peter had enough to do just to earn a living, but he consented to explore the technology. If what I wanted proved feasible, I would work with another UT graduate student to develop the maps. As it turned out, such maps were feasible, and Peter grew so intrigued that he agreed to work with me in producing them. They were shaded relief terrain maps, created on a computer screen by downloading data (numbers, basically) from the U.S. Geological Survey. Every terrain elevation had its own number and thus its own shade, and we used specialized software to lay in the rivers, cultural features, and other depictions wanted on a particular map. We spent hours in front of the computer in the little office he occupied at the back of his Georgetown home.

When printed in color, the maps not only clearly delineated the topography and other features but looked stunning as well. We envisioned an inset of these maps in color but doubted that Holt would find it financially feasible. Nonetheless, we sent the color portfolio to Jack Macrae and urged him to consider using color. He did, and at length he agreed that the maps would be printed in color directly from a computer disk. Peter and I suffered through a nightmarish process in pressuring Holt to find a printer who could get it right, but he finally succeeded. We are both proud of these maps, and they have gained widespread admiration among readers of the book.

But still no title, even as publication date approached in the spring of 1997. Jack, Carl, and I kicked around various possibilities, but none seemed to work. Finally Jack came up with a quotation from Francis Parkman, who observed the mountain men when he visited Fort Laramie in 1846: "I defy the annals of chivalry to furnish the record of a life more wild and perilous than that of a Rocky Mountain trapper." We three agreed, I think somewhat unenthusiastically; and the dust jacket, adorned with a colorful painting by John Clymer of a Green River rendezvous, bore the title *A Life Wild and Perilous: Mountain Men and the Paths to the Pacific*.

I wanted to unveil the book at the Western Writers of America convention in Cheyenne, Wyoming, late in June. The delays incident to acceptable printing of the color maps placed that hope in jeopardy. Melody and I drove to Cheyenne resigned to the book's absence among the other works on my table at the traditional ceremony in which members autograph their books. As it turned out, the first thirty books emerged from the bindery on June 25, 1997, and were stacked on my signing desk at Barnes and Noble on June 26.

I think this book is a good read with some fresh insights and groundbreaking maps. Melody is less enthusiastic. The sales record tends to support her judgment. It has not done well at all. We both agree that, aside from content, an important flaw is the title. Although the subtitle conveys the content, the title does not. In retrospect, because the book was published at the height of the success of Stephen Ambrose's *Undaunted Courage*, a much better title would have been *After Lewis and Clark: Mountain Men and the Paths to the Pacific*. (At this writing, Holt has licensed the paperback rights to the University of Nebraska Press, whose director agreed to retitle it *After Lewis and Clark*.)

A Life Wild and Perilous had not even cleared the bindery when the subject arose of what next. In New York in May 1997 Melody and I lunched separately with Carl Brandt and Jack Macrae. My proximity to Texas sources made a history of the Texas Rangers an appealing project, one that Jack said he would like to do. As Carl and Jack worked over the contract, however, it grew apparent that the new management at Holt, headed by Michael Naumann, preferred to spend money on corralling all the works of Salmon Rushdie rather than on creating a diversified list. Holt offered an advance of $80,000, $10,000 less than for the mountain men. That incensed both Carl and me, and without actually counseling against acceptance, Carl signaled his discontent.

At the October 1997 session of the Western History Association in St. Paul, I was approached by Peter Ginna. He had recently joined Oxford University Press with a mandate to develop a trade publishing arm to go head-to-head with the other big New York houses. He said he would like to work with me on a book. When the negotiations with Holt for the Texas Rangers reached an impasse, I asked Carl to get in touch with Peter Ginna. Carl replied that Peter could not afford me and said the same thing when he talked with Peter, who answered, "Try me." Peter offered $95,000 and, of perhaps equal importance, a publisher of enduring stability in a publishing world of frenzied mergers, acquisitions, and bank-ruptcies. We signed a contract in March 1998.

Peter Ginna turned out to be a skilled editor, fully the equal of Jack Macrae but entirely different in style. We have worked well together. I value my relationship with Peter and with Oxford.

Television continued to be a sometime affair in my life. Greystone's *The Real West,* which eventually boasted sixty episodes, played and replayed on the new History Channel. *How the West Was Lost* enjoyed a revival on Discovery now and then, as did *A.K.A. Billy the Kid* on the Disney Channel. I liked and had worked well with Arthur Drooker in some *Real West* productions. In July 1996 he had an assignment from Greystone to produce a two-hour biography of Custer for the A&E Channel. I flew to Burbank for my talking-head filming. Art set me up in the Gene Autry Museum with Custer's Civil War battle flag as a backdrop. I talked a lot about Custer, but it was a bad day. I could not seem to speak clearly and thought I turned in a lousy performance. Art tried to reassure me that I had done nobly. But for the first time, I think, I had not. Even so, judicious editing extracted enough coherent sound bites to give me a role in the production.

In December 1997 Donna Lusitana at Greystone called to say that the History Channel wanted to do a two-hour documentary based entirely on *A Life Wild and Perilous*. It would be in the series presided over by Roger Mudd. Not until September 1998 did producer Greg Goldman and a camera crew arrive at our Georgetown home to film me. Greg set up an imaginative backdrop of our fireplace with fire flickering, coffee table bearing one of my Wrangler Award statues glinting in the firelight, and me seated in front of cameras set up in the dining area. The day was beastly hot and humid, and to offset the fire in the fireplace we ran the air conditioner constantly throughout the three-hour interview. This time, in contrast to the Autry Museum appearance, I did well.

The two-hour mountain man documentary aired on the History Channel on March 20, 1999. The camera zoomed in on my book, and Roger Mudd introduced the production by announcing that it was drawn from the book. My appearances all met my standards, but Greg Goldman had also taken his cameras to an annual "rendezvous" of mountain man reenactors at Pinedale, Wyoming. They afforded so many opportunities for live action shots that he let them take over the editing. The reenactors dominated the presentation, so much so that they became repetitious and even, with fake blood splashed on a fake Hugh Glass, overly contrived. Even so, I welcomed the publicity, then and afterward. It replays every few months on the History Channel.

I used to contend that the surest guarantee of immortality was entry in library card catalogues. Now I concede that *The Real West* and other documentaries offer an even surer immortality. Recycled over and over by the History Channel, hardly a week passes that I don't appear on the TV screen. Repeatedly, in airports, hotels, and even supermarkets, people recognize me from cable TV. *The West, The Way West, The Wild West, How the West Was Lost,* Custer and the mountain men—all have had their time, but *The Real West* seems destined to live forever.

In September 1993, the very month in which Bob Baker's regional office signed the secret memorandum of understanding with North Shield Ventures, Little Bighorn Battlefield at last got another superintendent. Barbara Booher had not done well as a park manager.

As an Indian, moreover, she was viewed by the Custer loyalists as an appointment dictated entirely by political correctness—as it was.

Bob Baker chose another Indian, this one with plenty of park experience. A Mandan-Hidatsa, Gerard Baker was an enormous strapping Indian experienced at park management but also strongly tied to his Indian heritage. He could expect full support from the new regional director, John Cook, who reveled in a Cherokee lineage that sometimes influenced his evaluation of Indians in the gray and green uniform. Baker's style should have elicited some gentle counseling from his chief.

The new superintendent found it difficult to balance his views as an Indian with Park policy and sound management of the Park. He could not curb his big mouth, which spewed outrageous but quotable commentary on Custer and the Little Bighorn. The media delighted in interviewing him. This kept him in constant trouble. He so antagonized the Custer loyalists that they barraged Congress and the president with petitions for his removal.

The interpretive program fell into a shambles, with interpreters mouthing pro-Indian tirades and butchering history in the cause of political correctness. Without the usual bidding, Baker contracted tours to Little Bighorn College in Crow Agency, a struggling young institution, and he barred all other tour buses from the park. The Indian bus guides were as bad as the park guides.

In 1996 I received numerous reports of egregious factual errors and interpretive distortions. They were so credible and specific that on October 8 I wrote a bitingly critical letter to Cook, an old friend and associate of many years' standing. "Interpretation at Little Bighorn stands in urgent need of major overhaul," I concluded, and "Gerard can't make this happen alone." For one thing, he needed a qualified historian to oversee what the interpreters were telling the visitors. I sent a copy of the letter to Baker and one to Chief Historian Dwight Pitcaithley.

Predictably, the letter angered both Cook and Baker. Cook enjoyed a close relationship with Bill Brown, my friend ever since Santa Fe days in the 1960s, and called him in his Alaska retirement to ask how to handle Utley. Bill said that Cook and Gerard ought to meet with me and talk about it. Instead, a month later Cook wrote me a conciliatory letter accepting my criticism. He had already arranged for a top-flight historian to join the park staff. (That did not happen; Gerard declined to select him.) Cook also planned to bring in not only a superior interpreter, Bill Gwaltney, but Bill Brown himself to assess what was wrong and how to fix it.

They did. By all accounts reaching me, the summer of 1997 featured a vastly improved program, addressing many of my complaints. But the true fix came in January 1998, when Gerard moved on and Cook, to his everlasting credit, appointed the first effective superintendent since Jim Court. Neil Mangum had served Court as chief park historian and interpreter and had done a fine job. Later he had worked for Melody in Santa Fe and succeeded her as regional historian when she went to LBJ. Now Cook brought Neil back to straighten out Little Bighorn. He performed admirably, as I confirmed during a visit in August 1998. He introduced professionalism and balance into the interpretive program, made peace with both the Custer loyalists and the Indian community, and embarked on innovative measures to improve operations, management, and especially, planning for the future. He worked well with the Crow tribe, long an obstacle to progress, in developing joint ventures for restructuring the park tour sequence and conveying the Crow heritage in a joint visitor center.

Neil's signal contribution was to put the Indian memorial on the final leg of its long and painful journey to its destination, a low hill west of the historic monument. He not only pacified the Sioux opposition but addressed the obstacle of funding. Basic to the committee report of 1989 was federal funding. The United States had paid for the monument to the soldiers. It could do no less for the Indians. Yet the authorizing legislation had thrown the burden to philanthropy, which had to produce the $2 million or so the project would cost. Philanthropy failed spectacularly. Neil then raised the entrance fee and devoted the increase to the memorial, a move that sparked controversy and was of doubtful propriety if not legality. Next he turned to the Montana congressional delegation and persuaded them to slip the needed money into an appropriations bill. In the end, therefore, the United States rightly paid for the Indian memorial.

The dedication took place on the anniversary date of June 25, 2003. Interior Secretary Gail Norton did not make the headlines. She was upstaged, in a reprise of 1976, by none other than Russell Means. In a bright red shirt and astride a fine mount, he took station next to the speaker's platform. As the program got underway, he jumped off his horse, ascended the platform, and seized the microphone. "I want to tell you a little bit of the history here before the government revises it," he declared, then launched into the familiar tirade he had spewed out at every opportunity. Although long since consigned to political irrelevance, the colorful old activist could still command the television cameras.

Neil Mangum had already surrendered the battlefield to a successor. When he transferred to Chiricahua National Monument in 2002, he left much undone, but he had rescued the park from almost two decades of bedlam and set it on a stable course into the future.

John Cook had opened his November 1996 letter to me with these words: "My old friend, this won't be the first time, and probably won't be the last time, that we'll have a major disagreement and feel the other hasn't a clue what he's talking about." That was an accurate statement, including "my old friend." We did have disagreements, from our first in the 1960s when he was superintendent of the new Hubbell Trading Post National Historic Site. Cook had a distinguished but rocky career—rocky because of an honesty, integrity, and fierce devotion to park values that kept him constantly at odds with successive Republican administrations. Beholden to special interests, they sought more than once to get rid of him altogether. But John Cook's retirement in 1999 left a huge void in the top management of the Park Service. Despite our occasional clashes, I regard him as one of a small handful of the very best.

On August 11, 2000, Custer popped unexpectedly into my life. It was a Friday evening after a hard week working on the Texas Rangers. John Drayton, director of the University of Oklahoma Press, called to say that Salamander Books of London was negotiating for the text of *Cavalier in Buckskin* to carry a large-format, lavishly illustrated book entitled *Custer: Cavalier in Buckskin*. That seemed a fine idea. Then over the weekend, I reread *Cavalier*, probably for the first time since its publication in 1988. The chapters held up well until the last two, dealing with the Little Bighorn and my judgments on it and Custer. My interpretation of those issues had changed radically since *Cavalier*, in part because of the work I did on Sitting Bull and in part the work of others, especially the late John Gray, Greg Michno, and Larry Sklenar. Larry in particular contributed some highly original new interpretations in *To Hell with Honor*. So on Monday I called Drayton back and told him revision would be necessary. He consented, but only if I did it by Labor Day. I did an almost total rewrite of the two chapters and e-mailed it to Drayton near the end of August.

My further contribution to this coffee-table book took the form of e-mail exchanges early in 2001 with Salamander's picture editor, who labored feverishly to meet unrealistic deadlines and whose knowledge of the subject lacked substance. He, not I, wrote the captions and arranged the illustrations. I received my copy in May, and despite a placement of pictures that somewhat deranged chronology, I had to admit it was a handsomely designed book. Three hundred illustrations, many in color, and my old maps professionally redrawn adorned the revised text. To my surprise, the book retailed for under $30, almost unique for a book of such magnitude.

The University of Oklahoma Press handled distribution in the United States and decided to put out the revised edition in paperback, designing a new cover but using the original format and title. It appeared on Oklahoma's fall 2001 list. Booksellers and buyers have yet to sort out the difference between *Custer: Cavalier in Buckskin* and *Cavalier in Buckskin: George Armstrong Custer and the Western Military Frontier*.

Monday June 25, 2001, marked the 125th anniversary of the Battle of the Little Bighorn. I was there for daylong ceremonies that featured both Indians and the Custer loyalists. They got along well, and all went smoothly, thanks mainly to the diplomacy of Superintendent Neil Mangum.

I was there for two reasons. First was that stack of stunning picture books entitled *Custer: Cavalier in Buckskin.* The day was beastly hot but the crowd large enough to provide a lot of book buyers for a squad of authors established behind long tables on the visitor center portico. To my surprise and delight, I autographed 150 copies of my big new Custer book, the park store's entire stock.

The second reason was a symposium the next day organized by the nonprofit Friends of the Little Bighorn Battlefield. Titled "Remembering the Battlefield," it called on five people who had served the battlefield at various times in the past. Representing the earliest period, I went first. I told the audience about Cap and Evelyn Luce and recounted stories about the battlefield during Luce's superintendency. I related how we presented a triumphalist interpretation of Custer and the battle, relegating the Indians to the enemy. I recalled Brice Custer and Larry Frost and the rough practical jokes they and Luce inflicted on one another. In short, I described a park, staff, and story told to the visitor very different from what followed. Some of what followed had been bad for the battlefield and for the Park Service. But some had registered genuine progress. Certainly interpretation under Neil Mangum reflected public attitudes and values befitting the twenty-first century. In my time we had reflected the public mood of the middle of the twentieth century, but the rocky road to fundamental change had reached a proper destination.

The audience vigorously applauded my reminiscences. Most had not even been born when I first stood on Custer Hill in the uniform of the National Park Service. As battlefield buffs, they had come of age long after Cap Luce hired an adolescent to tell the story of the battle to visitors. They loved the battle and the field on which it took place. So will the next generation and generations beyond counting.

This visit to the battlefield was both nostalgic and sad. Sad because so much had changed since my youthful tenure. However much the change marked progress, it was still change alien to the happy memories of more than four decades earlier. Nostalgic because the visit rekindled those happy memories, especially in the telling to a later generation.

As a young ranger in green, a badge on my chest and a "flat hat" Stetson on my head, I had mingled with the throng at the seventy-fifth anniversary of the battle, June 25, 1951.

As an assistant director of the National Park Service, I had helped face down Russell Means and addressed a troubled audience on the centennial anniversary, June 25, 1976.

And now, as an elder survivor of a long-ago era, I autographed books at the 125th anniversary.

The third major anniversary seems to mark some kind of personal ending. I do not know if I shall ever return to the Little Bighorn Battlefield. I am almost certain I shall never write another book about Custer. But I am fully certain that, however many years are left to me, I have not ended the story of Custer and me.

Books and Brochures by Robert M. Utley

BOOKS

Custer and the Great Controversy: Origin and Development of a Legend. Los
Angeles: Westernlore Press, 1962, 1980. Reprint, Lincoln: University
of Nebraska Press, 1998. In print.

The Last Days of the Sioux Nation. New Haven: Yale University Press, 1963.
2nd ed., 2004. Award of Merit, American Association for State and
Local History. Buffalo Award, New York Westerners. In print.

(ed., with annotations) *Battlefield and Classroom: Four Decades with the American Indian, 1867–1904,* by Richard Henry Pratt. New Haven: Yale University Press, 1964. Reprint, Lincoln: University of Nebraska Press,
1987. Reprint, Norman: University of Oklahoma Press, 2004.

Frontiersmen in Blue: The United States Army and the Indian, 1848–1865. New
York: Macmillan, 1967. Reprint, Lincoln: University of Nebraska Press,
1981. History Book Club selection. In print.

Frontier Regulars: The United States Army and the Indian, 1866–1891. New
York: Macmillan, 1973. Reprint, Bloomington: Indiana University
Press, 1977. Reprint, Lincoln: University of Nebraska Press, 1984. Mili-
tary Book Club edition, Garden City, N.Y.: Doubleday, 1974. Pub-
lished in England as *Bluecoats and Redskins.* London: Cassell, 1975.
History Book Club selection. In print.

(with Wilcomb Washburn) *The American Heritage History of the Indian
Wars.* New York: American Heritage, 1977. American Heritage Library

edition, New York: Houghton-Mifflin, 1985. Published in France as *Guerres Indiennes du Mayflower à Wounded Knee.* Paris: Albin Michel, 1992. Library edition in print. New edition, fall 2001.

(ed., with annotations) *Life in Custer's Cavalry: Diaries and Letters of Albert and Jennie Barnitz, 1867–68.* New Haven: Yale University Press, 1977. Reprint, Lincoln: University of Nebraska Press, 1987. History Book Club selection. Recommended reading, Book of the Month Club. In print.

The Indian Frontier of the American West, 1846–1890. Histories of the American Frontier Series. Albuquerque: University of New Mexico Press, 1984. History Book Club selection. Book of the Month Club selection. Revised edition, retitled *The Indian Frontier, 1846–1890.* University of New Mexico Press, 2003. In print.

If These Walls Could Speak: Historic Forts of Texas. With paintings by J. U. Salvant. Austin: University of Texas Press, 1985. In print.

Four Fighters of Lincoln County, Calvin P. Horn Lecture Series of 1985. Albuquerque: University of New Mexico Press, 1986. Out of print.

High Noon in Lincoln: Violence on the Western Frontier. Albuquerque: University of New Mexico Press, 1987. Western Heritage Award, National Cowboy Hall of Fame, best nonfiction western of 1987. History Book Club selection. In print.

Cavalier in Buckskin: George Armstrong Custer and the Western Military Frontier. Norman: University of Oklahoma Press, 1988. Book of the Month Club selection. History Book Club selection. Military Book Club selection. French edition, 1997. Western Heritage Award, National Cowboy Hall of Fame, best nonfiction western of 1988. Revised paperback edition. University of Oklahoma Press, 2001. In print.

Billy the Kid: A Short and Violent Life. Lincoln: University of Nebraska Press, 1989; London: I. B. Tauris, 1990. Published in Spanish as *Billy el Niño: Una vida breve y violenta.* Barcelona–Buenos Aires–Mexico City: Ediciones Paidos, 1991. French edition, 1997. On tape, Frederick, Md.: Recorded Books, 1990. History Book Club main selection, 1989. Book of the Month Club selection. In print.

The Lance and the Shield: The Life and Times of Sitting Bull. New York: Henry Holt, 1993. History Book Club main selection. Book of the Month Club selection. Paperback edition, New York: Ballantine, 1994. Quality Paperback Book Club selection. Italian edition, Milan, 1994. French edition, Paris, 1997. English edition, London, 1997. Spur Award, Western Writers of America, best nonfiction of 1993. Caughey Prize,

Western History Association, best nonfiction of 1993. *New York Times* Notable Book, 1993. Books on Tape, 1994. In print.

A Life Wild and Perilous: Mountain Men and the Paths to the Pacific. New York: Henry Holt, 1997. History Book Club selection. Book of the Month Club selection. Recorded Books, 1998. Paperback edition, fall 1998. In print.

Custer: Cavalier in Buckskin. With 300+ illustrations. London: Salamander; Norman: University of Oklahoma Press, 2001.

Lone Star Justice: The First Century of the Texas Rangers. New York: Oxford University Press, 2002. History Book Club main selection. Book of the Month Club selection.

(ed.) *The Story of the West.* New York: Smithsonian Institution/DK Books, 2003.

BROCHURES

Custer's Last Stand, with a Narration of Events Preceding and Following. Dayton, Ind., 1949.

Fort Union National Monument, New Mexico. National Park Service Historical Handbook Series. Washington, D.C.: U.S. Government Printing Office, 1962.

Fort Davis National Historic Site, Texas. National Park Service Historical Handbook Series. Washington, D.C.: U.S. Government Printing Office, 1965.

(with Andrew Ketterson) *Golden Spike.* National Park Service Historical Handbook Series. Washington, D.C.: U.S. Government Printing Office, 1969.

Custer Battlefield. National Park Service Historical Handbook Series. Washington, D.C.: U.S. Government Printing Office, 1969. Revised edition, 1988.

A Clash of Cultures: Fort Bowie and the Chiricahua Apaches. National Park Service Historical Handbook Series. Washington, D.C.: U.S. Government Printing Office, 1977.

The Contribution of the Frontier to the American Military Tradition. Harmon Memorial Lectures in Military History, no. 19. Colorado Springs, Colo.: U.S. Air Force Academy, 1977. Also published in James P. Tate (ed.), *The American Military on the Frontier: Proceedings of the Seventh Military History Symposium, USAF Academy, 1976,* 2–14. Washington, D.C.: USAF, 1978. Reprinted as introduction to Paul A. Hutton (ed.), *Soldiers West:*

Biographies from the Military Frontier, 1–10. Lincoln: University of Nebraska Press, 1987.

Indian, Soldier, and Settler: Experiences in the Struggle for the American West. St. Louis: Jefferson National Expansion Memorial Historical Association, 1979.

(with Barry Mackintosh) *The Department of Everything Else: Highlights of Interior History.* Washington, D.C.: U.S. Department of the Interior, 1988.

Fort Union and the Santa Fe Trail, Southwestern Studies Series, no. 89. El Paso: Texas Western Press, 1989.

Fort Scott National Historic Site, Kansas. Tucson: Southwest Parks and Monuments Association, 1991.

Fort Larned National Historic Site, Kansas. Tucson: Southwest Parks and Monuments Association, 1993.

Changing Course: The International Boundary, United States and Mexico, 1848–1963. Tucson: Southwest Parks and Monuments Association, 1996.

Eastern National Park and Monument Association: The First Fifty Years, 1947–1997. Conshohocken, Penn.: Eastern National Park and Monument Association, 1997.

INDEX